Improving Reading Comprehension of Self-Chosen Books Through Computer Assessment and Feedback

Schools around the world use online programs like Accelerated Reader and Reading Counts to improve students' reading comprehension of real books, but how can such software be used most effectively? In this unique resource, researcher Keith Topping analyzes independent research studies and brings you best practices on quality implementation to enhance effectiveness. He explains the evidence base for the programs in a comprehensible way and addresses many common questions, such as "Does it work?," "How should it be implemented to make it work?," and "Is it cheaper and more efficient in teacher time than what we were doing before?" He also discusses best practices for using the assessment data, for tailoring implementation in elementary vs. high schools, and for working with disadvantaged students. Appropriate for teachers, literacy coaches, curriculum leaders, and other stakeholders, the book will provide you with a strong research foundation and easily accessible information to help you fine-tune your understanding of the reading programs and implement them more successfully in your schools and classrooms.

Keith James Topping is a researcher, educator, author, and international speaker. His interests are peer learning, parents as educators, social competence, computer-assisted assessment, and inclusion. Topping has written 27 books and over 400 other publications, including over 200 peer-reviewed journal papers.

Improving Reading Comprehension of Self-Chosen Books Through Computer Assessment and Feedback

Best Practices from Research

Keith James Topping

Routledge
Taylor & Francis Group
NEW YORK AND LONDON

Cover image: © Getty Images

First published 2023

by Routledge
605 Third Avenue, New York, NY 10158, USA

and by Routledge
4 Park Square, Milton Park, Abingdon, Oxon, OX14 4RN, UK

Routledge is an imprint of the Taylor & Francis Group, an informa business.

© 2023 Keith James Topping

The right of Keith James Topping to be identified as author of this work has been asserted in accordance with sections 77 and 78 of the Copyright, Designs and Patents Act 1988.

All rights reserved. No part of this book may be reprinted or reproduced or utilised in any form or by any electronic, mechanical, or other means, now known or hereafter invented, including photocopying and recording, or in any information storage or retrieval system, without permission in writing from the publishers.

Trademark notice: Product or corporate names may be trademarks or registered trademarks, and are used only for identification and explanation without intent to infringe.

Library of Congress Cataloging-in-Publication Data
A catalog record for this title has been requested

ISBN: 978-1-032-10558-1 (hbk)
ISBN: 978-1-032-07620-1 (pbk)
ISBN: 978-1-003-21588-2 (ebk)

DOI: 10.4324/9781003215882

Access the Support Material: www.routledge.com/9781032105581

Typeset in Palatino
by SPi Technologies India Pvt Ltd (Straive)

The Electronic Bookshelf was developed in 1981 by a school librarian named Rosalie Carter with her husband Jerry Carter. We celebrate Rosalie and Jerry's foresight. The Electronic Bookshelf went on to become Reading Counts, used only in the USA.

Without any knowledge of this, in Wisconsin in 1984, Judi Paul wanted her four children to love reading as much as she did. So, Judi listed her favorite novels and to inspire her children and ensure they were comprehending what they were reading, she wrote multiple-choice questions about each book and created a points system based on book difficulty and length. That was the birth of Accelerated Reader (AR), which was later developed by Terry Paul. Thirty-five years later, AR is used by over many thousands of schools in over 100 countries around the world. We celebrate Judi and Terry's foresight.

Contents

Acknowledgements ix
Executive Summary x

1 Introduction 1

2 What is Computer Assessment of Reading
   Comprehension of Real Books? 13

3 Disentangling Opinion and Fact 36

4 So, Does It Work? 49

5 How to Implement for Increased Student Success 98

6 How Have Schools Done with Implementation? 105

7 Increasing Student Achievement in Elementary
   and High School 118

8 Improving Outcomes for Low- and High-Ability
   Readers 129

9 Using Favorite Books as a Major Motivator 137

10 Encouraging Careful Reading of Non-Fiction Books 143

11 Working Effectively with Spanish-Speaking,
   Disadvantaged, Disabled or EFL Students 149

12 Electronic Reading and Out-of-School Reading 163

13 What Bang for Your Buck? The Importance of Cost-Effectiveness 170

14 Summary and Conclusions 181

Appendices

    Appendix A: Implementation Quality Checklist 197

    Appendix B: Reports Authored by the Manufacturers 200

    Appendix C: How to Use This Book in a Professional Development or Study Group 203

    Subject Index 208
    Author Index 211

Acknowledgements

My grateful thanks for giving permission to reproduce the screenshots in this book go to Renaissance Learning and Houghton Mifflin Harcourt (HMH).

My grateful thanks for providing new information and data go to:

Eric Stickney and Lindsay Haas (USA) and James Bell, Gareth Andrews and John Moore (UK) of Renaissance Learning

Renee Behring (Education Research Director) and Francine Alexander (Chief Research Officer) of HMH.

However, the analysis and interpretation of this information and data are entirely my own.

Executive Summary

This book is about improving reading comprehension of real self-chosen books through computer assessment and feedback. The software is used by about nine million school students in 100 countries. The book summarizes independent, peer-reviewed research evidence and new research on effectiveness. It also gives guidance on good-quality implementation which enhances effectiveness. Computer-based systems for managing independent book reading have students choose a real book (adequately challenging for age and ability), read it and then self-test comprehension with a quiz. Their performance is automatically scored, and results are swiftly fed back to the student. Results also feed back to the teacher, who can guide the student towards more-effective choices and manage the reading of the whole class. There are two main programs: Accelerated Reader (AR) and Reading Counts (RC). There are three other programs but no published literature on any of these. All the independent research studies in peer-reviewed journals, excluding studies by the manufacturers, were gathered. Books, chapters, doctoral dissertations and master's theses were also excluded. Five research databases were searched. AR had many hits, RC very few. However, Read 180 (a program for lower-ability readers in which RC is now embedded) had many hits. This book added new analyses of fresh data from 2018–19 (as later years had been disrupted by the pandemic). Better studies quoted effect size (ES) (a quantitative measure of magnitude of effect).

AR uses the Star Reading computer-based adaptive reading comprehension test to automatically indicate the student's starting reading difficulty level (but other tests will do this manually). A minimum of 30 minutes of daily independent reading time for elementary schools and 20 minutes for secondary schools is recommended. AR is not an instructional program and not a reward program, nor should it be linked to the grades. Over 200,000 quizzes are quite literal, essential for reliability. Book difficulty level is determined by ATOS (Advantage/TASA Open Standard for Readability). AR Bookfinder enables synchronization of a school's book stocks with AR quizzes. Students can set goals and rate favorite books. Feedback to parents is also encouraged. Training for teachers is readily available. RC is similar but has about 75,000 book tests and is based on the Lexile measure of difficulty. The Reading Inventory test gives starting levels, and Book Expert enables choice of books. Teachers can customize tests in various ways, but the proportion of teachers doing this is small. RC is mostly embedded in Read 180, a larger program which includes small group teacher instruction targeted to lower-ability readers. RC is not an instructional program (but Read 180 certainly is) and is not a reward program. So, AR and RC are not in competition but are different. AR and RC have been criticized, but criticisms are often based on misconceptions of what the programs do.

Overall, of 64 studies of AR, four reported no effects and four were not clear, so 56 (88%) reported positive effects. There were 14 reviews, seven randomized controlled studies and four controlled studies, yielding an average ES of 0.33, which is moderate but substantial compared with ESs for other educational interventions. There was only one very weak study of RC. However, Read 180 had many studies. Reviews gave average ESs of 0.59 and 0.10, but it was not possible to extract the effects of RC from this. New data were available for AR on 8,745,130 students. Quizzes Taken averaged 38, Quizzes Passed 33, and the Pass Rate was 87%. The average Difficulty Level was 3.61, Comprehension Quality 79%, and Engaged Reading Time per day 22 minutes. Females performed slightly better than males. There were differences between countries on these variables. RC-only data were available for 14,567 students, and the difference between initial and final Lexiles gave an ES of 0.23. In only 9% of cases did teachers allow retaking of tests, and only 7% were successful. The Difficulty Level averaged 4.03, Tests Passed were 16, Pass Rate was 72% and the Test Score was 71. Data for Read 180 were available for 26,921 students. Initial to Final Lexile gave ES 0.36, with much lower Tests Taken and Difficulty Level than RC Only (as would be expected given that Read180 targets lower ability students). Only 66% of tests were passed on first try, but fiction and non-fiction reads were equal in number.

RC seems more complex than AR. While RC's ability to customize might appear intuitively appealing to teachers, the amount of time needed to use these features is likely to prove prohibitive; indeed, the number of teachers using these features is very small. There was evidence of variability in implementation in both AR and RC, and there were special concerns about RC. Secondary schools showed the worst implementation. A checklist of implementation quality variables will be found in Appendix A.

AR was more effective in the elementary grades, less so in secondary. This may be due to differences in implementation quality or to changes in preferences of students as they grow older. However, some studies did find gains in secondary schools. AR was used maximally in grades 3 through 5 but much less after the first two grades of secondary. Book difficulty rose steadily through elementary school, much less in secondary school. Quality of comprehension was high through elementary school but declined at the secondary level. Engaged Reading Time was much higher in elementary than secondary schools. RC Only was even more erratic, plateaued in the early years and in secondary school, and rose steeply in upper elementary school. High-ability readers generally did better on AR than others. Low-ability readers could make large gains but probably only if participation and implementation quality are high. AR students in grades 1 through 4 read their Favorite books at a difficulty level far above their actual age while maintaining a high rate of comprehension quality. There was a marked difference after secondary school transfer, when favored books were no longer above chronological age and a rapid decline in difficulty set in. Voting for favorite books was much less common in secondary school than in elementary school.

Girls tended to prefer fiction and boys non-fiction, a tendency especially marked at secondary school. For AR, three times more fiction books than non-fiction books were read. Book Difficulty for non-fiction was markedly higher than for fiction. Boys' reading of non-fiction showed lower Comprehension Quality than girls. In RC Only, more non-fiction was read but still less than fiction. AR can be effective in schools with a higher proportion of students with social disadvantage, but high implementation quality might be needed. There were no direct comparisons of advantaged and disadvantaged students. Three studies mentioned disability, and two studies of AR with English as a Foreign Language students had positive results. Regarding race/ethnicity, one study found that Caucasians did best and Native Americans and African-Americans worst. However, new data showed Native Hawaiians doing very well, Caucasians not doing so well, but African-Americans still came out worse, although this appeared to relate to the amount of Engaged Reading Time the different groups were given. Some students tried books in the Spanish language (with quizzes in Spanish), but performance was poor and this dropped off quickly as students turned to English books and quizzes.

In regard to electronic reading, myON is software which can be downloaded onto any device the student possesses and gives access to the text of 13,000 books (2021 numbers) and AR quizzes which go with them. Four studies of myON all reported positive effects. Much the same was found in new data. The average ATOS of myON titles was somewhat higher than for regular books.

Considering cost-effectiveness, many studies by Yeh and Simon compare AR to a wide range of other educational interventions. Yeh found AR better than all others; Simon found AR only bettered by Classwide Peer Tutoring. In the USA, the cost of AR + Star Reading was $12.45 per student per year and in the UK was USD $11.65 per student per year in 2021. This represented 0.0008% of the annual expenditure on schools (2021 prices). Salaries and benefits for staff make up 80% of the annual expenditure on schools. RC Only (including the Reading Inventory) costs $12 per student per year and thus is more or less the same price as AR.

So, can AR and RC Only be compared? AR has more quizzes, more participating students, a higher quiz Pass Rate, a higher number of Quizzes Passed, higher Comprehension Quality, better implementation, a higher proportion of studies with a positive outcome, and a higher effect size. RC Only has a higher Book Difficulty level (which may partially account for the lower Pass Rate and lower Quality of Comprehension but not for the far lower number of Quizzes Passed) and a more equivalent ratio between fiction and non-fiction. AR and RC Only cost about the same. For both AR and RC Only, there was a decline in Book Difficulty in secondary school, at least partially due to poorer implementation. For RC Only, teachers were not using RC Only's greater flexibility to any great extent. Fiction/non-fiction ratios were very different between AR and RC Only, and RC Only had proportionately twice as many non-fiction books read. However, RC mostly operates as part of the wider Read 180 and System 44 programs, so AR and RC are not really in competition.

Recommendations are that the implementation of AR and RC could certainly be improved, especially in secondary schools, and hopefully the implementation checklist will encourage this. Establishing points clearly as a form of feedback rather than anything else should enhance student metacognition. More information about other kinds of quizzes testing higher-order thinking should be made available to schools. Vygotsky's name is misused and this should be clarified.

1

Introduction

This Introduction first talks about the aim of the book – what it is and what it is not. Then it gives a brief description of the programs described in the book. The main ones are Accelerated Reader (AR) and Reading Counts (RC) (and description of them is enlarged in Chapters 2 and 5). A comment on other, somewhat similar programs follows. Then the research methods used to gather information are broadly outlined, followed by a more specific section on search methods. Then a section on statistical analysis seeks to explain in simple language some of the methods that were used (but don't worry, it's easy to understand). The issue of who might read the book is discussed. Finally, an expanded version of this paragraph (structure of the book) gives more details about what readers might expect, to help them decide which chapters to read first.

The Aim of This Book

This book is about a single kind of software, made in different versions by different companies. It might seem extraordinary to propose a book about a single kind of software, but this is no ordinary software. It is used in about 100 countries worldwide and is the most widely used educational software in the world. Additionally, some versions have attracted a large number of evaluation studies – more than any other piece of software. Especially in the USA and other English-speaking countries, there is great emphasis on evidence-based education, and schools are looking for a single source of evidence to justify their use of such software. This book is such a single source of evidence for improving reading comprehension of real books through computer assessment and feedback.

The book is thus *not* a "how to do it" book for teachers, since the precise method of delivery is well covered in manuals for the software and in the training and coaching programs provided by the manufacturers (both of which, of course, change somewhat from time to time). However, the book does make some comment on the broad pattern of implementation desired and expected by the manufacturers (see Chapter 5), the variations in how the programs are actually implemented and what the effects of these variations might be (see Chapter 6). Teachers will glean important messages about implementation from these chapters, and an implementation checklist is provided to help this.

The book also offers a summary of the *independent, peer-reviewed* research evidence already completed and of new research freshly done. This addresses many of the major concerns of schools, which will have questions like "Does it work?", "How should it be implemented to make it work?" and "Is it cheaper and more efficient in teacher time than what we were doing before?" All of these questions are answered in this book.

This review of evidence leads to some suggestions for how the use of these programs can be improved. It will thus reassure schools that much if not all of their practice is evidence-based and well substantiated, lead them to improve their implementation of such programs, and enable them to state and defend their case in that regard to school district managers, local and national government, parents and other stakeholders. It will also be of interest to researchers, especially in areas where data are sparser or more difficult to track.

The book is thus intended to give the evidence base for these programs in an easy and comprehensible way. Within this, it focuses on special subtopics which may be of interest to particular readers.

What Are These Programs?

Of course, schools have long had programs to encourage independent reading of self-chosen books, such as Sustained Silent Reading (SSR), Uninterrupted Sustained Silent Reading (USSR), Drop Everything and Read (DEAR), Free Uninterrupted Reading (FUR), Free Voluntary Reading (FVR), SQUIRT (Sustained Quiet Uninterrupted Reading Time), Independent Reading Time (IRT) and Writing and Reading Time (WART) (to name a few). These programs could have an element of accountability, such as book discussion groups, book reports and so on, but this becomes a problem when students are choosing their own very diverse books and is, in any event, very consuming of time.

By contrast, computer-based systems for the management of independent reading encourage students to choose a real book of their own choice (within the boundaries of what would be considered adequately challenging for their age and ability), read it and then self-test their comprehension of it with a quiz on a computer. Their quiz performance is automatically uploaded for scoring and analysis and then the results are swiftly fed back to the student, indicating the level of success. The student can then consider whether they need to try an easier or harder book or just read with more care for better comprehension. The results are also fed back to the teacher, who can then guide the student towards more effective book choices. Teachers and librarians receive feedback on individuals or whole classes of students, which enables them to manage the reading experiences of students with far greater efficiency than before. One of the advantages is that the programs enable more efficient tracking of students' reading habits and progress while reducing the time commitment of the teacher or librarian to this task. It is also possible for results to be fed back to parents.

Thus, the programs are about practice in reading – specifically, successful practice on self-chosen books of an appropriate level of challenge. The program does not directly teach phonological skills, important as these are – but it does give students the opportunity to practice their phonological skills in the context of real books. It might be argued that this program could lead to students reading books only in order to take the quiz, but this seems implausible when reading the book takes so long, taking the quiz is so quick and there are so many thousands of quizzes. In fact, the intrinsic desire to read a book which seems especially interesting seems to be the motivating factor.

There are two main programs which deliver computer assessment and feedback on the reading of real books: AR (published by Renaissance Learning in the USA and the UK – https://www.renaissance.com and https://www.renlearn.co.uk) and RC (published by Houghton Mifflin Harcourt [HMH] in the USA – https://www.hmhco.com/programs/reading-counts and https://readingcountsbookexpert.tgds.hmhco.com/book-expert/default.asp).

Accelerated Reader

AR was developed around 1984 by Judi and Terry Paul and has always been owned by Renaissance Learning (although Renaissance Learning has been taken over by a larger company). Since then, very large numbers of students have become involved, especially in the USA and the UK but also in many other countries. Now there are 50,000 book quizzes for it in the UK and 205,000 in the USA (2021 numbers), and these numbers grow every year. A very large number of elementary and high schools are involved globally – representing a very large number of students.

AR is also one of the best-researched methods in the field of education. There are many independent peer-reviewed studies (including randomized controlled trials and control group studies). This research has been debated and sometimes criticized, but the alternative methods offered have often not been researched at all. AR has also met the highest review standards of reputable organizations, such as the National Center on Intensive Intervention, the National Center on Response to

Intervention, the National Dropout Prevention Center, and the Promising Practices Network. In the UK, AR is now marketed together with Star Reading, a computer-based adaptive norm-referenced multiple-choice reading comprehension test. In the USA, these two products can be purchased separately.

Reading Counts

The first reading management program, called the Electronic Bookshelf, was developed in 1981 by a school librarian named Rosalie Carter along with her husband Jerry Carter. This was taken over by Scholastic in 1998 and renamed RC (and switched to being based on Lexile measures of book difficulty). RC was then taken over by HMH in 2015.

In many ways, RC is similar to AR, but in some additional ways, it is different. RC has a default Pass Rate of 70%, but teacher users can adjust this to suit their requirements. However, only about 10% of teachers actually do this (see Chapter 4). Teachers can also allow retake of tests which are failed, as their book tests have a total of 30 questions by default and are adaptive, presenting a different, set of questions on each retake. Again, the number of teachers who actually do this is fairly limited (see Chapter 4). Teachers can also change the number of questions in a book test, making it longer for more able readers or shorter for less able readers. All of these features are quite different from AR.

RC is available as a stand-alone program but is also embedded in Read 180, a program that includes the same computer assessment and feedback but also small group teacher instruction and independent reading. Read 180 is mainly targeted on the second quartile of readers (i.e., 25th–50th percentile, below average but not the worst readers) (System 44 is for even lower-ability readers). Thus, Read 180 is not for average- to high-ability readers. It has an equal amount of fiction and non-fiction, although the tendency is to increase the non-fiction element.

In fact, only about 35% of RC operates as a stand-alone program (RC Only), but obviously this is the section that is of most interest to this book. Equally obviously, the cost of RC Only is much less than that of RC embedded in Read 180, but we will come to that in Chapter 13.

Given their rather different orientation, it seems that AR and RC are not in competition, but overall target rather different students in somewhat different ways. In addition, RC is about to be wholly integrated in much more complex and expensive programs, so it will then be impossible to disentangle its separate effect.

Similar Programs

There are three other programs which appear to do somewhat similar things to AR and RC.

One is Book Adventure by Sylvan Learning (https://bookadventure.com). This is said to have 40,000 quizzes and gives rewards for reading in the form of virtual "coins". It used to be free but now costs US $50 (2021 prices) per student per year – clearly much more expensive than AR or RC (see Chapter 13).

The other is ReadnQuiz (https://readnquiz.com), which is said to have 50,000 quizzes and allows retakes of tests (similar to RC). The quizzes are "written by librarians and teachers" (i.e., many different people who may or may not be experienced in test writing). There may be *up to* 40 questions per quiz, so quizzes may be unlike each other in length. ReadnQuiz seems to see itself more as a vehicle for home-schooling than for use in schools. It costs $30 per year for one student, $95 for one class for one year, and $250 per school plus $1.50 per student using the system (2021 prices). Thus, it is more expensive than AR and RC for small numbers of students but less expensive for larger numbers.

While Book Adventure is more expensive and ReadnQuiz cheaper for large numbers of students than AR and RC (unless it is used for home-schooling) (see Chapter 13), the third program seems to be free. Book It is operated for pre-K through sixth grade by Pizza Hut (https://www.bookitprogram.com), is targeted on home-schoolers as well as schools, and essentially offers extrinsic rewards of pizza for completing reading tasks.

It "recommends" books and offers complementary activities. Book It seems to be the most easily criticized program of them all, but paradoxically it does not seem to have been criticized.

However, when these three companies were contacted to request their cooperation in producing this book, they declined to participate. Actually, they just didn't reply. There is no published literature on any of the programs. Consequently, I was unable to include them any further in this book.

In addition, there were two somewhat similar programs which have since disappeared: BookSharp and That's a Fact, Jack!

Research in the Book

A large number of research reports have been produced by the manufacturers of these programs, but more importantly, there have been many independent research studies, particularly of AR. The present book gathers together all the independent research studies in peer-reviewed journals on all versions of these programs while only listing in an Appendix and not otherwise mentioning studies done by the manufacturers, which might be considered biased. Books, chapters and doctoral dissertations and master's theses were also excluded, as they had not been subject to peer review and were very diverse in quality. The book also adds new analyses of many of the areas under consideration, using fresh data supplied by the relevant companies but analyzed independently.

Clearly (given the numbers of schools involved), these programs are very popular with teachers, but there is a fair amount of misinformation in circulation about them, often promoted by those who have no experience of using them. This book should do much to make information and evidence, as opposed to opinions, more readily available. Its purpose is to give teachers easily accessible information that should enable them to fine-tune their understanding and implement the program more successfully in their classrooms. It also aims to provide a coherent research foundation not only for teachers but also for school managers and educational researchers.

Search Methods

The literature search began by asking all product manufacturers for their descriptions of their programs and how they worked. They were also asked to supply lists of both externally authored research reports of which they were aware and in-house research reports. Only Renaissance Learning and HMH replied. Five relevant research databases (ERIC, JSTOR, Scopus, Web of Science and Google Scholar) were then searched using the terms "Accelerated Reader" or "Reading Counts". The first term generated many hits, the second very few. However, Read 180 (in which RC is now embedded) generated many hits.

There were over a hundred master's theses and doctoral dissertations on AR and a few on RC. However, the quality of these was so various that it was felt safer to exclude them from the literature review. Of course, peer-reviewed journal articles are also various in quality but less so. Chapters in books and books were also excluded on the grounds that they had not been peer-reviewed, as were unpublished research reports (although research reports were included if they had appeared in peer-reviewed journals or were from other authoritative source such as the US government or a university). Studies of either AR or RC which combined the programs with some other intervention and did not disentangle the effects of the various aspects were also excluded. The full text of each retrieved item was then read to ensure that it met the criteria for inclusion.

Renaissance Learning and HMH were also asked if they could supply data which might cast light on the issues to be investigated. As the years 2019–2020 and 2020–2021 had been severely disrupted by the covid pandemic, it was decided that such data should come from the academic year 2018–2019, which was a "normal" year. In the event, HMH could provide data for 2015–2016 only. These data were provided at the level of individual students, averaging performance for each student over the year. The data were then independently analyzed by the author of this book.

Statistical Analysis

Descriptive statistics are often given for some of the analyses that follow. First there is the *number* of observations, usually indicated as n or N. Then there is the arithmetic *mean* or *average* (the sum of all observations divided by the number of observations). For simplicity, this will be called average rather than mean. There is also the *standard deviation* (s.d.) (a measure of the amount of variance in the data) – a simple average does not tell you how widely the data were spread, but s.d. does. Very often, you will see the figure for the mean is followed by the s.d. in brackets. Sometimes, you will also see the *range* – the distance between the smallest and largest observation. *Percentiles* are a way of expressing where an observation falls in the range of other observations. If you arrange all your observations in ascending order of size and divide them into 100 groups with an equal number of observations in each group, each group is a percentile. Thus, for example, if an observation is at the 20th percentile, this means that 20% of all the scores recorded are lower and 80% are higher. Some of the percentiles have special names – for example, the 25th, 50th and 75th percentiles are called the first, second and third *quartile*, respectively.

In some analyses, you will see that the difference between two means or averages is tested for statistical significance. One way of doing this is with the *t-test*, which compares the means with reference to their s.d.'s and n's and sees if the value of the resulting statistic t is large enough to be statistically significant. *Statistical significance* is a quantification of whether what you see is likely just due to random chance or whether it is more probably the result of some influential factor you are studying. Usually, a criterion of probability of 0.05 or 5% is set as the limit of statistical significance, below which what you see is more likely due to your factor of interest and above which is more likely due to random chance. In this book, the new data sample size for an analysis is often very large. One result of this is that even very small differences appear statistically significantly, as statistical significance is strongly affected by sample size – the larger the sample, the more likely statistical significance becomes.

An alternative way of looking at this is via effect size (ES) (a quantitative measure of the magnitude of effect). The larger the ES, the stronger the relationship between two variables. ES is also affected by sample size, but in the opposite direction and not to the same extent; that is, small samples tend to give larger ESs. Clearly this does not apply to the data here, so ESs will be used more than statistical significance and thus any error will be on the side of conservatism. ES can also be influenced by the degree of variation in the sample (samples with high variability tending to show lower ESs). There are different kinds of ESs, but here Hedges' g is used (which is the most widely used). (Hedges' g *is* weighted according to the relative size of each sample and is used where there are different sample sizes). ESs are often approximately categorized according to their size: very small = 0.01, small = 0.20, medium = 0.50, large = 0.80, very large = 1.20, huge = 2.00 (Sawilowsky, 2009). However, these categorizations are very approximate and depend on the context in which the ESs were calculated.

For AR, you will see reference to *student growth percentiles* (SGPs). These describe a student's growth over a period of time compared with other students with similar prior test scores. An SGP is a number between 1 and 99, so it has some similarities with regular percentiles. For example, if a student has an SGP of 85, we can say that she showed more growth than 85% of her academic peers (Betebenner, 2011).

Audience

The primary audience for this book is pre-service and in-service school teachers as well as teacher educators and those involved in supporting the ongoing professional development of educators. In addition, school principals, district superintendents, and managers will seek to use the book as a reference source. Officials and politicians at local and national government are also likely to use the book, as are researchers in computerized assessment and literacy.

Structure of the Book

The book starts with an Executive Summary, a rather unusual venture for a book. However, many administrators and politicians (and even some teachers) may wish to absorb the contents of the book but will not have time to read the full text, so the Executive Summary allows them a brief overview (which hopefully will stimulate them to read other sections of the book in more detail).

An Introduction gives a less brief overview. Each subsequent chapter is divided into potentially five elements: research literature on AR, research literature on RC, new data on AR (if available) and new data on RC (if available). Then chapter after this one ends with a Summary. Generally, within chapters, systematic reviews and meta-analyses are reviewed first, followed by randomized controlled trials, followed by control group studies, and these three kinds of studies are given the most detailed analysis. The remaining studies are categorized according to whether they included many schools or only one school and whether they included reading tests or not. Then the new data are analyzed and summarized. Wherever possible, these data are summarized in tables and figures for ease of access by teachers.

Chapter 2 defines exactly what each program is and what it is not (encompassing *inter alia* how quizzes are developed and how the difficulty of books is determined). A third chapter looks at negative perceptions and opinions of these programs and seeks to disentangle opinion from evidence. The fourth chapter looks at the evidence on whether these programs work – do they actually raise student reading attainment? A fifth chapter on how the program *should* be implemented follows, outlining best implementation practices in schools. The sixth chapter considers how well the program actually *is* implemented, and shows that the more best implementation practices are followed, the higher is student attainment.

A chapter (7) on differences in performance between elementary and high schools follows. The eighth chapter considers whether the program is effective with low-ability readers (a challenging population for raising reading attainment) and high-ability readers (who might be considered too competent at reading to be able to benefit from the program). Readers can also vote for their Favorite books after completing a reading, and Chapter 9 analyzes whether these Favorite books generate a different kind of performance from students. Chapter 10 considers the difference between fiction and non-fiction reading, asking whether performance differs by type of reading and gender.

Then we look at whether the program works better or worse with disadvantaged students (defined by proportion of free/reduced lunch or free school meals), with students of different races/ethnicities, with students reading in Spanish (relating performance in reading Spanish books with Spanish reading quizzes), with students with some kind of Disability or Special Educational Need, and with English as a Second Language (ESL) students. After this, we investigate the expanding role of electronic reading (Chapter 12). Of course, the program costs something, so a chapter about relative cost-effectiveness follows (Chapter 13). The final Chapter 14 offers an overall Summary and Conclusions. An extensive list of references and Appendices follow, the Appendices including the Implementation Checklist.

References

Betebenner, D. (2011). *A technical overview of the Student Growth Percentile methodology: Student Growth Percentiles and percentile growth projections/trajectories*. ERIC Document retrieval number ED583125. https://files.eric.ed.gov/fulltext/ED583125.pdf

Sawilowsky, S. S. (2009). New effect size rules of thumb. *Journal of Modern Applied Statistical Methods*, 8(2), Article 26. doi: 10.22237/jmasm/1257035100. http://digitalcommons.wayne.edu/jmasm/vol8/iss2/26

2

What is Computer Assessment of Reading Comprehension of Real Books?

This chapter defines exactly what these programs are and what they are not. It covers, among other things, goals and purposes, how quizzes are developed and how the difficulty of books is determined. We will look first at Accelerated Reader (AR) and then at Reading Counts (RC).

Accelerated Reader

Goals and Purposes
Traditional methods to account for and manage book reading (e.g., reading logs, reading journals or diaries, oral and written book reports, parent reports of their child's reading) take a great deal of teacher time to moderate and are not reliable as they are essentially subjective. AR was designed to make the job of managing book reading easier and more reliable whilst motivating students to read more books for pleasure.

AR is a personalized practice and progress-monitoring system that helps teachers accurately and efficiently monitor student progress in quality (comprehension), quantity and difficulty of books read. AR enables instant feedback and monitoring by both student and teacher of independent book-reading practice with both fiction and non-fiction reading for prekindergarten through 12th grade. Quick feedback leads to better performance (e.g., Kettle & Häubl, 2010; Samuels & Wu, 2003), and positive feedback fosters positive self-image, which in turn is likely to improve future performance. The feedback to students leads them to reflect on their own thought processes and strategies (encouraging metacognition) and take appropriate action when choosing their next book. AR keeps track of all aspects of student book reading, such as titles of books, authors, book readability levels and quiz scores. This information is also passed back to the teacher, who can look at patterns for the whole class (or indeed the whole school) and take whatever action is needed (e.g., shape subsequent reading instruction, guide individual students, discuss choosing books with the whole class and motivate students to continue reading).

Points are awarded based on the difficulty of the books; the more difficult the book, the more points it is worth. Students can set goals for themselves in terms of successful reading and see if they reach those goals. Students can have different points goals for the term or school year, depending on initial reading level and previous performance. This avoids the situation where weaker students may always feel they are at the bottom of the list (Cox, 2012; Yeh, 2010). For beginning readers, the emphasis is on reading to or with students rather than on completely independent reading. AR has a system for peers to read books together in a kind of peer tutoring known as Duolog Reading. Usually, one member of the pair is more able than the other. When the book is completed, both members of the pair can take the quiz independently. You would expect the more able member of the pair (the tutor) to pass the quiz more easily or with a higher score than the weaker member of the pair (the tutee). Students also have the opportunity to rate the book they have read (after they have read it), and data are recorded on student choices of these Favorite Books.

The Star Reading computer-based adaptive reading comprehension test can be used to indicate the student's starting reading level. It takes 10 minutes and because of its adaptive and item-banked nature can be used frequently during the year (students are never presented with the same set of test items). Results are used to determine a starting difficulty level and "zone of proximal development" for each student. This describes "the readability range from which students should be selecting books to achieve optimal growth in reading skills without experiencing frustration". However, this should not be used as a definitive guide, as students can often read books above their official level with good comprehension if they are motivated to do so.

Reports for parents can also be generated. Home Connect is one of the features of AR that allows parents and guardians to monitor what their children are reading (see Figure 2.1).

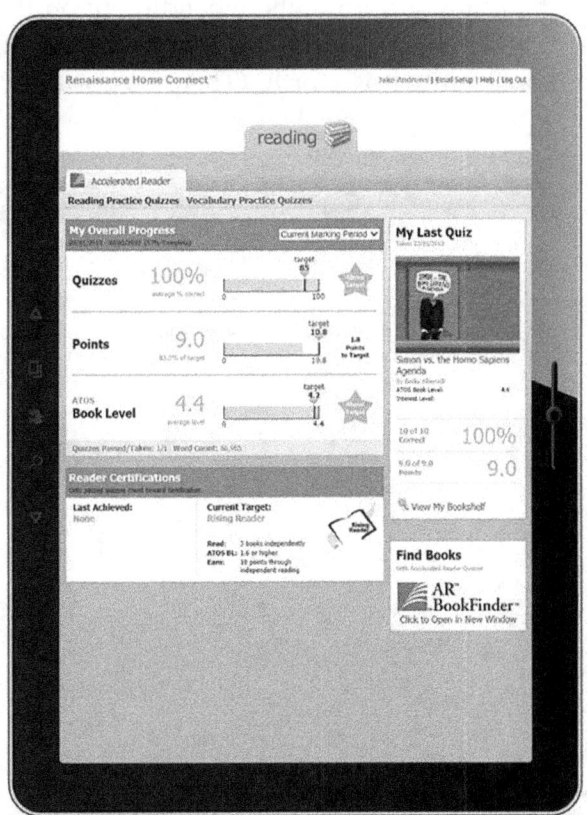

FIGURE 2.1 Screenshot of Home Connect

How Quizzes are Developed

Reading Practice Quizzes assess comprehension of the book through multiple-choice questions (see Figure 2.2). These quizzes comprise 5, 10 or 20 items (the number of questions increasing with the difficulty level and length of the book), about significant events, characters, and literal features of a book, and are presented in line with the chronology of the book. Reading Practice quiz questions are literal rather than open-ended and are presented in multiple-choice format but cannot be answered on the basis of having read a summary or seen an associated film. They are literal because this was found to give the most stable and reliable results. Renaissance Learning has a dedicated team of quiz development specialists. In total, quizzes are available for more than 200,000 books, many of which are non-fiction. Each book is worth a certain number of points depending upon the reading level, length and complexity of the book; the more difficult the book, the more points it is worth. (There is, however, an issue

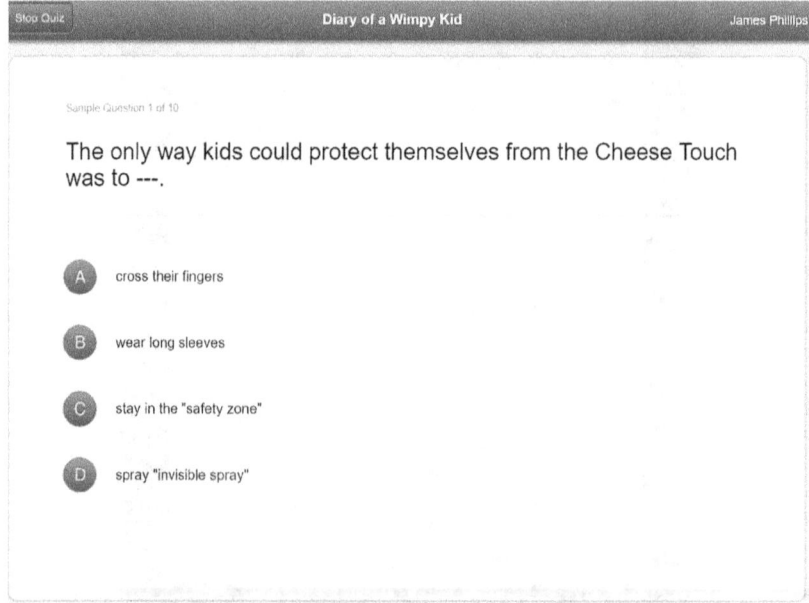

FIGURE 2.2 Screenshot of a Reading Practice Quiz

about whether the points provide sufficient feedback on correctness for the student.)

Pass rates are set at 60% for shorter quizzes and 70% for longer ones. Unless the quiz is passed, there are no points allocated and the student is not able to see which questions they got right or wrong. An 85% accuracy rate is approximately the level at which optimal reading growth starts to happen – where texts are challenging but are understood. AR has been criticized in the past for narrowing the reading of books to those for which quizzes were available, but the number of quizzes is now so large and all are available to all students, so this seems unlikely to still be the case. About 200 new reading practice quizzes are added to the program every month.

Recorded Voice quizzes are also available for beginning readers and students learning English. Every short quiz has a recorded voice quiz available. These quizzes are professionally recorded by a narrator who reads the quiz questions and answer choices as they appear on screen. Vocabulary Practice Quizzes measure a student's command of vocabulary words encountered while reading. These quizzes are designed to reinforce vocabulary acquisition, assist with individualizing vocabulary instruction and generate student interest in words through authentic, in-context literature experiences. Such quizzes include 5, 10 or 15 words from a particular book as well as review words from previously read books.

Additionally, AR Literacy Skills Quizzes are designed to give teachers information on 24 specific higher-order comprehension and thinking skills (Figure 2.3), but these are not so reliable and not that popular with teachers. Questions are randomly generated from a 36- or 60-item bank, resulting in 12 or 24 quiz questions. Owing to item-bank technology, Literacy Skills Quizzes can be taken up to three times. Additional quiz types include Spanish quizzes (based on Spanish books, for Spanish bilingual and Spanish language learning students).

Available titles are found using AR Bookfinder (https://www.arbookfind.com), which enables search by Lexile or ATOS (Advantage/TASA Open Standard for Readability) level as well as by title and author. Bookfinder makes book selection easy

18 ◆ What is Computer Assessment of Reading Comprehension

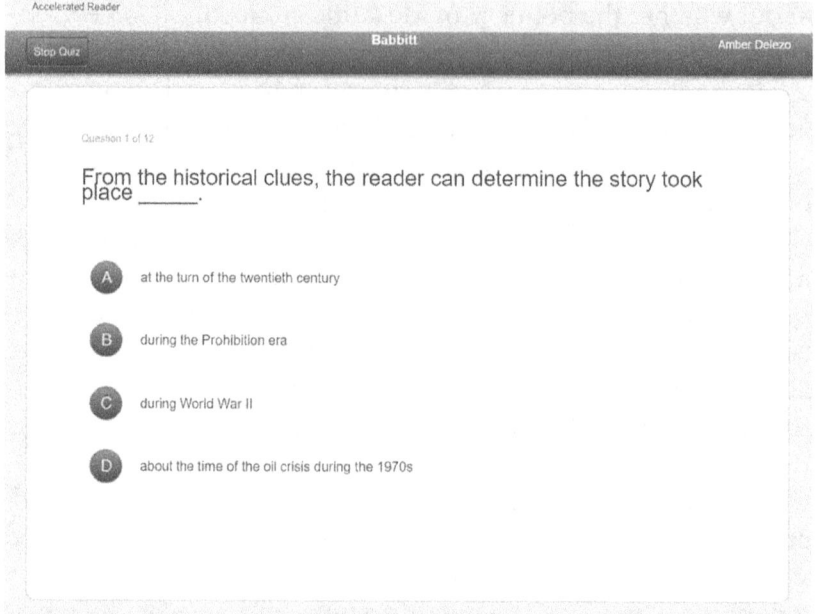

FIGURE 2.3 Screenshot of a Literacy Skills Quiz

for students (as well as teachers, parents and librarians) by providing descriptions about each book for which an AR quiz is available as well as having specialized search tools so students can, for example, identify award-winning books or match particular interests in other areas (see Figure 2.4).

Leveling of Books

Book difficulty level is determined by the ATOS formula. This helps students, teachers and parents with the book selection process. It is usually marked on the book, so students can make sure that they are choosing books that are not too easy or too hard – challenging without causing frustration or loss of motivation. ATOS uses four factors to determine readability: average sentence length, average word length, word difficulty level and the total number of words in the book. The entire book is scanned and the formula applied to the whole book – not a small sample of text as with other formulae. ATOS gives a figure which is directly related to grade levels. In order to relate the ATOS levels to the

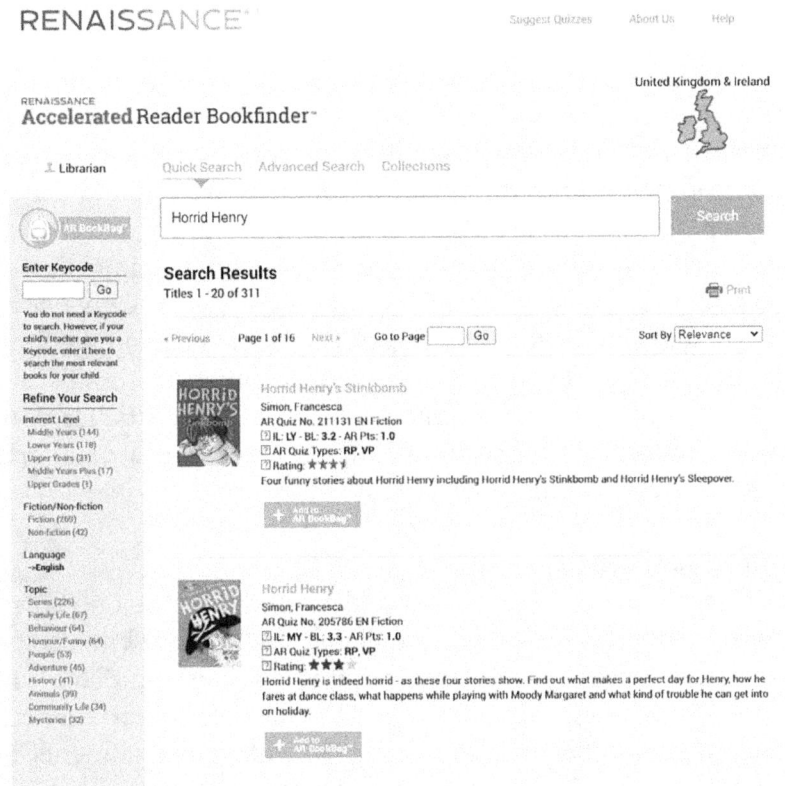

FIGURE 2.4 Screenshot of AR Bookfinder

British system, '1' would have to be added to bring the difficulty level up to English, Welsh and Northern Irish Years and '2' added to bring it up to Scottish P years. Other text can be analyzed for free at https://www1.renaissance.com/Products/Accelerated-Reader/ATOS/ATOS-Analyzer-for-Books. It is important to note that readability formulas typically produce an estimate of a book's text difficulty but not the suitability of a book's content or literary merit for individual readers. Additional information to support book selection (such as interest level and student ratings) can be found in AR Book Finder.

The utility of levelling books has been debated by Houston (2008). In 2012, Benjamin (2012) published a review of readability, finding that "for general reading of connected text, the New Dale-Chall Readability Formula, Lexile and ATOS have been widely tested and proven to be largely reliable and valid for predicting comprehension of texts among readers of wide-ranging ages and abilities." ATOS had strengths in "its extensive development phase and the large databank of student reading performance that the company was able to use in developing it". Nelson, Perfetti, Liben and Liben (2012) analyzed Lexiles and ATOS and also Degrees of Reading Power (Questar Assessment, Inc.), REAP (Carnegie Mellon University), SourceRater (Educational Testing Service), the Pearson Reading Maturity Metric (Pearson Knowledge Technologies) and Coh-Metrix (University of Memphis). ATOS performed better than Lexiles or Degrees of Reading Power on most measures, and REAP was particularly poor.

Training and Support
AR "Best Practices" recommend that students not only read books at appropriate levels of challenge and interest but also be given free choice in what they read. It is likely that students will frequently be assigned books to read as part of the core curriculum at their school, but it should be more likely that students be able to choose to read books about topics, characters, locations and so forth that are of interest to them. Once students learn to read, having choice over what they read is motivational.

AR is used because it saves time, motivates students to read and is more reliable and accurate than traditional methods of monitoring student book reading. However, it may require changes in teacher, classroom and even school practices. More time for in-school reading, establishing individualized target setting and careful monitoring of student reading comprehension are required. As a basic minimum, Renaissance Learning recommends 30 minutes of daily independent reading practice for elementary schools and 20 minutes of daily independent reading practice for secondary schools.

Renaissance Learning strongly recommends AR Best Practices to help ensure fidelity of implementation. Extensive research has shown it is not just the quantity of reading or time spent reading that helps students read well and become well-read.

It is also the level or degree of challenge in the book and the quality of comprehension or how carefully they read. The more carefully students read, the more they comprehend and the more their reading practice leads to improved reading achievement.

Reading Renaissance was a supplementary optional professional development program, but Renaissance Learning now markets AR + Star Reading + a professional development package as a single item. An in-person training session could be as short as one full school day (six hours) with no follow-up, and the number of participants is unlimited. Remote sessions occur via telephone and internet and can be scheduled on an hourly basis. A one-day training session with some ongoing contact has been a common choice amongst schools. The main purpose of training is to work with teachers on classroom implementation. (For example, introductory topics include goal setting, use of assessment tools and reports to monitor progress, and data use including diagnosis of problems and intervention and program evaluation. Advanced topics include book selection, working with struggling readers, and using quizzes to improve critical thinking skills.) Other training sessions are targeted towards librarians and to teachers working with special populations, such as English language learners, at-risk readers, or gifted students. Finally, training workshops are offered for teachers working with AR in summer school, after-school programs, and non-traditional environments.

In addition to receiving formal training, schools may purchase a contract to communicate with trainers or consultants on request via telephone. Subscribers may also access asynchronous, pre-recorded webinars and tutorials via the Renaissance Learning website.

What the Program Is Not

Renaissance Learning are very clear that AR is not an instructional program or method and that it is not a reward program. Renaissance Learning does not recommend that AR be linked to or associated with grades in schools.

In 1996, McQuillan reviewed the effects of extrinsic incentives on reading and found that, despite their popularity, reading incentives had not been critically examined as to their effectiveness in promoting more positive attitudes toward reading, more frequent reading, or increases in reading proficiency. He examined the available evidence on the effect of incentives on reading in school and public library programs for elementary and secondary students. It was concluded that there was no clear causal relationship in any of the studies between the use of rewards and an improvement in reading attitudes, achievement or habits. Putman (2005) demonstrated that students who accumulated the largest number of points on AR reported increases in reading self-efficacy but that students in groups who accumulated fewer than 35 points showed decreases. This underlines the importance of the teacher emphasizing the importance of enjoying reading than merely accumulating points and the importance of goal-setting for individuals.

A series of school-based field experiments in over 200 urban schools across three cities was reported by Fryer (2011), investigating the impact of financial incentives on student achievement. In Dallas, students were paid to read books. In Chicago, students were paid for classroom grades. In New York, students were rewarded for performance on interim assessments. The impact of financial incentives on student achievement was zero in all three cities. Only English-speaking students in Dallas showed the slightest effect. Similarly, Bettinger (2012) examined the utility of financial incentives for grade 3 through 6 students to pass their high-stakes tests. He found that math scores improved by about effect size (ES) 0.15 (a very small increase when compared with the cost of the program) but that reading, social science, and science test scores did not improve.

More specifically to the AR program, Brindger (2009) used extrinsic rewards allied to AR points with 56 gifted middle school students. *Even though both groups of students made some gains from the pretest to the post-test, the group that did not receive extrinsic motivation actually gained more than the group that did receive extrinsic motivation.* Gardiner (2014) offered an overview of rewards (mentioning AR) and concluded that they had no positive effect and often a negative effect, but he offered no new data.

Funding

Schools that implement both AR and its professional development program meet federal criteria for comprehensive school reform, resulting in eligibility for government grants as large as $225,000 over three years. From a financial perspective, this may provide a means and an incentive to introduce the program. Indeed, many schools wishing to fund the installation of AR seek external funding from the following: Title I, gifted and talented programs, English as a second language programs, grants, community foundations, parent groups, literacy partnership programs, school fundraisers, local business, philanthropists or charities. Renaissance Learning offers a kit to support schools in soliciting funds from business and civic leaders.

How It Is Used in Schools

One of the issues with AR is that it is possible to cheat, as only one version of the quiz questions is available (unlike RC, where several versions of the quiz questions are available to be used adaptively). Thus, if only one student has read the book and another student wants to be credited with the points, it is possible for students to tell each other the answers (if their memory is so good or they are quick and devious at taking notes). A quick search of YouTube will reveal that there are many videos which give the answers to quizzes on AR books, and Google also has many sites which encourage students to cheat. Teachers should be very careful if students want to take AR tests at home or out of school or otherwise away from supervision. All of these are further reasons not to link AR to extrinsic rewards.

Chapter 5 looks at what implementation should look like, and Chapter 6 at what evidence there is on actual implementation.

Reading Counts

Goals and Purposes

RC is a program that supports the independent reading of K–12 students and provides educators with actionable data to monitor effort and progress. For students, RC encourages independent reading through the following: personalized, leveled reading recommendations; quizzes to explore understanding of books; direct performance feedback; and recognition and acknowledgement. As students engage in the program, they gather points for their reading effort and receive targeted reading recommendations to help broaden their interests and improve their reading levels. Point allocation can be adjusted by the teacher. The Points Multiplier allows teachers to double or triple the normal point values if needed. There are about 75,000 quizzes related to high-quality books.

For teachers, RC provides the following: measurement tools that track student effort, progress and success; customized features for personalization and individual goal setting; and program flexibility to support a variety of implementations. RC automatically tracks students' reading choices, reading (in and out of school) and progress throughout the year. Reports can also be produced for parents or carers. The time-consuming tasks of creating and scoring quizzes, gathering data, and keeping records are automated. Educators can view student records at any time and receive alerts if an intervention is needed.

The point value for each book is determined by the number of words (length), text complexity and interest level. Points are awarded based upon the percentage of quiz questions answered correctly. The pass rate is set at 70% by default, but students are encouraged to aim for 80% as being the level at which the book is really understood. Teachers and students can set reading goals in terms of the point system. Struggling readers have the opportunity to retake quizzes – students are able to take the 10-question quiz three times because there are 30 questions in the item bank. Quiz settings can be customized based on individual students' needs for extra support or challenge. Books are labelled with the Lexile and grade-equivalent level to make it easy for students to identify suitably challenging books. The school needs to consider if RC will be reflected in grades and, if so, to what extent. Schools also need to consider if they will attach extrinsic rewards to points, but as we have seen in the AR section, this is unlikely to be effective and may be damaging.

RC includes a number of features to help encourage and motivate independent student reading. These features include congratulations screens, student reading reports, the Read-O-Meter device for indicating the extent to which they liked the book (which can be discussed with peers), points and certificates. There are reports for administrators, teachers and parents. Reading goals can be set. "Book Expert", a database of thousands of books (https://readingcountsbookexpert.tgds.hmhco.com/bookexpert/default.asp), enables search of books by title, author, language (English or Spanish), book type (fiction or non-fiction), Lexile measure, genre and topic. RC helps students select reading options that match their Lexile scores and personal interests. RC is the current name, but this might change in the future.

RC is available as a separate program, but mostly it is embedded in Read 180, a program that includes computer assessment and feedback but also small group teacher instruction and independent reading (thus being much more complex than RC alone). Read 180 is mainly targeted at the second quartile of reading ability (i.e., 25th–50th), not the whole range of readers. System 44 is for even lower-ability readers. Read 180 is equally balanced between fiction and non-fiction.

Read 180 is an evidence-based intervention for striving readers (reading two or more years below grade level) in the late elementary, middle, and high school grades. It provides blended learning instruction (i.e., combining digital media with traditional classroom instruction), student assessment, and teacher professional development. Read 180 is typically delivered in 45- to 90-minute sessions that include whole-group instruction, three small-group rotations, and whole-class wrap-up. Small-group rotations include individualized instruction using an adaptive computer application, small-group instruction with a teacher, and independent reading.

System 44 is an intervention program designed to build foundational reading and decoding skills for the most challenged readers (the bottom quartile). This blended learning solution includes daily reading, writing, talking, and critical-thinking exercises. Materials feature modeled and independent reading with age-appropriate books that target decoding skills and strategies to promote comprehension, build vocabulary, and increase content-area knowledge. Using adaptive technology, students complete a personalized learning progression through five strands that include the code, word strategies, sight words, success and writing.

So, AR and RC are not competition but are different.

How Quizzes are Developed

First, the classroom teacher or librarian administers the computer-adaptive Reading Inventory (https://www.hmhco.com/programs/reading-inventory) as a reading placement test to all students. It measures student reading levels by assessing understanding of authentic text passages. It is a computer-adaptive test – when a student answers a question correctly, the next question will be more difficult; but if the student answers a question incorrectly, the next question will be easier. This process continues until a strong level of certainty of the test taker's ability has been established – then the test ends and a scale score is provided. This test provides a Personal Lexile score for each student. The reports also list the students' optimal Lexile text readability levels (a numerical range).

Once students know their reading levels, they can select books from Book Expert (https://readingcountsbookexpert.tgds.hmhco.com) within these reading levels. Book Expert is a searchable database which provides information about books supported by RC tests, enabling searching by title, author, grade level, Lexile measure and other criteria to obtain annotated descriptions and key metrics. Although RC is a Lexile-based program, it also includes grade-level equivalency and guided reading levels in the search engine. Additional filters include grade-level interest (K–2, 3–5, 6–8, high school, and high interest/intervention), fiction and non-fiction, subject areas, genre, and curriculum-integrated books.

Quizzes are the most critical component of RC, testing independent basic reading comprehension. Scoring is automatic and feedback is immediate (see Figure 2.5). Quizzes are cheat-proof because each quiz is made up of a randomly selected set of questions from the 30-item database, which means that no two tests

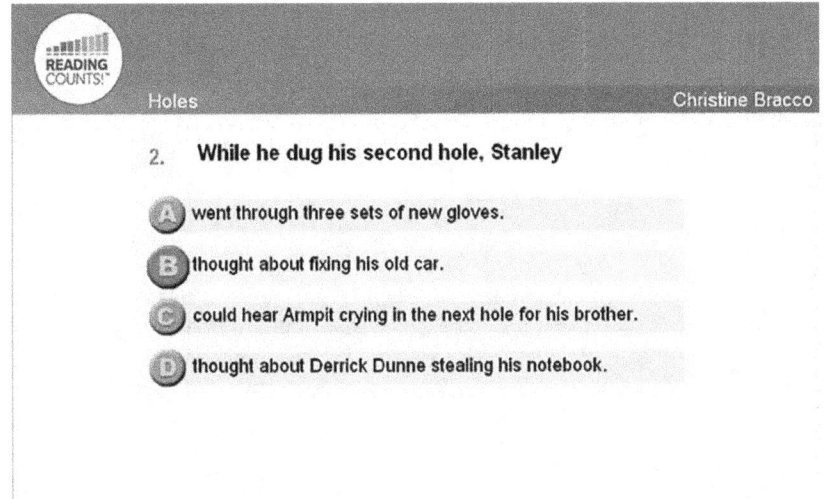

FIGURE 2.5 Reading Counts Quiz

are alike. Multiple-choice quizzes feature the following: straightforward presentation of questions with non-ambiguous answers; highlighted answer choices so students know when they have selected the correct answer; customization that allows educators to adjust the length of quizzes to support students with low frustration levels; and varied quiz question formats to include embedded cloze, modified cloze, direct questions, and complete-the-stem questions to help students think about responses.

Teachers can customize the quiz by doing the following: modifying the number of questions per quiz (5–30; default is 10); establishing a passing rate for the quiz (0%–100%; default is 70%); determining the number of quiz attempts allowed (1–6 times; default is 3); and deciding on the number of days between retakes (default is 24 hours). RC also allows teachers and students (with teacher supervision) to develop custom quizzes. Teachers can create quizzes to do the following: support books of local interest, assess students on specific skills or content, create chapter quizzes for longer titles, and provide assessment for books that are part of the curriculum.

Congratulations screens provide immediate feedback to students after completing a quiz successfully. On the Book Interest

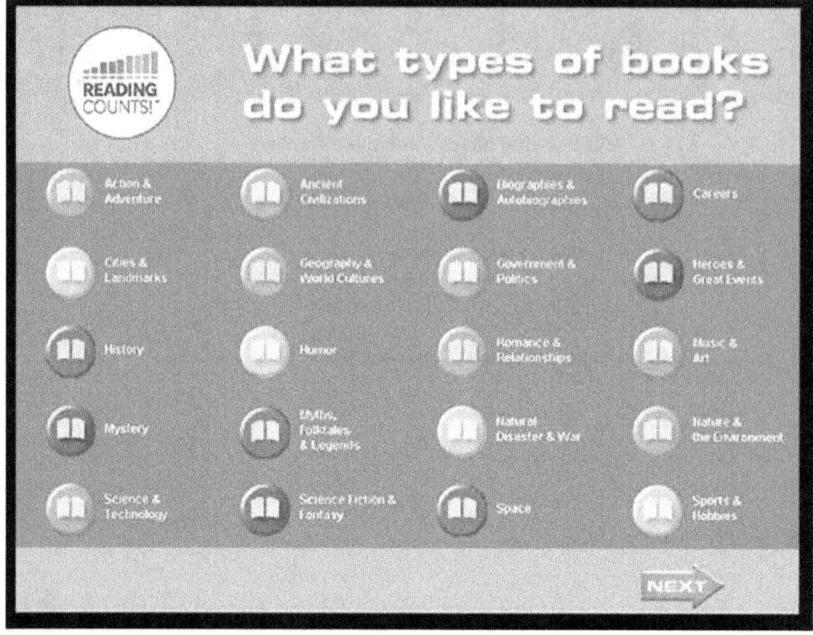

FIGURE 2.6 Book Interest Screen

Screen, students are asked to select three topics of interest. These interests will be reflected in the Recommended Reading Report (Figure 2.6).

When students pass a quiz, they use the Read-O-Meter to give a personal rating of the book (Figure 2.7). The Student Achievement Manager (SAM) records these student ratings in the Book Frequency and Rating Report.

RC also supports group reading and literature circles. Students can work together but be assessed separately.

Levelling of Books

RC is based on Lexiles, which range from 0 to 2000 (rounded to the nearest 10) and are based on measures of word frequency (the semantic variable) and sentence length (a proxy for syntactic complexity) for the whole text. Lexiles corelate highly with reading comprehension tests ($r = 0.84, 0.93$). Each book has a Lexile measurement. For example, *Harry Potter and the Prisoner of Azkaban*

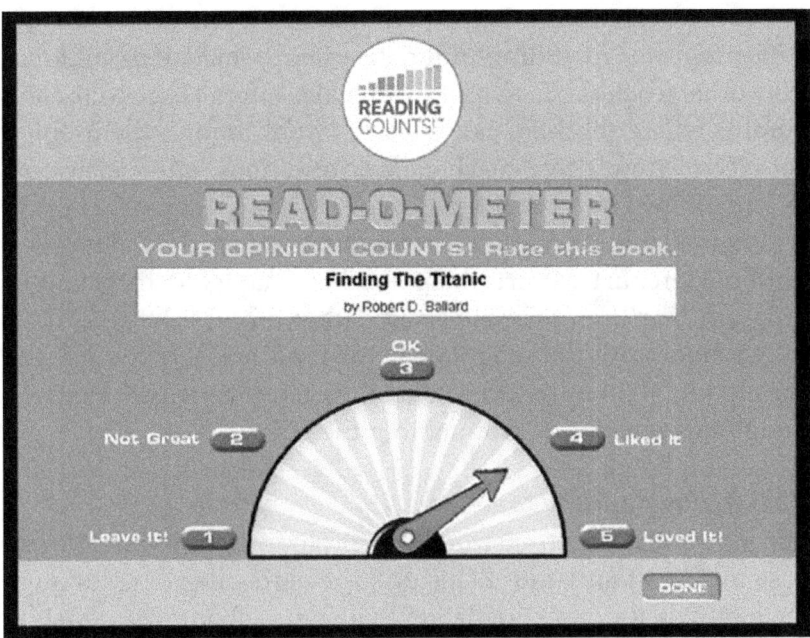

FIGURE 2.7 Read-o-Meter

has a Lexile measurement of 880L. A student also gets a Lexile reading measure from a reading test (e.g., 880L). The match or otherwise between the book measure and the student measure indicates whether that book is currently suitable for that student in terms of reading difficulty, and if it is, a comprehension rate of 75% can be expected. Readers tend to make the most progress when they are provided with books that match their reading level. Reading books that are too easy results in little challenge, and reading books that are too difficult can result in frustration. However, some students can read books above their level with high comprehension if they are highly motivated.

Training and Support

RC has a number of supporting professional development sources and resources. Ed is a learning platform focused on successful program implementation. Teachers' Corner provides teachers with a library of professional learning resources designed to help them maximize the effect of their new program, including authentic classroom videos and tips from other teachers. Teacher's Corner also offers a Facebook community where teachers can discuss issues among themselves, get advice from other teachers, ask questions, and participate in live Office Hours and other live sessions. Technical support is also available on request. Free webinars hosted by Houghton Mifflin Harcourt experts help teachers navigate their online program. The Professional Services team discusses the needs of each school with the school. It helps if all teachers are already enrolled in RC so the professional development can focus on actual data emanating from within the school.

What the Program Is Not

RC is not of itself an instructional program, but Read 180 and System 44 certainly are. RC is not a reward program, although the manuals for it acknowledge that some schools may wish to use extrinsic rewards, and some of the literature cited under AR applies here also.

Funding

Subscription Licenses allow a school or district to do the following: access the program software and all quiz assets online through a browser; host RC remotely on Houghton Mifflin Harcourt servers; automatically receive quiz updates monthly; automatically receive new versions and technical updates; and renew annually to receive continued access to the entire program, including all currently published quizzes. Whereas RC alone is relatively inexpensive, Read 180 or System 44 are considerably more expensive. Schools sometimes use funds from philanthropists or charities to purchase these packages.

How It Is Used in Schools

Like AR, RC is theoretically open to cheating, and an internet search will show that there are sites dedicated to this. However, the number of sites is much less than with AR, partly because the program is not so widely used as AR and partly because RC has quizzes which are item-banked, so it is much more difficult to cheat on them.

Chapter 5 looks at what implementation should look like, and Chapter 6 at what evidence there is on actual implementation.

Chapter Summary

Accelerated Reader

AR enables computer-based individual assessment of comprehension of self-chosen independently read real books and provides instant feedback to the student. AR covers both fiction and non-fiction reading for prekindergarten through 12th grade. The feedback to students enables them to reflect on their own thought processes and strategies (encouraging metacognition) and take appropriate action when choosing their next book. AR is also a progress-monitoring system that helps teachers accurately and efficiently monitor student progress in comprehension (quality), quantity, difficulty of books read and quiz scores. Through many different kinds of reports, teachers can look at patterns for the whole class (or school) and take whatever action is needed (e.g., shape subsequent reading instruction, guide individual students, discuss choosing books with the whole class, and motivate students to continue reading).

The Star Reading computer-based adaptive reading comprehension test is often used to indicate the student's starting reading level and a "zone of proximal development". Renaissance Learning recommends a minimum of 30 minutes of daily independent reading practice for elementary schools and 20 minutes for secondary schools. Renaissance Learning is very clear that AR is not an instructional program or method and that it is not a reward program. Nor does Renaissance Learning recommend that AR be linked to or associated with grades in schools.

Reading Practice Quizzes comprise 5, 10 or 20 multiple-choice items (the number of questions increasing with the difficulty level and length of the book), are literal rather than open-ended (for stability and reliability), but cannot be answered on the basis of having read a summary or seen an associated film. Quizzes are available for more than 200,000 books, and 200 new quizzes are added every month. Pass rates are 60% for shorter quizzes and 70% for longer ones, but an 85% accuracy rate is recommended for optimal reading growth. AR allows teachers to develop custom quizzes. There are also Recorded Voice quizzes, Vocabulary Practice quizzes, Literacy Skills quizzes (covering 24 specific higher-order comprehension and thinking skills) and Spanish quizzes (based on Spanish books, for Spanish bilingual and Spanish language learning students). Available titles are found using AR Bookfinder, which enables search by Lexile or ATOS level as well as title and author.

Book difficulty level is determined by the ATOS formula, usually marked on the book, so students can be sure they are choosing books that are not too easy or too hard. ATOS scans the whole book and uses four factors to determine readability: average sentence length, average word length, word difficulty level and the total number of words in the book. Points for success on book quizzes are based on the difficulty of the books. Students can set goals for themselves in terms of successful reading. For beginning readers, the emphasis is on reading to or with students. Students also have the opportunity to rate the book after they have read it, and student choices of Favorite Books are recorded. Reports for parents can also be generated. Home Connect allows parents and guardians to monitor what their children are reading.

Initiating AR involves dedicating more time for in-school reading, establishing individualized target setting and careful monitoring of student reading comprehension. Both remote and face-to-face training sessions, varying in length and frequency, are available. It is possible to cheat with AR. Teachers should be very careful if students want to take AR tests at home or out of school or otherwise away from supervision.

Reading Counts
In many ways, RC is similar to AR but has some additional features. RC has about 75,000 book tests (RC tends to call them tests rather than quizzes). The program is based on Lexiles, which range from 0 to 2000 and are based on word frequency

and sentence length for the whole text. Books are labelled with the Lexile and grade-equivalent level. Points are awarded based upon the percentage of quiz questions answered correctly. The pass rate is set at 70% by default, but students are encouraged to aim for 80%. Reading goals can be set.

First, the teacher administers the computer-adaptive Reading Inventory as a placement test. Once students know their reading levels, they can select books from the Book Expert information database within these. Quizzes are cheat-proof because each quiz is made up of a randomly selected set of questions from the 30-item database, which means that no two tests are alike. Varied quiz question formats include embedded cloze, modified cloze, direct questions, and complete-the-stem questions. Teachers can customize quizzes to suit the needs of individual students by doing the following: modifying the number of questions per quiz (5–30; default is 10); establishing a passing rate for the quiz (0%–100%; default is 70%); determining the number of quiz attempts allowed (1–6 times; default is 3) (because there are 30 questions in the item bank, struggling readers can take the 10-question quiz three times); deciding on the number of days between retakes (default is 24 hours); and adjusting point allocation. Many of these features are not found in AR, but the proportion of teachers using them is small. RC allows teachers and students (with teacher supervision) to develop custom quizzes. RC has congratulations screens, student reading reports, certificates and the Read-O-Meter device for indicating the extent to which students liked the book.

RC is available as a separate program, but mostly it is embedded in Read 180, which includes computer assessment and feedback, but also small group teacher instruction and independent reading, and is mainly targeted on lower-ability readers. In terms of supportive professional development sources, RC offers a range of mostly online initiatives, access to which is driven by the enquiring teacher. The kind of training courses associated with AR do not seem to be offered. Securing funding for RC does not seem to be as well supported as is the case for AR. RC is theoretically vulnerable to cheating, but partly because of the adaptive nature of RC quizzes, this is not such a problem as with

AR. RC is not an instructional program, but Read 180 and System 44 certainly are. RC is not a reward program. So, AR and RC are not in competition but are different.

References

Benjamin, R. G. (2012). Reconstructing readability: Recent developments and recommendations in the analysis of text difficulty. *Educational Psychology Review*, *24*(1), 63–88.

Bettinger, E. P. (2012). Paying to learn: The effect of financial incentives on elementary school test scores. *The Review of Economics and Statistics*, *94*(3), 686–698.

Brindger, C. (2009). The effects of Accelerated Reader (AR) as an extrinsic motivation tool for improving gifted students' reading levels. *The Corinthian*, *10*, Article 5. https://kb.gcsu.edu/thecorinthian/vol10/iss1/5

Cox, D. (2012). Is Accelerated Reader best practice for all? *The California Reader*, *46*(1), 14–22. https://www.researchgate.net/profile/Donna-Cox-4/publication/309604377_Is_Accelerated_Reader_Best_Practice_for_All/links/5819354108ae50812f5de729/Is-Accelerated-Reader-Best-Practice-for-All.pdf

Fryer, R. G. Jr. (2011). Financial incentives and student achievement: Evidence from randomized trials. *The Quarterly Journal of Economics*, *126*(4), 1755–1798.

Gardiner, S. (2014). Stop the pay, stop the play. *Phi Delta Kappan*, *95*(8), 39–42.

Houston, C. R. (2008). The use of reading levels as alternative classification in school libraries. *Cataloging & Classification Quarterly*, *45*(4), 65–80. DOI:10.1300/J104v45n04_05

Kettle, K., & Häubl, G., (2010). Motivation by anticipation: Expecting rapid feedback enhances performance. *Psychological Science*, *31*(2), 545–547.

McQuillan, J. (1996). The effects of incentives on reading. *Reading Research and Instruction*, *36*(2), 111–125. DOI:10.1080/19388079709558232

Nelson, J., Perfetti, C., Liben, D., & Liben, M. (2012). *Measures of text complexity: Testing their predictive value for grade levels and student performance. Technical Report to the Gates Foundation.* https://

achievethecore.org/content/upload/nelson_perfetti_liben_measures_of_text_difficulty_research_ela.pdf

Putman, S. M. (2005). Computer-based reading technology in the classroom: The affective influence of performance contingent point accumulation on 4thgrade students. *Reading Research and Instruction, 45*(1), 19–38. DOI:10.1080/19388070509558440

Samuels, S. J., & Wu, Y. C. (2003). *The effects of immediate feedback on reading achievement.* Minneapolis, MN: University of Minnesota. https://web.archive.org/web/20060423031356/http://www.tc.umn.edu/~samue001/web%20pdf/immediate_feedback.pdf

Yeh, S. S. (2010). Understanding and addressing the achievement gap through individualized instruction and formative assessment. *Assessment in Education, 17*(2), 169–182. DOI:10.1080/09695941003694466

3

Disentangling Opinion and Fact

Any new development which becomes large enough to be significant, in education and in other fields, soon attracts onlookers who have an opinion about it. Unfortunately, some of these onlookers do not stop to consider the evidence or they look at the evidence through very tinted glasses, and sometimes their opinions do not stand up to investigation. This chapter will consider such perceptions and opinions (generally negative ones) and consider how closely related they are to the evidence. Curiously, most of the complaints are about Accelerated Reader (AR), and there has been very little about Reading Counts (RC) and nothing about the other three programs, although they all follow a somewhat similar model.

One of the main complaints is that AR is a "reward program", so students read only for extrinsic reward and as soon as the reward is no longer available, they stop reading – so the argument goes that AR is certainly not a way to ensure a sustained interest in books. This is all based on a misapprehension and relates to the way AR has sometimes been implemented in a particular country – the USA. In the US, some schools have in the past certainly chosen to link AR success to extrinsic rewards, such as pizza – regardless of whether all the readers actually needed such an artificial device to motivate them. In other countries, this has been much less likely and is used (if at all) only with students

DOI: 10.4324/9781003215882-3

with a reading disability who might otherwise never pick up a book of any sort. It is unsurprising that many of the complaints about AR emanate from the US rather than any other country.

Renaissance Learning's position on this is clear and has been stated repeatedly – they say that AR is NOT a rewards program but a way to motivate and encourage student independent reading by providing swift feedback on the success of reading comprehension. Giving extrinsic rewards to the students who perform the best in the class will do nothing for the weaker readers, who are likely never to earn any rewards, feel disenfranchised and learn to dislike the AR system. Ah, you might say, but what about giving rewards in an individualized manner, to each student depending on whether that student has achieved their personal goals? Well, that might make a bit more sense, assuming that weaker readers can set appropriate goals for themselves, but it still leaves many readers being "rewarded" when it is not necessary and indeed may be counter-productive. Another idea is the awarding of books as prizes for increased reading, and at least that is more closely connected to the behavior to be improved, but again many students will earn prize books that they do not need and which have no effect – has the education system got that much spare money?

However, students do like feedback, especially if it is quick in relation to the performance being appraised, and AR gives them quick feedback without their having to wait for the teacher to get round to it. Some commentators disagree with the idea of any kind of "test" of understanding of a book, arguing that attaching such a test to a book is likely to lead to students focusing on passing the test rather than enjoying the book. That may be true up to a point, but the quiz is so quick compared with the long amount of time spent reading the book that it seems unlikely that many students will dwell on the test, especially in educational times when they are surrounded by other, weightier, tests. And the quiz certainly sorts out those who have read the book from those who have read a bit of it or seen the film and are essentially trying to hoodwink the teacher. However, the "points" that are awarded as a form of feedback might not be understood by all students since they are not necessarily in the form of percentage correct, which would be more readily understood. Perhaps the designers of these programs could give more attention to the nature and comprehensibility of feedback that the programs give.

Another cause for complaint has been that the quiz questions are all literal – they do not explore higher and more complex responses to the book. It is perfectly true that the main quiz questions are literal, and as Renaissance Learning explains, this is because literal questions are the only kind that give reliable and valid answers. Asking for students' extended speculative thoughts about a book is all very well and certainly desirable, but it cannot be done reliably within the context of a multiple-choice quiz. Teachers may well seek to elicit this kind of response, as well as have students use AR, but they will have time to do it on only a very few books. Renaissance Learning does also produce measures which seek to elicit more speculative and extendedly thoughtful responses from students (e.g., Literacy Skills quizzes), but these are not nearly so reliable and teachers have not chosen to use them very much.

Some commentators in the past have complained that where a school did not have many "AR books" which had quizzes, students were often diverted from other books (in which they might have been more interested) because the teachers told them to read the "AR books". These days that complaint is not relevant as such a huge number of quizzes are available and schools are charged per student, not per batch of quizzes. Nonetheless, Renaissance Learning is very clear that students should be allowed to read any book they want to read, whether it has a quiz or not.

Over the years, at least 18 authors have critiqued AR, and it has become something of a way to build a career. It started with Alfie Kohn (1993) (but this was a book "Punished by Rewards" and so will not be discussed here). Kohn's (2010) more recent ideas are not that different, however. He notes that reward and punishment are associated with power – power that the teacher has but the student does not have. He asserts that reading should not be surrounded with commands and that requiring book reports demotivates students. Instead, he encourages peer feedback and developing a community of readers. He is very negative about extrinsic rewards for reading and (mistakenly) mentions AR as promoting this. He discourages a total focus on teaching the skills of reading. Teachers should not over-test or spend time preparing students for tests (easier said than done in some countries like the USA). Students should have free choice of books, and teachers need to realize that education is done *with* students rather than *to* them. Kohn has published very few peer-reviewed journal articles but many books. His publications make little reference to research literature, and he is famous for his opinions rather than his contribution to science.

While one can sympathize with some of Kohn's opinions, a more complete lambasting of AR and Electronic Bookshelf (later to become RC) was offered by Betty Carter (1996), a librarian who might have known what she was talking about. Although the programs increased library circulation and reading test scores, they "devalued reading, diminished motivation, limited title choice, restricted materials selection and collection development, discouraged independent selection of books, and emphasized testing rather than needs". While limited title choice might have been a problem when she was writing, it is not now. Otherwise, it is very difficult to see what these complaints actually mean, and as no evidence is offered, we are left in the dark.

Jean Stevenson and Jenny Camarata (2000) compared AR to a "whole language program" (although AR was never intended to comprise the whole of reading instruction in a classroom and is perfectly compatible with a whole language approach). The authors argued that AR involves "earning points toward prizes" and implied that reading is an isolated and competitive activity – none of which is true. The "evidence" offered was anecdotal selected classroom stories. These authors later offered a further commentary (Stevenson & Camarata, 2005) which argued that AR "controls the curriculum by determining what books children read and what books teachers use" – clearly not true. They added that "AR is fast becoming the primary reading program in many school districts" – clearly not true. They continued: "students, teachers, and schools within a district are often encouraged to compete with each other" – if this is the case (and no evidence for this statement is offered), there is nothing within the AR program that suggests it. They also complained about "inaccurate and inappropriate leveling of books", even though the ATOS (Advantage/TASA Open Standard for Readability) levelling system used by Renaissance is recognized as at least equal to the best available.

They raised the question "what will have to be dropped from the curriculum in order to incorporate the program?", which is perfectly reasonable as, of course, something needs to go to make way for anything new. The issue is whether what is dropped was actually less effective than AR and had fewer advantages and more real disadvantages even when properly implemented. If not, there was no point dropping it. Any school considering implementation of AR would be well advised to operate a small pilot first to evaluate the program before launching into larger-scale investment. Stevenson and Camarata (2005) also commented on teachers who did not wish to participate since they were feeling pressured by students who wished to be involved because otherwise, they were missing out on extrinsic rewards. Clearly, extrinsic rewards are a major problem, but one that is peculiar to the USA. Students voicing their opinions is not an issue of concern, but voicing their opinions in this narrowly focused way clearly is.

Some of these complaints were echoed by Deborah Biggers (2001) but in a much more balanced way. Biggers argues that the implementation of AR in schools may lead teachers to believe that reading is somehow "taken care of" and this may cause them to pay less attention to other aspects of the reading process which they had previously pursued. This may be true (no evidence is given), but it is difficult to see why AR should be blamed since this could equally apply to any other innovation. Biggers also noted (as did Stevenson and Camarata above) that Renaissance Learning does not interpret the Zone of Proximal Development (ZPD) precisely as Vygotsky (1978) had described it, but nonetheless take Vygotsky's name in vain in passing. Vygotsky's idea of the ZPD was that it represented the zone in which a student could not learn unaided but could learn with the help of others, while Renaissance Learning (and, to some extent, Houghton Mifflin Harcourt) interprets it as the range of difficulty in which individual growth is possible (i.e., the book is not too easy). Greater acknowledgement of this difference would certainly be welcomed.

Goodson, Tardrew, Kerns, Pavonetti and Cipielewski (2003) features an interesting exchange of letters to the editor of the journal, Tardrew and Kerns responding to Pavonetti and Cipielewski's article (which is not discussed here but in Chapter 4). Tardrew and Kerns argued that the article contained several mistruths which were not substantiated by the evidence in the article. The authors responded by saying that they did not think AR would ever replace teachers. Well, of course not – actually AR, when properly implemented, makes considerable demands on the teacher, who is certainly irreplaceable.

McCarthy (2003) offered a more balanced perspective, describing AR accurately and pointing out that *some* schools (in the US) choose to link points to prizes (which we have already debated above). She concludes that AR should not be the determining factor of what books are in school library media collections (of course not, although the number of quizzes is now so large that almost every book a student would want to read has a quiz) nor influence what books students can select and read independently from those collections. (It is not clear how AR is supposed to do this – if it is done, it is done by the teachers of their own volition.)

A more evidence-based approach was offered by Stephen Krashen (2003, 2005). Unfortunately, there was an error in the first paragraph of his 2003 paper – "children can exchange their points for prizes". Krashen was happy that students had more access to books and had more time to read books. He further analyzed a number of studies not published in peer-reviewed journals (and so not discussed in this book), but he emphasized the value of studies which used a control or comparison group. These included Peak and Dewalt (1994), Pavonetti et al. (2002), and Vollands, Topping and Evans (1999). He notes that Peak and Dewalt (1994) found positive effects. Vollands et al. (1999) found some positive effects, but the study had several methodological problems, as the authors acknowledge. Krashen concludes by berating the use of extrinsic rewards, even though none was used in the study by Vollands et al. Pavonetti et al. (2002) did not find positive effects (but there was no evidence of implementation quality). The limited amount of research discussed in the 2003 paper has since been overtaken by a great deal more, a little of which was addressed by Krashen in an update (2005). This referred to the study by Malette, et al. (2004), which found that AR improved attitudes to academic reading but not recreational reading (but see the definitions of these in Chapter 4) and that low-ability students had a lower self-mage with AR (which may well have been due to the use of extrinsic rewards).

Cheri Triplett (2004) offered a qualitative case study of a struggling reader, focusing on the emotions experienced by the student. "Mitchell" reported "feeling bad" when he "never got the prizes" offered by AR. He also reported that he "felt bad for his friends" from other classes who weren't good readers because they never got their points and they "hated Accelerated Reader." However, he was now really happy that his teacher set individual goals that everyone could reach. Apart from the problems of arguing from a sample of one, this study also assumed that extrinsic rewards are part of AR but pointed a way out of this dilemma – with teacher behavior varying, not AR. Triplett attributed various undesirable elements to AR which were, in fact, in the purview of the teacher.

Joette Stefl-Mabry (2005) describes AR accurately as it was in 2005 (although it is now very different). She refers to Krashen (2003, 2005) for a "more thorough" evaluation of the research evidence and goes on to repeat much of it and add some studies which are mostly outside the scope of this book (e.g., master's theses). Stefl-Mabry usefully discusses the problem of time allocated to reading – which is usually insufficient – and notes that Sustained Silent Reading (SSR) has been making the same plea for many years – except SSR does not include the element of accountability. Overall, this paper is one of the more balanced papers cited in this chapter.

"Teacher implementation of the AR program is as widespread as it is diverse", noted Robin and Eric Groce (2005) as a first sentence in one of the few papers so far in this chapter to raise the issue of implementation quality. However, they went on to cite many of the papers referred to above. Their own survey indicated that about half of their teachers were not implementing AR as suggested by Renaissance Learning. They concluded that students may be missing out on critical-thinking, higher-order, and aesthetic activities, although why AR might be to blame for this is never explained.

The other famous name in the anti-AR camp is Jim Trelease (2001), and although this was a book, we nevertheless feel obliged to mention it. Like Alfie Kohn, Trelease has virtually no peer-reviewed journal articles to his name – he is famous for his opinions. Unfortunately, he starts with a misconception: "Passing the computer quiz earns points which can be redeemed for prizes". Nonetheless, Trelease offers a list of eight positive outcomes from the use of AR and RC (but no evidence to support them). He concedes that he hears ten times more positives than negatives and adds "Where's the problem here? Certainly, it's not with the computer program." Much of what follows discusses the misuse of AR and RC.

Renita Schmidt (2008) repeats the faulty assumption about AR: "students take AR tests and are rewarded with points, which may be used to purchase awards, toys, snacks, stickers, or other rewards deemed suitable by individual schools". She had realized that she valued "the cultural or discourse model" of reading and saw AR as "emphasizing numbers and efficiency and encouraging a positivist and more behaviorist way of reading". While this philosophical (epistemological) stance is, of course, justifiable (albeit stated here in terms which could well be contested), this is clearly a teacher who is content to impose her own philosophy on classrooms full of students with no concern as to what their philosophical stance might be. She quotes student survey responses favorable to AR but criticizes these as inappropriate.

Gail Thompson, Marga Madhuri and Deborah Taylor (2008) focus on the effects of AR with high school students, having used interviews and focus groups with a small group of them – but they were students from an under-performing school that had only recently purchased the program and AR was tied to course grades. Students complained that the amount of reading required was unrealistic and too time-consuming; they did not like being "forced" to read; they did not enjoy the book selections; they resented their course grade being tied to earning points for reading; and they disliked having to pass tests. Apart from the AR-to-grade link (which was the school's choice and not a sensible one at the point of introduction of the program), the students were, in fact, not "forced" to read and were free to choose their own books. More time spent reading is, of course, a key requirement (as it would be with SSR), and it is perhaps unsurprising that these students were resistant at this stage. Likewise, taking quizzes is a key feature of AR – why did these students not want to be accountable for what they had read (or had not actually read, as the case might be)? Why did the school not make participation voluntary to start? The students' complaints revealed that part of the problem with the program was its implementation, which caused it to be ineffective in the students' eyes. The authors conclude with a plea to "listen to the students".

By contrast, Mariana Souto-Manning (2010) studied AR with seven-year-old students – emergent readers, who nonetheless made similar complaints – that they were not being listened to. She accused AR of "limiting choice and disregarding teacher expertise (a software program makes reading assignments based on multiple-choice tests)". Quite apart from this not being true, the studies of implementation variation above clearly show that AR does not disregard teacher expertise. The "evidence" in this article consists of selected quotes from a very small number of students.

An interview with Ruth Small is reported by Susan Fulgham, Michael Shaughnessy and Ruth Small (2012). Small repeats the usual inaccuracies about rewards and complains that AR stipulates what books students should read. All not true. Nicole Willekes (2014) repeats the AR fallacy: "The foundation of AR is the point system; students strive to earn points in order to gain rewards such as public recognition, snacks, or small toys". She adds, "AR strips students of control, mismanages task complexity, fails to provide clear and useful objectives, offers no useful feedback, and mistakes extrinsic motivation for intrinsic." No evidence is offered and it is difficult to see how these extraordinary claims can be justified. A different perspective is offered by Luz Murillo and Janine Schall (2016), who report the views of 80 first-year university students, most of whom were females of Mexican origin, in relation to their readiness for college-level literacy (they were paid for participating). There was said to be a dislike of AR but this was not evidenced except for a quote from one student.

Summary

Many of the papers attacking AR and RC are based on misconceptions of what the program does and often attribute defects of implementation to the programs when, in fact, they reflect independent decisions about implementation by teachers (often despite advice to the contrary). Paradoxically, at the same time, there is complaint that the program robs teachers of their right to make decisions about education. Many of these papers cite only other papers antagonistic to AR and RC as "evidence", and almost all are conspicuously lacking in anything which to any independent observer would pass as evidence.

To dispel any false illusions, we state:

1. AR and RC are not the whole main reading program, just a supplement to it.
2. AC and RC do not stipulate what books students should read – this is purely a free choice.
3. Students should be allowed to read any book they choose, whether it is quizzed or not.
4. AR and RC are not reward programs. Most countries do not use extrinsic rewards, and this is always the choice of the individual school.
5. If extrinsic rewards are used, they should be based on individual goal-setting and be related to reading (e.g., a book).
6. Students might not like quizzes (especially when they fail them), but they do like more or less immediate feedback.
7. Literal quiz questions are necessary because they are reliable and valid.

8. There are so many quizzes available now that the school book collection is not narrowed or restricted.
9. Implementation quality is crucial – deviations from what is recommended are purely the responsibility of the school.
10. AR does not replace teachers – it actually requires more from teachers.
11. Teachers should not over-teach reading – some instruction plus the opportunity to practice is what is needed.
12. Teachers need to be very careful they are not imposing their own philosophical position or power status on their students in regard to reading.
13. Adopting AR or RC clearly involves leaving something else out – what is left out should be based on estimates of its relative effectiveness.
14. AR can improve attitudes to reading, but these have to be generalized out of school.
15. Introducing AR or RC to a school (especially an underperforming school) should be done slowly and thoughtfully and seek to involve the students.
16. Cost is now based on students participating, not number of quizzes, which seems more appropriate.

On the side of improvements that could be made:

1. Points could be made more clearly into a representation of the degree of success in reading, to emphasize their feedback purpose.
2. The misinterpretation of Vygotsky is unfortunate and this should be clarified.
3. More information about the other quizzes which test higher-order thinking should be made available to schools.

References

Biggers, D. (2001). The argument against Accelerated Reader. *Journal of Adult & Adult Literacy*, 45(1), 72–75.

Carter, B. (1996). Hold the applause!: Do Accelerated Reader (TM) and Electronic Bookshelf (TM) send the right message? *School Library Journal*, *42*(10), 22–25.

Fulgham, S. M., Shaughnessy. M. F., & Small, R. V. (2012). Interview with Ruth V. Small. *Educational Technology*, *52*(5), 39–42.

Goodson, F. T., Tardrew, S., Kerns, G. M., Pavonetti, L. M., & Cipielewski, J. (2003). Accelerated Reader: Lasting effects. *Journal of Adolescent & Adult Literacy*, *47*(1), 4–7.

Groce, R. D., & Groce, E. C. (2005). Deconstructing the Accelerated Reader program. *Reading Horizons, A Journal of Literacy and Language Arts*, *46*(1), 17–30.

Kohn, A. (1993). *Punished by rewards: The trouble with gold stars, incentive plans, A's, praise, and other bribes*. Boston, MA: Mariner Books.

Kohn, A. (2010). "EJ" in focus: How to create nonreaders: Reflections on motivation, learning, and sharing power. *The English Journal*, *100*(1), 16–22.

Krashen, S. (2003). The (lack of) experimental evidence supporting the use of Accelerated Reader. *Journal of Children's Literature*, *29*(2), 16–30.

Krashen, S. (2005). Accelerated Reader: Evidence still lacking. *Knowledge Quest*, *33*(3), 48–49.

Mallette, M. H., Henk, W. A., & Melnick, S. A. (2004). The influence of Accelerated Reader on the affective literacy orientations of intermediate grade students. *Journal of Literacy Research*, *36*(1), 73–84. DOI:10.1207/s15548430jlr3601_4

McCarthy, C. A. (2003). Is the tail wagging the dog? An analysis of Accelerated Reader and the influence of reading rewards on learning and library media centers. *School Library Media Activities Monthly*, *20*(3), 23–26.

Murillo, L. A., & Schall, J. M. (2016). "They didn't teach us well": Mexican-Origin students speak out about their readiness for college literacy. *Journal of Adolescent & Adult Literacy*, *60*(3), 315–323.

Pavonetti, L. M., Brimmer, K. M., & Cipielewski, J. F. (2002). Accelerated Reader: What are the lasting effects on the reading habits of middle school students exposed to Accelerated Reader in elementary grades? *Journal of Adolescent & Adult Literacy*, *46*(4), 300–311. https://www.jstor.org/stable/40013588

Peak, J. P., & Dewalt, M. W. (1994). Reading achievement: Effects of computerized reading management and enrichment. *ERS Spectrum*, *12*(1), 31–35.

Schmidt, R. (2008). Really reading: What does Accelerated Reader teach adults and children? *Language Arts*, *85*(3), 202–211. https://www.jstor.org/stable/41962268

Souto-Manning, M. (2010). Accelerating reading inequities in the early years. *Language Arts*, *88*(2), 104–113.

Stefl-Mabry, J. (2005). Accelerated Reading: Silent Sustained Reading camouflaged in a computer program? *School Library Media Research*, *8*, 1–15.

Stevenson, J. M., & Camarata, J. W. (2000). Imposters in whole language clothing: Undressing the Accelerated Reader program. *Talking Points*, *11*(2), 8–11.

Stevenson, J. M., & Camarata, J. W. (2005). Held hostage by the Accelerated Reader program. *Talking Points*, *16*(2), 16–23.

Thompson, G., Madhuri, M., & Taylor, D. (2008). How the Accelerated Reader program can become counterproductive for high school students. *Journal of Adolescent & Adult Literacy*, *51*(7), 550–560. DOI:10.1598/JAAL.51.7.3

Trelease, J. (2001). *The read-aloud handbook*. New York & London: Penguin Books. https://web.archive.org/web/20060103105402/http://www.trelease-on-reading.com:80/rah_chpt5_p3.html

Triplett, C. F. (2004). Looking for a struggle: Exploring the emotions of a middle school reader. *Journal of Adolescent & Adult Literacy*, *48*(3), 214–222.

Vollands, S. R., Topping, K. J., & Evans, H. M. (1999). Computerized self-assessment of reading comprehension with the Accelerated Reader: Action research. *Reading and Writing Quarterly*, *15*(3), 197–211 (themed issue on Electronic Literacy).

Vygotsky, L. S. (1978). *Mind in society: The development of higher psychological processes*. Cambridge, MA: Harvard University Press.

Willekes, N. (2014). Disrupting the flow: The detrimental effects of Accelerated Reader on student motivation. *Language Arts Journal of Michigan*, *29*(2), Article 7. DOI:10.9707/2168-149X.2011

4

So, Does It Work?

This chapter considers the evidence on whether the program works – for example, does it raise student reading attainment on reading tests? For both Accelerated Reader (AR) and Reading Counts (RC), emphasis is first placed on reviews of the research literature, then on studies comparing intervention and control groups which are randomized, then on control group studies which are not randomized. Other studies are then considered, looking first at studies of many schools which used a reading test, then at studies of single schools that used a reading test, then at studies of many schools that did not use a reading test, and then at studies of a single school that did not use a reading test. (I do not consider that a reading test is essential or even valuable, but this does give a way of breaking down the studies.) Within each subsection, studies are reported in chronological order. A table is then provided indicating the number of different types of study and the country of origin by location of the authors, together with average effect sizes (ESs) (where these are available). After this, the chapter considers new data on AR and RC which have not previously been available. Finally, a summary is offered of the whole chapter (probably much needed, as this is by far the longest and most intense chapter).

DOI: 10.4324/9781003215882-4

Research Literature on Accelerated Reader

Reviews

There are 14 reviews of AR, of various sorts: 10 from the USA and four from the UK.

Topping (1999) offered a review of the advantages and disadvantages of AR, but unfortunately the International Literacy Association has lost this paper. The Education Commission of the States (2000) reported a number of studies of effectiveness, including papers by the Idaho Statewide Implementation, not reported in this book. The Florida Center for Reading Research (2004) reviews Peak and Dewalt (1994) and Samuels and Wu (2003). The following were described as being weaknesses of AR: while an extensive list of book titles and quizzes is provided, students are limited to the books available in their school, and quiz items do not assess inferential or critical thinking skills. These criticisms are dealt with in the previous chapter.

Three state-wide analyses of reading management program implementation in 7,240 schools were reviewed by Kulik (2003), and schools that owned AR had higher reading scores. Results of three controlled comparisons also suggested that AR had positive effects on students' reading. One of the studies found a strong AR effect, one found a moderate-size effect, and one found a trivial effect. Median AR impact in the three studies was an ES of 0.43, equivalent to an increase from the 50th to the 67th percentile.

In the UK, Rudd and Wade (2006) reported an independent evaluation of AR and its corresponding mathematics program in Specialist schools (state secondary schools that aimed to be local centers of excellence in their chosen specialism, which could be technology, language, arts, sports, business and enterprise, engineering, mathematics and computing, science, humanities and music, benefitting from public funding under the "Specialist Schools Programme" and from private sector sponsorship). They matched schools using AR (n = 14) with comparable schools that did not (n = 7). Standardized tests, interviews and questionnaires were used. In the elementary schools, average test scores for reading improved in five out of six treatment schools; in two comparison schools, one saw a decline in average score and one saw an improvement. In secondary schools, two treatment schools returned their tests, and in both cases the average standardized score declined, as did one comparison secondary school. This suggests that implementation of the tests in secondary schools had its problems, which implies that AR implementation might also have been in doubt. There was some evidence that students in AR schools had more positive attitudes to reading than did their peers in non-program schools. In all the AR schools, the staff interviewed had a positive attitude about using AR and agreed that it motivated students. All said they would recommend the program to colleagues in other schools. No ESs were reported.

Balajthy (2007) provided a wide-ranging review of digital technology in education, which included AR and Star Reading, but he did not provide empirical data for any of the programs he mentioned. The What Works Clearinghouse (WWC) (2008) reviewed 100 studies of AR and found two that met its criteria (one a PhD dissertation and so not reported here, and the other a controlled study – Ross, Nunnery & Goldfeder, 2004; see below). The WWC then reported that the evidence for AR was medium to large for comprehension and small for reading fluency and general reading achievement, reporting an ES of 0.31 for comprehension and 0.43 for general literacy attainment. The absurdity of eliminating 98 studies (which is typical of WWC reviews; see later) was criticized by Slavin and Madden (2008). Additionally, WWC did not consider the costs of any program.

A review of effective reading programs for middle and high schools was offered by Slavin, Cheung, Groff and Lake (2008). This included a review of only two studies of AR (one of which was a PhD dissertation, the other Ross et al., 2004), so the critique of WWC by Slavin et al. did not seem to have resulted in any different outcomes in their own study. The average ES was 0.09. Slavin et al. (2008) did point out that whereas a few programs do have evidence of effectiveness, the vast majority do not (and they listed those that did not). A review of effective reading programs for the elementary grades followed (Slavin, Lake, Chambers, Cheung & Davis, 2009). Two studies of AR had a mean ES of + 0.06, but both were PhD dissertations and not eligible for inclusion in this book.

Hansen, Collins and Warschauer (2009) provided a more thorough review of reading management software programs and had a particular focus on quality of implementation and the balance between intrinsic and extrinsic motivation. Implementation of reading management programs was influenced by a range of actors, including administrators, librarians, computer resource teachers, classroom teachers, parents and students, and a strong school-wide commitment to the program was needed. Four studies found positive effects for AR, and none found negative effects. However, improved attitudes were important, as they might be the vehicle for a longer-term love of reading. There was some evidence that girls might have better attitudes than boys and that high-frequency readers might have better attitudes than low-frequency readers (but, again, implementation quality was important). The authors commented that longitudinal or follow-up studies were sorely needed, as it might be that gains made in the elementary grades were washed out in the secondary grades.

Yeh (2010) conducted a review of 22 approaches to raising cost-effectiveness in schools, which suggested that "rapid assessment" (by which he meant AR) was more cost-effective with regard to student achievement than the following: comprehensive school reform, cross-age tutoring, computer-assisted instruction, a longer school day, increases in teacher education or teacher experience or salaries, summer school, more rigorous classes, value-added teacher assessment, class size reduction, a 10% increase in per-student expenditure, full-day kindergarten, Head Start (pre-school), high-standards exit exams, National Board for Professional Teaching Standards (NBPTS) certification, higher teacher licensure test scores, high-quality preschool, an additional school year, voucher programs or charter schools. This study is discussed further in Chapter 13.

A further report from the WWC (2016) identified 71 studies, of which only two met the WWC standards. One of these was the PhD dissertation that had been cited in the previous WWC report. The other was by Shannon, Styers and Siceloff (2010) (see below). The ES for the latter was 0.18.

Gorard, Siddiqui and See (2017) summarized the evidence from randomized controlled trials of seven popular literacy "catch-up" schemes for Year 6 through Year 7 students (i.e., transitioning to secondary school) in England. In regard to AR, four individual secondary schools with a high proportion of disadvantaged students evaluated AR over a period of 20 weeks. Students (n = 323) were individually randomly assigned to groups (180 to treatment, 163 to control). The findings were based on the New Group Reading Test. Switchon Reading (a form of Reading Recovery) and AR were the most promising (both having an ES of 0.24) (although Switchon Reading was 70 times more expensive than AR).

A review of literacy interventions in primary (elementary) schools was then offered by See and Gorard (2020), who found that AR, Fresh Start, Butterfly Phonics and Switch-on Reading (Reading Recovery) were the most effective. However, for AR this was based on only two studies of "medium quality" (Ross, Nunnery & Goldfeder, 2004; Siddiqui, Gorard & See, 2016). The average ESs were 0.25 for AR and 0.23 for Switchon Reading.

After these 14, the remaining studies are divided into groups reflecting their credibility as scientific studies. There are seven randomized controlled trials, four otherwise controlled studies, and 38 other studies. Thus, in total, there are 64 peer-reviewed studies of AR (excluding doctoral dissertations and master's theses and studies done by Renaissance Learning).

Randomized Controlled Trials

Studies with control groups can randomize participants to these groups at the student level, at the class level, or at the school level. Studies randomizing at the student level are rare, as randomization at this level would cut across classroom organization and have a high risk of contamination between groups. There are seven randomized trials: six from the USA and one from the UK.

Peak and Dewalt (1994) reported an early study of ninth graders in two very similar high schools in the USA, when only 900 quizzes were available (n = 100). Randomization was by student. Fifty ninth graders were randomly selected from each school and their third-grade, sixth-grade, and eighth-grade California Achievement Test (CAT) reading scores inspected. The intervention school had an average CAT score of 715.6 in third grade, rising to 788.0 in eighth grade. The control school had an average CAT score of 724.3, rising to 766. Thus, intervention students were lower at the beginning but higher at the end. Surveys indicated that intervention students checked out more books, read for longer, were pleased to be relieved of writing book reports and that three quarters of the students liked the program.

A more sophisticated six-month study for grades 3 and 5 (n = 74) was reported by Samuels, Lewis, Wu, Reininger and Murphy (2003) in a highly disadvantaged school with high levels of ethnic minorities in the USA. Four classes/teachers were randomly assigned to treatments (all teachers were experienced), independent reading time was held constant for both treatments (at 15 minutes per day), teacher reading time to students was the same, and all the students had access to books that were appropriate for their level of reading skill. Pre-test to post-test scores on the Group Reading Assessment and Diagnostic Evaluation showed that the intervention group outperformed the control group on comprehension and that results were stronger for fifth-grade and lower-ability students. Intervention students also outperformed control students on vocabulary.

A study varying reading ability (low, moderate and high) in the USA was reported by Samuels and Wu (2003). It also sought to evaluate immediate (from AR) versus delayed (book reports to the teacher) feedback effects on reading performance measures such as sentence and passage comprehension, as well as reading speed, in a highly disadvantaged school with a high proportion of ethnic minorities. Sixty-seven students in the third and fifth grades participated in a study that lasted for six months, with four classrooms randomly assigned to conditions. All students had the same amount of time devoted to reading, including 15 minutes of being read to by the teacher and 15 minutes of independent reading. Students in the immediate feedback condition were significantly superior on measures of passage comprehension (ES 0.95) and composite comprehension (ES 0.90) and this difference was almost three times as large. The low-ability group had significantly higher gain scores than the other two groups on sentence and composite comprehension. However, the moderate group had the greatest gain score in speed of reading.

Ross, Nunnery and Goldfeder (2004) reported two experimental studies of AR. Study 1 involved 76 kindergarten to sixth-grade teachers in 11 Memphis City schools and their 1,665 students, in a district in which 71% of all students were eligible for free/reduced-price lunch. In each school, a minimum of two teachers at the same grade level volunteered to be randomly assigned either to implement AR or to serve as a control teacher. Three quarters of the AR teachers had less than one year of experience with AR. The Star Reading Test was administered at the start, mid-point and end of the school year. The ESs were large (0.71) for kindergarten, 0.36 for first grade, 0.25 for second grade and 0.33 for third grade but not significant for grades 4 to 6 (ESs 0.01–0.14, so AR students still did better than controls). Of participating teachers, 95% were positive to AR.

The second study involved 978 students in grades 3 (n = 250), 4 (n = 381), 5 (n = 215) and 6 (n = 132). The students were 90% African-American, 83% were eligible for free or reduced-price lunch, and 3.3% had a specified learning disability. The quality of implementation was measured (based on researcher observations and then subject to factor analysis). Students in AR classrooms had higher average growth rates than students in control classrooms for all grades except 5th grade, in which growth rates were about equal. ESs were higher in the lower grade levels: +0.34 in third grade, +0.15 in fourth grade, +0.10 in fifth grade and +0.07 in sixth grade. This was a first-year implementation in a difficult setting (with many implementation issues raised with the consultants). Average Percent Correct (APC), which Renaissance Learning recommend to be at 85%, ranged from a low of 42% to a high of 86% among the 24 treatment classrooms, of which only three met the program standard. These "high" implementation classrooms significantly reduced the negative impact of learning disability status on growth in reading when compared with control classrooms or "low" implementation classrooms. Overall implementation levels of AR were low compared with

Renaissance Learning benchmarks. This second study was reported again in Nunnery, Ross and McDonald (2006).

A cluster randomized controlled trial was used to evaluate AR with 344 first- to fourth-grade students in three middle-class schools in a large Midwestern US city (Shannon et al., 2015). Within each grade and school block, researchers randomly assigned participating classrooms to intervention or comparison conditions. Less than 1% of students had special education status or were eligible to receive free or reduced-price lunch, and none of the participating students had limited English proficiency. AR was used for 24 weeks. None of the participating teachers had previously used AR. Implementation quality was assessed through teacher logs, which (unsurprisingly) reported high levels of implementation. Intervention classes read for a little longer than control classes. The Star Reading Test used pre-post showed statistically significant gains for the AR group compared with the control group (ES 0.38, a moderate ES). The authors conclude that their study "provides strong evidence that computer-assisted learning using AR with fidelity has a positive impact on elementary students' reading achievement".

Finally, Siddiqui, Gorard and See (2016) evaluated AR with 349 students in the UK in the first year of secondary school who had achieved poor results in English, located in four schools of high disadvantage, three of which had received recent poor inspection reports. Of the students, 35% had Free School Meals and 23% had special educational needs. They were randomly assigned into two groups (three schools randomly assigned by student and one school randomly assigned by classes). Baseline equivalence was established on the basis of prior English scores. The intervention group (n = 166) was exposed to AR for only 20 weeks, after which they recorded higher literacy scores on the online New Group Reading Test (sentence completion and passages) than the control group (n = 183) (ES 0.24). The ES for Free School Meals students was 0.38. However, students did more independent reading during the trial than they normally would have done, although in the case of one school this was after school time.

Control Group Studies

There are four control group studies where allocation to groups was not randomized: three from the USA and one from the UK. Studies examining the reading/written language abilities of 30 intellectually superior students who resided in supportive home environments and had been identified as Accelerated Readers at the age of four years were reported by Burns and Collins (1987) and Burns, Collins and Paulsell (1991). However, these studies are not about AR and are not relevant to our discussion of the literature.

Vollands, Topping and Evans (1999) conducted a pilot research project in two disadvantaged elementary schools in the UK. The teachers were completely new to the program and had one day of initial training. The pilot UK version of the software covered only 100 AR titles. Intervention time was six months.

In the first project, the AR group had 30 minutes reading time plus 30 minutes of being read to by the teacher. Students could and did test on books read *to* them, and the rate of success was high. Teacher monitoring and intervention were initially slow, but on average 84% of test items were answered correctly. The control group had regular classroom teaching of reading, which included 30 minutes of reading time per day and book reports. On the Shortened Edinburgh group reading test of silent reading comprehension, standardized scores for the AR group showed a statistically significant increase but those of the comparison group did not (ES 0.72). On the Neale individually administered test of oral reading accuracy and reading comprehension, a random sample of 12 students showed a statistically significant increase in reading accuracy over the experimental period (ES 0.30) but the comparison group did not. Two measures of attitude to reading were utilized: the Elementary Reading Attitude Survey and a locally devised Reading Interest Scale. The AR group showed greater improvement in attitude to reading than the comparison group on both measures, but these differences did not reach statistical significance. Girls performed better than boys at pre-test and this difference was even more marked at post-test.

In the second project, the AR class (n = 24) consisted of 11-year-old (sixth grade) students and the comparison class was a year younger but actually more able at reading. There was poor implementation and little reading time. However, on average, 84% of quiz items were answered correctly. The comparison group had regular classroom teaching supplemented by 15 minutes of individual silent reading time per day and group oral reading on a restricted selection of novels. On the Edinburgh test, the comparison group shower a larger gain from a higher baseline, but the AR ES was still 0.18. On the Neale test, the AR and comparison groups showed no significant difference, but the AR group ES was 0.13. On Neale comprehension, the AR group was much higher, reaching statistical significance (ES 0.28). On the two different reading attitude scales, the AR group was higher on one and the comparison group higher on the other. Girls were better than boys on both.

Holmes and Brown (2003) reported a study of four elementary schools in the USA: two intervention and two control. The intervention schools had shown evidence of good implementation of AR. One had 88% African-American students and 92% eligibility for free lunch, the other 99% Caucasian students and 52% eligibility for free lunch. Control schools were closely matched to each. Test scores were available for intervention students after the first year for 214 students and after the second year for 386 students. The control group numbered 132 students. Implementation of AR was assessed through an observation checklist of 24 desirable behaviors (see Chapters 5 and 6 for another checklist of desirable implementation behaviors). The average percentages of desirable behaviors observed were 53% for intervention schools and 39% for control schools. In all standardized test comparisons (Iowa Test of Basic Skills, Georgia Criterion-Referenced Competency Test and Star Reading Test for grades 2 to 4) in reading, language arts, and mathematics, the AR students (ES 0.50) outperformed controls (ES 0.05). The ESs were 0.71 for language arts and 0.75 for mathematics. First-year differences were maintained and increased in the second year. AR appeared to produce the largest gains with lower-achieving students. This study was reported again in Holmes, Brown and Algozzine (2006).

A six-year study in an urban, Title I elementary school in the USA where 36% of students received free or reduced-price lunch was conducted by Brem, Husman and Duggan (2005) to explore the long-term effects of AR. Over a three-year research period, data sources included Stanford Achievement Test ninth edition (SAT9) reading scores over a 6-year period; interviews with librarians and reading specialists; focus groups with teachers, students and parents; survey data from about 20 teachers, 150 parents and 300 students; measures of student motivation from about 300 students; and data for about 1150 students from AR. SAT9 Reading data and interviews with librarians and reading specialists were also conducted at a "control" school that had not implemented AR, located in the same district and geographical location, of similar size and student composition. From 1997 to 2002, the AR school showed a statistically significant 18% increase in SAT9 reading scores (ES 0.57). There were no significant changes in performance at the control school and this difference was significant. Mastery orientation was initially high and remained high throughout study. Extensive focus groups and surveys explored the perceived affective and motivational effects of AR on students' orientation towards independent reading. Almost all parents, teachers and students were favorably inclined towards AR. Students' motivation was enhanced by the program.

Nunnery and Ross (2007) reported a quasi-experimental study of AR on student achievement in grades 3 through 8 in a suburban Texas school district over four school years. There were 11 AR schools (nine elementary with grades 3 to 5 and two middle with grades 6 through 8). Free lunch eligibility ranged from 0% to 59%. Each was matched to a comparison school (n = 11) on the basis of school performance, poverty and ethnic composition. Measures used were reading scores which were part of the Texas Assessment of Academic Skills. Program effects on reading (and mathematics) were studied, and the impact of implementation fidelity examined. AR showed statistically significant, positive effects on reading achievement for elementary students in nine schools (ES 0.20, although this might be an underestimate) but not for middle school students in two schools (although the tendency was for AR to do better than non-AR). Students attending high-implementation AR schools scored significantly higher than students attending comparison schools or low-intensity schools. ESs were 0.14 for high-intensity schools and 0.11 for low-intensity schools. The effect of treatment was constant across years. Although the ES estimates reported here are smaller than those in other studies, they are relatively substantial compared with average effects for school reform models.

Many Schools + Reading Tests

Penuel (1997) studied longitudinal data on norm-referenced tests of reading and language administered state-wide for 19 elementary schools in a metropolitan area that reportedly had "used" AR for an average of almost two years (no information was presented on AR implementation). Students in both third and fourth grades made higher-than-expected gains in both language and reading, though these differences reached statistical significance in language only. The unit of analysis was the school rather than the class or the student, and details of the statistical analysis were missing. Nonetheless, Penuel concluded that the longer the AR program had been in the school, the greater were the gains in language.

Stiegemeier (1999) reported that the Language Integrated Technology Grant Project (LIT) consortium selected AR, Star and the Sentence Master computer-based programs for investigation. In 23 participating schools (17 elementary, two middle and four high), each school was provided with the software, hardware and staff development necessary to use the software. School dropout among high schools was much greater than among elementary schools. Many schools noted that their book collections were not large enough to accommodate the student demands for books once the program was implemented. After four to six months of operation, each school identified one evaluation classroom (we do not know how these choices were made). Usable data were collected from 579 students that included pre- and post-Star testing and AR information. Overall, students gained 2.0 Normal Curve Equivalents (NCEs) and 2.5 in percentile rank. Participation in the AR program was most beneficial for students in the lowest two quartiles – those with the greatest need to improve their reading skills. Students in the lowest quartile (25th percentile or lower) gained an average of 7.6 NCEs and had a mean gain of 9.7 in percentile rank. Students overwhelmingly noted that they liked AR and consistently agreed that they liked reading books aligned to AR quizzes, they liked earning AR points, and AR helped them to be a better reader. Teachers reported that, in a relatively short period of time, students were more excited about reading than before and demonstrated high motivation and engagement in reading. The project demonstrated that AR and STAR coupled with focused staff development efforts can create environments with significant impact on reading motivation and achievement.

Topping and Paul (1999) gathered AR data for over 659,000 students in 2,193 schools in kindergarten through 12th grades in one school year. The ethnic and socioeconomic status of students in these schools approximated to that of US schools generally. Twenty states for which AR data were available for at least 3,000 students were grouped into high (top quartile), average and low (bottom quartile) categories on National Assessment of Educational Progress (NAEP) reading test results. High-performing states (such as Wisconsin, Iowa, Indiana, Minnesota and Utah) had an average NAEP score of 221.4 and an AR points per student average of 39.2. Average-performing states (such as Missouri, Pennsylvania, North Carolina, Virginia, Tennessee, Texas, New York, Kentucky, Alabama and Georgia) had an average NAEP score of 213.3 and average AR points of 25.1. Low-performing states (such as Florida, South Carolina, Mississippi, Louisiana and California) had an average NAEP score of 202.0 and average AR points of 24.7. Obviously, many factors other than AR will have contributed to these findings. The difference in AR points acquired between NAEP high-performing quartile and low-performing quartile students at each grade level was at a factor of between three and four times. When the top 5% of readers were compared with the bottom 5%, the difference was even greater: the difference in AR points was 144 times more, suggesting the top 5% had vastly more reading practice. The time allocated in school to independent reading practice on self-selected materials declined after grade 6.

The data also suggested that the longer AR had been on campus, the more students read. Average points per student in schools where AR had been in school for less than one year were 9.78, 17.68 for one year, 20.91 for two years, 24.94 for three years, and 28.95 for four or more years. Across all grade levels, there was a 64 percent higher level of reading practice in schools using AR for four or more years as compared with schools using AR for just one year. The quantity of AR points was negatively correlated with school size. Data for elementary grades 3 through 6 in public schools were isolated and showed differences in mean AR points per student: 30.36 in schools <200 students, 24.73 in schools of 200–400 students, 23.43 in schools of 400–600, 20.09 in schools of 600–800, 14.3 in schools of 800–1000, and 13.93 in schools of over 1000. The 608,338 public school students in the sample logged average AR points of 19.34, while the 50,876 private school students logged 32.24. Students in private schools performed half a grade level equivalent higher in reading than their public-school counterparts, but this did not explain the difference in points gained. Thus, it seems possible that a major factor in reading disability is simply that weak readers get less practice.

The Tennessee Value-Added Assessment System (TVAAS), reported by Topping and Sanders (2000), used the largest longitudinally merged database of student achievement data in the USA to generate estimates of school system, school and teacher effects on indicators of student learning in a number of subjects, including reading comprehension. All students in grades 2 through 8 were tested annually with the Tennessee Comprehensive Assessment Program (TCAP). This covers five areas, including reading. TVAAS uses multivariate, longitudinal statistical analysis of several millions of records, merged longitudinally for all students tested over the last several years. TVAAS uses each student as their own control and estimates the "value added" each year to the student's academic profile. It seeks to provide the best linear unbiased estimates and predictors of the influence of school systems, schools and teachers upon student learning rates while allowing for differences in socioeconomic status and other in- and out-of-school factors. Schools known to possess and be implementing AR in Tennessee were invited (n = 379) and 313 (83%) responded with AR data, amounting to data on about 80,000 students. Of these, 62,739 could be successfully merged with TVAAS.

Value added rose with increased numbers of books read by students. However, the number of books read per grade declined as expected (older students read longer but fewer books) and the difficulty level increased – but not at the same rate as the actual grades were increasing (from 2.5 to 5.4 over grades 2 to 8). Value added also rose with increasing percent correct on AR quizzes. The influence of overall student ability was then examined, dividing the students into six groups of ascending prior achievement on TCAP reading, language arts and math scores combined. In all grades (3–7), the lowest-ability group had the lowest percentage correct (72–74) and the highest-ability group the highest (89–92). Operation at low percent correct was particularly likely to be true of students of low overall ability, and this implied that teachers were not generating or not responding to AR At-Risk Reports. The recommendation is to sustain APC above 85%, and the data strongly supported this, as this was clearly the point at which positive value added emerged. Alarmingly, however, more than half of the students in the study were operating below this level.

Mean book level showed a statistically significant effect for four out of five grades. However, at the individual student level, beyond the third grade, students increasingly tended to read books below their actual grade level, and this applied to students of all reading abilities. There were no significant differences between males and females or fiction and non-fiction. Surprisingly, this analysis suggested that increasing reading challenge was associated with decreased teacher effectiveness at all levels of reading volume. The difference in teacher effectiveness between the top and bottom quartile was most striking in the lower grades (especially for students of lower ability), decreasing in the higher grades. High effectiveness in teaching the most able students was relatively rare. High percent correct and high reading volume were positively related to teacher effectiveness (most value added). Implementation quality was very likely to be various between schools, and there was undoubtedly a lot of noise in the data.

Johnson and Howard (2003) investigated the effect of a year-long AR program on the reading achievement and vocabulary development of 755 third through fifth graders from low socio-economic status schools where 85% were African-American. There were three categories of AR usage: Low participation (0–20 AR points, fewer than three books per year), Average participation (21–74 points, three to five books per year), and High participation (75 points and above, more than eight to ten books). Participants in all three groups improved their reading skills on the Gates–MacGinitie Reading Test. High AR users gained significantly more on reading comprehension (2.24 years) than average (1.52 years) or low (0.73 years) users.

Topping and Fisher (2003) explored the impact of AR on reading achievement in 13 schools of different types spread across the UK. Schools known to possess the AR software were invited to volunteer to participate and then selected to give some geographical and school type spread but also to include many (nine out of 13) in disadvantaged areas. Five were primary (elementary) schools, three were first schools (kindergarten through fourth grade), one was a junior school (third through sixth grade), one was a middle school, three were high schools and one was a 'city technology college' (a senior high school with extra funding for technology). Each school had only 1,000 AR quizzes. Two classes in each school were selected for participation. The intervention period was 0.66 of a year. Participants numbered 704 and were 7 to 14 years old. Pre-post norm-referenced group paper reading tests (the Primary Reading Test and the Group Reading Test II 6–14) and the Star Reading computer-based test were used. On the paper tests, the ES was 0.17; on the Star test, the ES was 0.41. The average percentage correct per student was only 76%, and only 64% of quizzes were passed – implementation integrity was very diverse. In particular, some teachers failed to intervene in response to AR data indicating that students were reading ineffectively.

Borman and Dowling (2004) investigated the AR reading records and Star Reading Tests of 45,108 students in 139 US schools in grades 1 through 12. Separate hierarchical linear modeling analyses were conducted for three clusters: second to fifth graders, sixth to eighth graders, and ninth to 12th graders. These analyses distinguished between student-level and classroom-level effects of a greater amount of reading, a high reading success rate, and the use of reading material that was appropriately matched to students' abilities. There were significant differences between schools in outcomes. Variability between classrooms accounted for 26%, 38% and 28% of the outcomes, much of the remainder being accounted for by student variability. Achieving the 85% correct standard was related to higher post-test scores in all grade clusters. Students who read more had higher post-test scores in all grade clusters. Students reading books below their optimum challenge level performed worse on post-test scores than students reading at the optimum level in all grade clusters. However, students reading books *above* their optimum challenge level tended to have higher post-test scores in all grade clusters. Interestingly, students in larger classrooms tended to have higher post-test scores than students attending smaller classrooms. There were also statistically significant positive effects for classrooms taught by "master" AR teachers in both the elementary and middle-school samples.

Does reading practice make perfect? Or is reading achievement related to the quality of practice as well as the quantity? To answer these questions, AR and Star Reading test data on 45,670 students in 2,365 first- through 12th-grade classrooms in 139 schools each containing between 12 and 30 students who read over three million books were analyzed (Topping, Samuels & Paul, 2007a). Points gained and APC on quizzes were totaled. The total number of points earned by a student is a proxy for Engaged Reading Volume (ERV) but not for mere exposure to books nor for time allocated to reading but not used for reading. ERV is an indicator not just of words read but of difficulty of words read successfully. ERV and APC both showed a positive statistically significant relationship with achievement gain at all levels of achievement. However, both high quantity and high quality in combination were necessary for high achievement gains, especially for older students. However, correlations were small and did not account for much of the variance. The positive relationship between ERV and reading achievement gain was curvilinear. Beyond a certain point, there was evidence of diminishing marginal returns in achievement for time spent engaged in reading. A striking interaction between quantity and quality was evident. Gains in achievement were found only with the combination of high ERV and high APC. Not until the threshold of 85% APC was exceeded did higher ERV begin to yield higher achievement. Both ERV and APC were strongly associated with the classroom in which the student was enrolled, and teacher implementation especially in guiding independent reading was important.

Topping, Samuels and Paul (2007b) explored the effects of variability in program implementation quality on achievement. Particularly, AR and Star Reading test data for one school year were analyzed for 50,823 students in 139 schools (2,365 classrooms containing 12–30 students) grades in 1-12 states in the US who read over three million books. The pre-post period was eight months. When minimum implementation quality criteria were met, the positive effect of AR was higher in the earlier grades and for lower achievement students. With higher implementation quality, reading achievement gains were higher for students of all levels of achievement and across all grades but especially in the higher grades. Very high gains were evident with very high implementation quality, particularly in the first through fourth grades. Given the association between the interaction of ERV (quantity) and APC (quality) and high achievement gains, a derived composite index of quality of implementation was used. This was the percentage of students in a class averaging above 85% APC multiplied by the percentage of optimal ERV the class had achieved (also see Chapters 5 and 6). This implementation quality index declined steadily as grade level increased. Analysis by ethnicity showed that Caucasians had the highest scores followed by Asians, and Hispanic, African-American and Native American students had the lowest scores.

Topping, Samuels and Paul (2008) then investigated whether different balances of fiction/non-fiction reading and challenge might help explain differences in reading achievement between genders. AR and Star Reading test data on 45,670 students in the first through 12th grades in 139 schools (in 2,365 classrooms containing 12–30 students) in 24 states in the US who independently read over three million books were analyzed. Overall, ERV (quantity) and APC (quality) were significantly positively related to reading achievement gain. At all grade levels, girls had higher ERV and higher APC than boys, and their initial reading achievement was higher. Boys tended to gain more in reading achievement than girls in the lower grades (but from a lower baseline), but girls gained more than boys in the higher grades.

Non-fiction book challenge levels were somewhat higher than fiction. Students reading a high proportion of non-fiction gained significantly less in reading achievement than the remainder of students. Non-fiction reading was negatively correlated to reading achievement gain, APC and ERV across all grades. Girls read proportionately more fiction than boys at all grade levels, and boys read more non-fiction than girls. Lower APC on non-fiction books was particularly pronounced for boys. APC for males on non-fiction consistently fell below the 85% criterion for reading achievement gain. Thus, boys generally appeared to read less than girls, but proportionately more non-fiction, but this less carefully—especially in the higher grades—and had lower reading achievement. Moderate (rather than high or low) levels of challenge were positively associated with achievement gain. However, classrooms characterized by particularly successful comprehension were almost equally good at achieving this with fiction and non-fiction. Classrooms not characterized by successful comprehension were particularly poor with comprehension of non-fiction. The minimum APC criterion of 85% required for reading achievement gain was found across all four quartiles for fiction, but only in the highest quartile for non-fiction, and this latter was associated with particularly high reading achievement gains.

Single School + Reading Tests
Goodman (1999) reported on AR use in the USA with 282 students in the seventh and eighth grade at a middle school, of whom 50% were Hispanic and 46% were eligible for free or

reduced-price lunch. On pre-post Gates–MacGinitie test scores, there was statistically significant improvement in vocabulary and comprehension. At the start of the intervention 82% of students were reading below grade level, and by the end this was down to 45%. Rodriguez (2007) investigated the impact of AR on the English language arts California Standards Test (CST) in the seventh and eighth grades of a Title I middle school with 50% eligible for free lunch. Of the school's population, 75% came from a Hispanic background and 15% from a Filipino-American background. This study tracked the AR and CST records of a structured sample of 180 students from three classes, representing one-third of the eighth-grade students (although all students were required to participate in AR). Reading time of 45 minutes per day was assigned plus 20 minutes of homework time, and individual AR point goals were set. Ten percent of the student's English grade was based on AR. Overall, AR had a significant effect on CST scores for both reading comprehension and literary analysis, and higher AR participation increased CST scores. Subgroups with higher AR participation outperformed groups with higher reading levels but lower AR participation rates.

Middle school students in one school were studied by Huang (2012). A total of 211 sixth- to eighth-grade students completed a survey (387 were requested, response rate was 55%). Thirty of these were randomly selected to participate in semi-structured interviews and classroom observations over one semester. The selected students' AR pre-test and post-test scores on the Star Reading Test were collected. Almost all students were near their grade level in reading. The pre-test to post-test differences were negative (i.e., scores went down). Very few books had an AR quiz as only a basic package had been purchased. There appeared to be no designated time for reading books in class. Students were not under any supervision when they took the AR tests and many students were taking AR quizzes and sharing answers with other students. Clearly there are questions here about the quality of implementation.

Foster and Foster (2014) collected data for three years from about 100 students each year in grades 2 through 8 in a school in the US. AR points earned over the course of a year were correlated with reading growth scores as determined by a standardized test. The median rose from 30 points in grade 2 to 150 points in grade 8, and there was no evidence of a plateau at the secondary level. The data showed that a student who did no additional AR reading would continue to fall behind the US average each year. The authors argue strongly for more use of reading goals and closer monitoring of reading behavior by the teachers.

Many Schools, No Reading Tests

The reading attitudes and self-perceptions of 358 students in the fourth (n = 167) and fifth (n = 191) grades in two school districts of similar socioeconomic status (low to moderate family incomes) were compared by Mallette, Henk and Melnick (2004). Students in the school(s) of one district (n = 235) used AR intensively and student grades were based upon it. By contrast, students in the control school (n = 123) had been exposed to AR but only in a limited and varied way according to the inclinations of each class teacher. Measures were the Elementary Reading Attitude Survey and the Reader Self-Perception Scale. The intensive AR group scored higher on a reading test. AR yielded statistically significantly higher attitudes toward Academic Reading than the Control condition but not for Recreational Reading. No ESs were given.

Everhart (2005) reported studies of three schools: two in Scotland (one elementary and one secondary) and one (elementary) in England, representing different levels of implementation (the secondary was worst). Methods included the following: observation, structured interviews with students and teachers, videotaped student focus groups, a student survey on self-reported reading, and administration of the Motivation for Reading Questionnaire. Teachers in the Scottish schools were eager to show that they had implemented AR "American-style" by using extrinsic rewards, but they also set AR goals and students were also rewarded by the performance feedback inherent in the program and teacher praise. Some students also read a large number of non-AR books. Students liked using the computer, taking quizzes, and the question format of AR. Dislikes included question difficulty, seeing mistakes, and quizzes being boring.

The majority of students (66 percent) liked AR, 21 percent did not like it, and 13 percent had no opinion. A greater proportion of females liked AR, and girls seemed to favor the social aspects while boys favored the competitive aspects. Of the 30 available reports, teachers commonly used only two. However, diagnostic use of these reports was not observed. These data were restated and linked to the US in Everhart, Dresang and Kotrla (2005).

Chase (2010) described the use of AR in Chesapeake elementary and middle schools. No tests were apparent. Smith and Westberg (2011) administered questionnaires completed by 1,365 students in grades 3 through 8 in four schools. Most students perceived the AR program as being helpful in motivating them to read and acquiring reading skills; however, older students had significantly less favorable attitudes toward the program. Then eight to ten students were selected by their teachers from five schools (with 68 heterogeneous classrooms) to meet in focus group settings. Students' experiences with AR varied from school to school. However, students at all sites were given an AR point goal for each quarter. Some schools had reading time in classtime, while other schools had it only as homework. Cheating was reported to be quite common and (especially in schools where AR points were linked with grades), students read quickly to "get their points in", after which they could read what they liked. (This appears to be a result of a limited number of quizzes and an overemphasis on points; the former problem has now been resolved.)

Stringfield, Luscre and Gast (2011) reported the effects of a story map on AR quiz scores in students with high-functioning autism. Three boys who ranged in age from eight to 11 years with high-functioning autism who attended elementary schools were taught to use a graphic organizer called a Story Map as a postreading tool during language arts instruction. The effect of the intervention on story recall was assessed within the context of a multiple-baseline design across participants as measured by performance on AR quizzes. Positive effects were achieved quickly and maintained throughout the study. However, this study is more an evaluation of Story Map than of AR.

Grades 2 through 4 in two small elementary schools were studied by Long and Bonds-Raacke (2012). Both schools were 88% Caucasian, and 38% to 41% received free lunch. In both schools, the standards of reading performance were high, but there were differences in quizzes taken, Quizzes Passed (QP) and AR points earned. Correlation revealed a positive relationship between age in months and QP/quizzes taken only in fourth grade but not in second and third grades. These correlations were significant but small (0.26, 0.25), accounting for little of the variance. There were very few gender differences.

Do students who use AR think differently about reading, do they enjoy reading more, and do they read more often than students who do not use AR? Clark and Cunningham (2016) used data from a literacy survey in the UK in which more than 32,000 children and young people aged eight through 18 participated. Three in ten participating students said that they used AR. Significantly more students who used AR enjoyed reading either very much or quite a lot in comparison with students who did not use AR (59% vs. 52%). Compared with their non-AR peers, significantly more AR students read frequently outside class. For example, 84% of AR students read outside class at least once a week compared with 76% of non-AR students. AR students were significantly more likely to think positively about reading than their non-AR peers. For example, while 49% of AR students thought that reading was cool, only 37% of non-AR students thought the same.

Clark and Cunningham (2016) also followed 1,500 students who were seven or eight years old until they were 10 or 11. AR use was reported by 37% of these. Students who had done AR for four years (N = 82) enjoyed reading more, were more confident readers, read for longer and had more positive attitudes towards reading than students who had done AR for shorter periods. Reading enjoyment, reading frequency and reading attitudes in 2011 positively predicted reading attainment in 2012. This suggests that reading enjoyment has a strong bi-directional link with reading attainment, both predicting and being predicted by reading attainment.

Smith, Westberg and Hejny (2017) surveyed third- through eighth-grade teachers who used AR as a part of their literacy program. An online questionnaire gathered data in urban, rural, ex-urban and suburban school settings in both elementary and middle schools. Teachers were asked to respond to items based on a four-point scale from strongly disagree to strongly agree, and there was a final open-ended response question. Thirty-nine teachers responded; however, not every respondent completed the entire survey. We do not know how many teachers were sent the survey. The respondents had been using the program between one and 15 years. Most of the teachers indicated that their students enjoy the program and most teachers required their students to take the AR quizzes. Results indicated that most teachers believed that AR motivated their students to read; however, they also recognized that AR was largely an accountability measure ensuring that their students read independently. Additionally, teachers recognized that AR measures comprehension at knowledge-recall level and was not an indicator of overall reading comprehension.

Single School, No Reading Tests

Rosenheck et al. (1996) surveyed fifth-grade students in three matched (by socioeconomics, multiculturality, and achievement levels) elementary schools. One school had no AR, one had mandatory AR, and one had voluntary AR. A survey instrument was developed that included queries about the use of the media center, number of books checked out, enjoyment of reading, and favorite indoor activities. In total, 222 surveys were returned (we do not know how many were sent out). Results indicated no relationship between the use of AR and frequency of library use or attitudes toward reading and the media center, but the great majority of students in all three schools enjoyed reading.

Hamilton (1997) reported the use of AR with high school English as a Second Language students. She coupled this with writing tasks. There were changes in the students' reading habits. Lawson (2000) reported that in less than a year after first implementing AR, some students' reading grade levels increased by two to three years while the majority experienced more than a year's growth. The author also notes that reading motivation increased significantly. In addition, library circulation increased from 600–700 books a month to around 4,000. Anderson (2001) found AR most effective for struggling readers. Library circulation more than doubled, and students read for pleasure and recommended books to one another.

Chenoweth (2001) compared AR and RC and discussed school librarians' attitudes toward the programs. McGlinn and Parrish (2002) examined the AR program over three months with English as a Second Language students in the fourth and fifth grade in one school in rural North Carolina. Ten students had 45 minutes a day for independent reading. The quantity of student reading greatly increased, attitudes towards reading improved, and there was a moderate overall increase in student reading level. (But unfortunately, the measures of reading level were not the same pre and post, and half of the students were reading at too low a level.) No individual goals were set. No ESs were reported. Cuddeback and Ceprano (2002) discussed AR with emergent readers and concluded that AR did contribute to students' reading comprehension improvement when utilized in conjunction with other materials and teaching procedures.

Pavonetti, Brimmer and Cipielewski (2002–3) surveyed 1,536 seventh-grade students (some had used AR in elementary school) from 10 middle schools to determine their reading habits. The Title Recognition Test was administered but was based on "lists of books for teens and young adults", which suggests that books suitable for lower-ability readers did not feature. There was no significant difference between the elementary AR group and the elementary non-AR group, but the subgroup that continued using AR in the middle school did show positive results. This was thus a kind of follow-up study. Rejholec (2002) studied the effect of extrinsic rewards on the motivation of 32 eighth-grade language students in one urban middle school. During a baseline period, many students forgot to bring their AR book to class (an average of 12 remembered), but once rewards (candies) were made available for just remembering to bring the book to class, this rose to an average of 16.3 students. However, many students were still not remembering, and the study did not examine what was done with the books that were remembered.

A study in one elementary school with 36% eligible for free lunch and 24% from minority backgrounds was reported by Husman, Brem and Duggan (2005), who tracked 329 students from grades 3 through 6 for one semester. Teachers, parents and students generally held favorable opinions of AR. There had been a significant gain in reading test scores since its inception (when compared with a matched non-implementing school), library records showed far more books being checked out, and survey and interview data indicated that the vast majority of parents, teachers and students wanted the program expanded. Goal orientation was measured with the Patterns of Adaptive Learning scale, but scores declined from pre-test to post-test. Nonetheless, students showed a strong mastery orientation that persisted.

Esposito and Smith (2006) reported the use of interviews and focus groups with students who were initially very poor at reading. The teacher introduced AR and her students' end-of-the-year test results showed that 95% of students met or exceeded standards. Of course, other teacher actions might have had an impact. Moyer (2006) (a school librarian) reported the use of AR in one high school in New Jersey, but the report is wholly descriptive. Moyer and Williams (2011) then described how this school customized AR to the needs of disabled students. Pappas, Skinner and Skinner (2010) investigated the use of extrinsic rewards with AR with 32 fourth-grade students in three classes in an inner-city school where 90% were eligible for free lunch. Before the study, a student received a tangible reward after passing each AR quiz. With interdependent group-oriented contingencies, the entire group received a reward when they met a group-oriented goal (e.g., number of AR QP by the class). When this contingency was applied, the number of QP per week increased immediately but this increase was not maintained. The lowest-ability students showed the largest gains.

Another paper by a school librarian is from Pfeiffer (2011). She reports that with the adoption of AR, students at a middle school went from not making Adequate Yearly Progress in reading to making Standard of Excellence in reading each year from 2007

TABLE 4.1 Type and Frequency of Studies with Location of Authors and Average Effect Sizes

	USA	UK	UK/USA	Total	Average ES where given
Reviews	10	4	0	14	0.28
Randomized	6	1	0	7	0.35
Controlled	3	1	0	4	0.35
Many schools, reading tests	4	1	5	10	
Single schools, reading tests	4	0	0	4	
Many schools, no reading tests	8	1	0	9	
Single schools, no reading tests	16	0	0	16	
Totals	51	8	5	64	

to 2010. Finally, Solley (2011), another school librarian, offered a descriptive article about how she was sent to Renaissance Learning training and came back with many good ideas about implementation.

Table 4.1 summarizes the categories of study with country of location and their outcomes in ESs (where given).

Research Literature on Reading Counts

Very little research literature about RC which met the inclusion criteria was found (except for two studies, below). There were five PhD dissertations and master's theses on this topic, which, of course, were excluded. No other papers were found in any of the databases searched.

Greer's (2003) paper is interesting as it was the only one which directly compared AR and RC. However, consisting largely of passing observations, it offered no data. A middle school study (Biggers, 2010) reported linking RC points to 10% of school grades, which the authors acknowledge was controversial. Most teachers were positive towards the program, but only 24% of students met the requirements and 71% of teachers reported that the students were still not motivated to achieve reading points, although RC did improve student accountability. There was no attempt to investigate student perceptions or to investigate any further data from RC. Thus, both of these papers are of little use.

However, a great deal of literature was found about Read 180, in which RC is now embedded. Slavin, Cheung, Groff and Lake (2008) reviewed evaluations of intervention programs for secondary education, including Read 180. They found nine studies of Read 180 which met their inclusion criteria, yielding ESs between −0.12 and +1.58 (average 0.39 but this was obviously a wide range). Proctor, Daley, Louick, Leider and Gardner (2014) evaluated Read 180 with 76 middle school students who were both native English-speaking and otherwise. Self-efficacy was positively and significantly associated with reading comprehension, while intrinsic motivation and extrinsic motivation were not. The effect of self-efficacy was not moderated by English as a Foreign Language (EFL) status.

The WWC reported on Read 180 in 2010 and 2016a. In 2010, WWC identified 56 studies of Read 180 for students with learning disabilities; these studies included reports from schools and PhD dissertations and were published or released between 1989 and 2009 (WWC, 2010). However, none of these met the WWC criteria for inclusion, so no conclusion was drawn. In 2016a, however, WWC identified 156 studies of Read 180, of which 117 did not meet their inclusion criteria. Of the remaining 39 studies, 30 did not meet the WWC design standards. Nine studies of students in grades 4 to 12 did meet the WWC criteria. Again, 147 studies were discarded – typical of WWC. The WWC considered the extent of evidence for Read 180 on reading achievement to be "medium to large" for comprehension and general literacy achievement. However, when we look at the average ESs, comprehension was only 0.10 and literary achievement was only 0.10, both of which would be considered "small". Reading fluency had "potentially positive effects" but only two studies reported this and only one had positive effects. Thus, WWC reports small effects for Read 180 but excluded 147 studies in arriving at this conclusion.

In addition, the Read 180 website reports over 50 studies from schools around the US, including evaluations with English learners, students with disabilities, economically disadvantaged students, and students of various ethnicities. (Although these are excluded from this book, teachers may wish to consult them.)

Thus, while it certainly appears that Read 180 is an effective program, it is impossible to extract the independent effect of RC from these data.

New Data on Accelerated Reader

Data were available for 8,745,130 students for the academic year 2018–2019, which was the year before the Covid pandemic disrupted schools. AR data were available regarding gender and ethnicity but not social disadvantage.

Quizzes Taken averaged 37.83 (standard deviation [s.d.] 49.37, range 0–4,404), while QP averaged 32.77 (s.d. 44.84, range 0–3,175). The Pass Rate was 86.6%. The Average Book Level (ABL) was 3.61 (s.d. 1.34, range 0.10–20.00). The APC was 0.79 (79%) (s.d. 0.17, range 0.00–1.00). The Average Engaged Reading Time (ERT) was 21.91 minutes per student per day (s.d. 27.40, range 0.00–2332).

Gender

Seventy-five percent of cases reported the gender of the participant. Of these, there were slightly more males than females (Table 4.2).

Star Reading student growth percentile (SGP) results were available for 1,487,977 females and 1,532,291 males. The female average was 49.41 (s.d. 28.66), and the male average was 48.99 (s.d. 29.86). This difference appears small, but because the sample size was so large, it was statistically significant at $p < 0.001$ ($t = 12.73$). This is equivalent to an ES of 0.02, which would be considered very small.

TABLE 4.2 Gender of AR Participants Where Known

Gender	Number	Percentage
Female	3,212,478	36.73
Male	3,324,887	38.02
Unknown	2,207,765	25.25
Total	8,745,130	100.00

For the following analyses, data were available for 1,486,428 female students and 1,530,729 male students, about 46% of the total.

Quizzes Passed
The female average was 33.69 (45.69), and the male average 32.50 (44.85); that is, females passed more quizzes than males. However, the ES was 0.03 (very small).

Average Percent Correct
APC is an indication of how successfully participants were reading and comprehending. The pass rate for tests was 60% for shorter tests and 70% for longer tests, and longer tests had more questions. The female average was 0.81 (0.15), and the male average was 0.78 (0.16); that is, females had better comprehension than males. The ES was 0.19 (still small).

Engaged Reading Time
The female average was 24.91 (27.32), and the male average was 23.15 (26.56); that is, females spent longer reading than did males. The ES was 0.07 (very small).

Average Book Level
Books were levelled by ATOS (Advantage/TASA Open Standard for Readability), and the ATOS figure indicates the ABL in terms of grade level (which can easily be related to chronological age). The female average was 3.59 (1.32), and the male average was 3.62 (1.35); that is, boys tended to read harder books. However, the ES was only 0.02 (very small). Nonetheless, this may to some extent explain the female superiority on QP and APC (above).

Countries
In 2018–2019, the main countries participating in AR were English-speaking countries: the USA, the UK, Australia, Canada and New Zealand (see Table 4.3). In recent years, the number of other countries using AR has grown, but these are largely countries where English is not the native language, and the students

TABLE 4.3 English-speaking Countries Participating in AR

Country	Number of students	Percentage
USA	7,629,981	87.25
UK	1,014,757	11.60
Australia	60,312	0.69
Canada	38,745	0.44
New Zealand	1,335	0.02
Total	8,745,130	100.00

TABLE 4.4 Star Reading SGP Scores by Country

Country	N	Percent of total	SGP average	s.d.
Australia	50	0.1%	45.78	29.74
Canada	12,900	33.3%	51.65	28.90
Great Britain	657,078	64.8%	50.34	29.08
USA	3,105,520	40.7%	49.21	29.34

involved are those learning English as a Second Language, so they have not been included here. By far the largest number of participating students were in the USA, followed by almost 12% in the UK, followed by less than 1% in each of Australia, Canada and New Zealand.

Star Reading SGP scores were not available for New Zealand, hardly any were available for Australia and only 33% were available for Canada. Indeed, only 41% were available for the USA, while the UK attained 65%. Nonetheless, averages have been calculated (Table 4.4).

Discounting Australia, there is limited variation between countries, from 49.21 in the USA to 51.65 in Canada. The ES is 0.08, categorized as small.

The percentage of students who yielded QP, APC, ERT and ABL data varied considerably, from 95% in the UK to 41% in Australia (see Table 4.5).

QP varied from 7.29 in New Zealand to 37.66 in the USA. While the New Zealand result might be accounted for by small and possible age-biased numbers in the sample, this cannot be said of other countries. For example, the difference between the

TABLE 4.5 Quizzes Passed, Average Percent Correct, Engaged Reading Time and Average Book Level by Country

Country	N	Percent of total	QP average	QP s.d.	APC average	APC s.d.	ERT average	ERT s.d.	ABL average	ABL s.d.
Australia	24,804	41.1%	11.21	15.62	0.77	0.19	10.77	20.26	3.99	1.19
Canada	22,169	57.2%	25.74	35.14	0.82	0.15	24.44	32.15	4.02	1.22
UK	965,028	95.1%	17.73	20.88	0.76	0.18	14.98	21.19	4.08	1.16
New Zealand	822	61.6%	7.29	7.56	0.75	0.19	12.60	17.87	4.86	1.01
USA	5,248,277	68.8%	37.66	47.90	0.80	0.16	23.24	28.21	3.56	1.31

USA and the UK is very large. The ES of the difference between the largest and the smallest was 0.63, well above "moderate".

APC varied from 0.75 in New Zealand to 0.82 in Canada. Again, the New Zealand result might be accounted for by the small sample. ES between the highest and the lowest was 0.46 (moderate).

ERT varied enormously, from 10.77 in Australia to 24.44 in Canada. The ES between highest and lowest was 0.52 (moderate).

ABL also varied considerably, from very low in the USA (3.56) to very high in New Zealand (4.86). ES was 0.99 (large going on very large).

Thus, all of these implementation variables varied considerably between countries, even allowing for variation in overall numbers between countries. We will consider this further in Chapters 5 and 6 on implementation quality.

New Data on Reading Counts

Some RC settings are customizable by the teacher, who may choose to hide such results, so the data may not be complete. For RC, data regarding gender, ethnicity, social disadvantage and country were unfortunately not available as they had not been collected (the latter is unsurprising given that RC was used almost entirely in the USA). Some data were available for the academic year 2015–2016; data for later years were not available.

In total, 41,488 students took RC. Of these, 20,367 took RC as part of Read 180, 5,213 took RC as part of System 44, and 1,341 took RC with Read 180 and System 44 together. Only 14,567 students (35%) took RC on its own. In subsequent analyses, we will take the RC-only students as one set and the RC with another intervention (regardless of whether it was Read 180 or System 44 or both) as another.

Reading Counts Only

Initial Lexiles were available, taken mainly in late August, September and October 2015. Final Lexiles were available, taken mainly in April and May 2016. For the RC-only students, 13,602 had data for both initial and final Lexile. The initial Lexile average was 629.72 (424.41) and the final Lexile average 726.34 (s.d. = 392.45), a difference of 96.63 (163.43), yielding t = 68.96, d.f. = 13,601, p <0.001, and ES = 0.23. Thus, on average, the RC-only students had certainly made a substantial improvement in the Lexiles of the books they were reading, in terms of both statistical significance and the ES, which however could be described only as "small".

Tests Taken overall were 307,912, the average was 21.09 (31.01) and the range was 1–474. Clearly there was a good deal of variance. However, this included tests that were retaken, so a more accurate statistic is probably the number of *unique* tests taken. Here the number was 278,495, 90.66% of the previous figure. It seems that although teachers can allow students to retake tests, this does not actually happen except in 9% of test cases. The unique test average was 19.12 (28.27) and range was 1–463. (You would expect the success rate on unique tests to be lower than for all tests including re-takes.) Let us now see if this differed by grade (Table 4.6).

Again, grade 0 and grades 10–12 can be disregarded as numbers are very small. The number of books read and uniquely quizzed declined steadily by year, as one would expect since books for younger readers tend to be shorter. By grades 8 and 9,

TABLE 4.6 Unique Tests Taken by Grade

Grade	N	Minimum	Maximum	Average	Std. deviation
0	78	3	167	26.87	33.16
1	557	1	276	48.62	48.56
2	1,336	1	463	36.89	48.13
3	2,636	1	394	27.84	35.76
4	1,950	1	177	18.92	22.22
5	1,691	1	275	15.69	17.25
6	2,141	1	93	11.44	10.95
7	1,978	1	111	10.07	9.61
8	1,410	1	72	8.31	7.94
9	457	1	104	8.32	11.52
10	186	1	123	10.92	16.60
11	107	1	38	8.67	8.71
12	40	1	26	8.75	7.32

only eight books were being read and quizzed each year, which is less than one per month, so perhaps this reflects a decline in student motivation as well as the effect of book length.

In regard to Tests Passed (in relation to tests taken), the average was 16.04 (24.81) and range was 1–440. Comparing this with Unique Tests Taken overall (above), Tests Passed was 70.44% of the total of unique tests – a rather low figure.

In regard to Pass Rate, the percentage of tests taken that were passed (whether at the standard and most common pass rate of 70% or at some other pass rate defined by the teacher; see below) averaged 72.02 (24.10) and the range was 3%–100%.

Table 4.7 reports the findings by grade. Again, grades 0 and 10–12 can be disregarded. Grade 1 does particularly well with the highest pass rate, and grade 9 rather poorly as it is the only average below 70%, which is the nominal pass rate for these quizzes. Of course, only the average is around 70%, which means that many quizzes are failed, and many scored at much-higher-than-average rates.

Turning now to Average Test Score, the percentage at which the tests were passed, which includes all tests whether taken for the first, second or third time and ranges from 1 to 100, we find that the average is 71.23 (18.27). Table 4.8 looks at this by grade.

TABLE 4.7 Pass Rate Percentage by Grade

Grade	N	Minimum	Maximum	Average	Std. deviation
0	78	24	100	80.63	17.37
1	537	10	100	78.41	19.34
2	1,274	10	100	72.70	22.00
3	2,467	5	100	70.70	22.97
4	1,818	6	100	72.54	23.49
5	1,602	6	100	73.56	24.15
6	1,976	3	100	70.95	25.39
7	1,831	5	100	70.40	25.82
8	1,239	8	100	72.77	24.24
9	385	6	100	68.01	27.19
10	165	5	100	74.84	24.80
11	91	14	100	71.77	29.97
12	36	14	100	75.32	27.56

TABLE 4.8 Average Test Score by Grade

Grade	N	Minimum	Maximum	Average	Std. Deviation
0	78	45	100	83.17	11.12
1	557	1	100	78.13	15.33
2	1,336	1	100	72.84	17.05
3	2,636	1	100	70.67	17.66
4	1,950	1	100	71.74	17.85
5	1,691	1	100	73.20	17.07
6	2,141	1	100	70.43	18.53
7	1,978	1	100	69.95	18.94
8	1,410	1	100	69.42	19.47
9	457	1	100	66.20	20.81
10	186	1	100	70.70	19.05
11	107	1	100	65.48	24.95
12	40	20	100	72.68	19.56

Again, grades 0 and 10–12 can be disregarded. Otherwise, there is not much difference between grades, expect for a slight tendency to decline from elementary grades to high school grades. However, all secondary school grades are below the 70% criterion.

Looking now at QP (n = 216,098) (which could be first failed and then passed at a later quizzing), we see that 201,623 were passed on first try (93%) by 13,344 students (average = 15.11 [23.69], range 1–425). By contrast, 12,228 were passed at the second try (6%) by 5,175 students (average = 2.63 [2.46], range 1–31). Beyond this, 2,247 (1%) were passed at the third try by 1,524 students (average = 1.47 [1.04], range 1–12). It seems that although teachers can offer students the opportunity to retake quizzes, this does not happen successfully in more than 7% of cases.

Looking now at the Average Reading Level of Books, we find that the average for 13,499 students was 4.03 (2.18) and range was 0–123, but these data were available for only a limited number of students. Similarly, the Average Lexile of Books Read was available for only a limited number of students (13,481), giving an average of 603.74 (229.99) and range of 0–1,350.

Data were also available on Fiction vs. Non-fiction reading (in both cases only when the quiz was passed, on whatever try).

Fiction reads were recorded for 12,774 students (62%); the average was 13.44 (20.35) and range was 1–276. By contrast, Non-fiction reads were recorded for just 7,702 students (38%); the average was 5.88 (10.04) and range was 1–173. Obviously, Fiction reads were much more frequent than Non-fiction reads in RC only, and comparing the two with an independent samples t-test yielded t = 45.34, p <0.001, df = 6,976, and ES = 0.59, which is above moderate and heading towards large. Thus, there was much more Fiction than Non-fiction reading, at a ratio of 3:2.

Reading Counts + Other Intervention

For the RC + Other Intervention students (n = 26,827 with both Initial and Final data), the Initial Lexile average = 487.95 (324.48) and the Final Lexile average = 603.20 (313.20). The difference was 115.25, t = 108.89, d.f. = 26,826, p <0.001, ES = 0.36 (somewhere between small and moderate, again affected by the large variance). Thus, where RC is used with another intervention, the effect on reading books independently is greater than when RC is used on its own. Given that the ESs per grade for RC only were not very different by grade, the same analysis has not been conducted for RC + Other Intervention data.

Quizzes Taken overall were 26,921; the average was 11.07 (13.22) and range was 1–330. As these figures included quizzes that were retaken, the number of Unique Quizzes was investigated. The average was 9.57 (11.23) and range was 1–328. Thus, it seems that for the RC + Other Intervention, teachers do not exercise their judgement in regard to allowing students to retake quizzes. This Unique Quizzes figure is considerably lower than that for RC only, but, of course, RC + Other Intervention is targeted on students in the lower ranges of ability, so that might be expected. The range is also lower for RC + Other Intervention, again as would be expected as lower-ability students are likely to read a more restricted range of books.

In regard to QP (in relation to quizzes taken), n = 24,764, average = 7.82 (9.22) and range = 1–324. Again, this is much lower than for RC only, with a more restricted range, as would be expected. Comparing this with Quizzes Taken Overall (above), QP was 91.99% of this total. In regard to Pass Rate for RC + Other Intervention students, the percentage of quizzes taken that were passed (all at the standard pass rate of 70%) (n = 24,766) averaged 70.26 (24.67). In regard to Average Test Score for RC + Other Intervention, which includes all quizzes whether taken for the first, second or third time and ranges from 1 to 100, the average was 69.94 (17.38). Thus, RC + Other Intervention brings this score up almost to the same level as RC only (71.23), but we must bear in mind that the former is targeted on low-reading-ability students.

Looking now at QP (n = 216,098) (which could be first failed and then passed at a later quizzing), we see that 168,666 were passed on first try (66%) by 24,065 students (average = 7.01 [8.53], range 1–319). This is much less than for RC-Only students (93%). Looking now at the Average Reading Level of books, we find that the average for 24,766 students was 3.03 (1.56) and range was 1–78. This is considerably less than for RC-Only students and has a more restricted range. The Average Lexile of Books Read was available for only a limited number of students (24,728), giving an average of 478.25 (211.57) and a range of 0–1,200. This was again considerably less than for RC-Only students.

Data were available on Fiction vs. Non-fiction reading (in both cases only when the quiz was passed, on whatever try). Fiction reads were recorded for 20,484 students (50%); the average was 4.73 (6.70) and range was 1–309. Non-fiction reads were recorded for 20,286 students (50%); the average was 4.78 (5.14) and range was 1–100. For RC + Other Intervention students, relatively far more non-fiction was read than for RC-only students. This reflects the nature of the System 44 and Read 180 curricula, which are more prescriptive about what students read and strive to establish a balance between fiction and non-fiction. While the fiction reads are much less than for RC-Only students, the non-fiction reads are approaching the same level. Thus, Fiction equated to Non-fiction reading, the ratio being 1:1. The ES was 0.01, showing no difference at all.

Chapter Summary

This chapter on What Works is divided into sections. First, AR and RC have separate sections to report the research literature on them. Then, AR and RC have separate sections reporting new data.

AR Research Literature

Within the AR research literature section, previous studies (n = 64) are divided into the following: Reviews (n = 14), Randomized Controlled studies (n = 7), Controlled studies Not Randomized (n = 4), studies of Many Schools with Reading Tests (n = 10), Single Schools with Reading Tests (n = 4), Many Schools with No Reading Tests (n = 9) and Single Schools with No Reading Tests (n = 16). Of these, 51 originated in the USA, eight in the UK, and five resulted from collaborations between the UK and the USA. The average ESs (where given) were +0.28 for Reviews, +0.35 for Randomized Controlled studies and +0.35 for Controlled studies Not Randomized, but many studies did not give ESs, so this should not be taken as definitive.

The AR Reviews section was largely disappointing, as many so-called reviews included very few studies, some of which were student theses which were not included in this book. Only five of these have much value, and it is left to the reader to decide which ones. The Randomized studies are much more satisfactory in quality, and all reported positive effects for AR. The Controlled but Not Randomized studies were equally satisfactory in quality, and all reported positive effects for AR. The Many Schools with Reading Tests section were equally satisfactory in quality, and all reported positive effects for AR. The Single Schools with Reading Tests section was generally satisfactory, and three out of four reported positive effects for AR, the exception being a study with very poor implementation. Many Schools with No Reading Tests were generally satisfactory, although in two studies the focus was not really on evaluating AR. Otherwise, all reported positive effects for AR, sometimes tempered by differences with older students. The Single Schools with No Reading Tests section was large and extremely various, and several studies showed severe design or methodology problems. Three studies showed no difference between AR and other conditions, and in the case of two studies, the results were not clear. The remaining 11 studies reported positive effects for AR.

Overall, of 64 studies, four reported no effects for AR and four were not clear. Thus, 56 (88%) out of 64 studies reported positive effects for AR. This high percentage will perhaps be surprising for those readers who have been unduly influenced by the largely opinion pieces reported in Chapter 3. In many of the subsections, there was frequent comment on the importance of implementation quality, a topic we will return to in more depth in Chapter 6.

RC Research Literature
Then, within the RC literature section, there was very little research literature about RC alone which met the inclusion criteria (except for two studies). Greer (2003) directly compared AR and RC but offered no data. Biggers (2010) offered a very weak study in a school with very poor implementation. However, Read 180 (in which RC is embedded) had a good deal of literature. Reviews by Slavin et al. (2008) indicated an average ES of 0.59, while a WWC review indicated an ES of only 0.10 (both reviews included nine studies). Thus, while it certainly appears that Read 180 is an effective program, it is impossible to extract the independent effect of RC from these data.

AR New Data
Data were available for 8,745,130 students for the academic year 2018–2019. Quizzes Taken averaged 37.83, while QP averaged 32.77. The Pass Rate was 86.6%. The ABL was 3.61. The APC was 0.79 (79%). The average ERT was 21.91 minutes per student per day. There were slightly more males than females, but females performed slightly better on the Star Reading test. Females also passed slightly more quizzes than males, their ERT was slightly higher than males, and the difficulty of books read by females was slightly higher. However, female quality of comprehension (APC) was markedly higher than males. In regard to differences between countries, Canada had the highest score on the

Star Reading tests, followed by the UK, the USA and Australia. Differences in QP were very large; the USA was highest, Canada was next and the UK was much lower. Differences in APC showed the US high and the UK low. Differences in ERT also showed the US high and the UK low, although both were low in relation to recommended reading time. However, in difficulty of books read (ABL), the UK was well ahead of the USA, which partially explains the difference in QP. Canada did well on all these variables.

RC New Data

Data for RC only were available for 14,567 students for the academic year 2015–2016. The difference between initial and final Lexiles gave an ES of 0.23. Tests Taken overall were 307,912 and *Unique* Tests Taken were 278,495, so in only 9% of cases did teachers allow students to retake tests. Unique Tests Taken declined steadily over the grades, as might be expected. The average for Tests Passed was 16.04, 70% of Unique Tests. The Pass Rate (whether at the default pass rate of 70% or at some other pass rate defined by the teacher) averaged 72. The Average Test Score was 71. For QP (n = 216,098), 201,623 (93%) were passed on the first try by 13,344 students. Although teachers can allow students to retake quizzes, this did not happen in more than 7% of cases. The Average Reading Level of books for 13,499 students was 4.03, and the Average Lexile of books read was 603.74. There was more Fiction than Non-fiction reading, at a ratio of 3:2 (ES = 0.59).

Data for RC + Other Intervention were available for 26.921 students, again for 2015–2016. Initial to Final Lexile gave an ES of 0.36, larger than for RC only students. Quizzes Taken overall averaged 11.07, while the Unique Quizzes average was 9.57, both considerably lower than for RC only. Compared with Quizzes Taken, QP were 92% of the total. The Pass Rate averaged 70. The Average Test Score was 70, only slightly less than RC only. On QP, 168,666 were passed on first try (66%), much less than for RC only. The Average Reading Level of books was 3.03, considerably less than for RC Only (as was the Average Lexile). Fiction and non-fiction reads were 50% each, so relatively far more non-fiction was read than for RC only students.

References

Anderson, J. (2001, July 31). What works: A skeptic is sold: A high school librarian finds reasons to love Accelerated Reader. *School Library Journal*.

Balajthy, E. (2007). Technology and current reading/literacy assessment strategies. *The Reading Teacher, 61*(3), 240–247. DOI:10.1598/RT.61.3.4

Biggers, P. S. (2010). Reading counts toward success: A program evaluation. *Paper prepared for Vila Rica Middle School*. http://stu.westga.edu/~sayers1/8480_FinalReport_psb.docx

Borman, G. D., & Dowling, N. M. (2004). *Testing the Reading Renaissance program theory: A multilevel analysis of student and classroom effects on reading achievement*. Madison, WI: University of Wisconsin-Madison. https://doc.renlearn.com/KMNet/R00405242EE3BD7A.pdf

Brem, S. K., Husman, J., & Duggan, M. A. (2005). *Findings from a three-year study of Reading Renaissance in a Title I urban elementary school: The effects of Reading Renaissance on students' standardized reading performance and motivation towards independent reading*. Tempe, AZ: Arizona State University.

Burns, J. M., & Collins, M. D. (1987). Parents' perceptions of factors affecting the reading development of intellectually superior accelerated readers and intellectually superior nonreaders. *Reading Research and Instruction, 26*(4), 239–246.

Burns, J. M., Collins, M. D., & Paulsell, J. C. (1991). A comparison of intellectually superior preschool Accelerated Readers and nonreaders: Four years later. *Gifted Child Quarterly, 35*(3), 118–124.

Chase, E., Goodin, P., & Nichols, W. R. (2010). Evaluation of the Accelerated Reader program in Chesapeake, VA, public schools. *ERS Spectrum, 28*(1), 25–32. https://www.learntechlib.org/p/55120/

Chenoweth, K. (2001). Keeping score. *School Library Journal, 47*(9), 48–51.

Clark, C., & Cunningham, A. (2016). *Reading enjoyment, behaviour and attitudes in pupils who use Accelerated Reader*. London: National Literacy Trust. https://files.eric.ed.gov/fulltext/ED570684.pdf

Cuddeback, M. J., & Ceprano, M. A. (2002). The use of Accelerated Reader with emergent readers. *Reading Improvement, 39*(2), 89–96.

Education Commission of the States (2000). *Accelerated Reader/Reading Renaissance*. Denver, CO: E.C.S. https://web.archive.org/

web/20050414213152/http://www.ecs.org:80/clearinghouse/18/79/1879.htm

Esposito, J., & Smith, S. (2006). From reluctant teacher to empowered teacher-researcher: One educator's journey toward action. *Teacher Education Quarterly, 33*(3), 45–60.

Everhart, N. (2005). A crosscultural inquiry into the levels of implementation of Accelerated Reader and its effect on motivation and extent of reading: Perspectives from Scotland and England. *School Library Media Research, 8*. https://files.eric.ed.gov/fulltext/EJ965628.pdf

Everhart, N., Dresang, E. T., & Kotrla, B. (2005). Accelerated Reader and information policy, information literacy, and knowledge management: U.S. and international implications. *International Association of School Librarianship Annual Conference*, Hong Kong. DOI: 10.29173/iasl8030

Florida Center for Reading Research. (2004). *Accelerated Reader*. Tallahassee, FL: FCRR. https://web.archive.org/web/20060210094815/http://www.fcrr.org/FCRRReports/PDF/Accelerated_Reader.pdf

Foster, D. K., & Foster, D. P. (2014). Estimating reading growth attributable to Accelerated Reader at one American School in the Caribbean. *Reading Psychology, 35*(6), 529–547. DOI:10.1080/02702711.2013.789764

Goodman, G. (1999). *The Reading Renaissance/Accelerated Reader program. Pinal county school-to-work evaluation report*. Tucson, AZ: Creative Research Associates, Inc. https://files.eric.ed.gov/fulltext/ED427299.pdf

Gorard, S., Siddiqui, N., & See, B. H. (2017). What works and what fails? Evidence from seven popular literacy 'catch-up' schemes for the transition to secondary school in England. *Research Papers in Education, 32*(5), 626–648.

Greer, J. (2003). Point: A positive experience with Accelerated Reader. *Teacher Librarian, 30*(4), 32.

Hamilton, B. (1997). Using accelerated reader with ESL students. *MultiMedia Schools, 4*(2), 50–52.

Hansen, L. E., Collins, P., & Warschauer, M. (2009). Reading management programs: A review of the research. *Journal of Literacy and Technology, 10*(3), 55–80. http://citeseerx.ist.psu.edu/viewdoc/download?doi=10.1.1.491.3652&rep=rep1&type=pdf

Holmes, C. T., & Brown, C. L. (2003). *A controlled evaluation of a total school improvement process, School Renaissance.* Paper presented at the National Renaissance Conference, Nashville, TN, February 7, 2003. https://files.eric.ed.gov/fulltext/ED474261.pdf

Holmes, C. T., Brown, C. L., & Algozzine, B. (2006). Promoting academic success for all students. *Academic Exchange Quarterly, 10*(3), 141–147.

Huang, S. (2012). A mixed method study of the effectiveness of the Accelerated Reader program on middle school students' reading achievement and motivation. *Reading Horizons: A Journal of Literacy and Language Arts, 51*(3), 5.

Husman, J., Brem, S., & Duggan, M. A. (2005). Student goal orientation and formative assessment. *Academic Exchange Quarterly, 9*(3), 355–359. http://www.rapidintellect.com/AEQweb/5oct3047l5.htm

Johnson, R. A., & Howard, C. A. (2003). The effects of the Accelerated Reader program on the reading comprehension of pupils in grades three, four, and five. *The Reading Matrix, 3*(3), 87–96. http://www.readingmatrix.com/articles/johnson_howard/article.pdf

Kulik, J. A. (2003). *Effects of using instructional technology in elementary and secondary schools: What controlled evaluation studies say.* Arlington, VA: SRI International. (SRI Project No. P10446.001). https://www.ic.unicamp.br/~wainer/cursos/2s2004/impactos2004/Kulik_ITinK-12_Main_Report.pdf

Lawson, S. (2000). Accelerated Reader boosts student achievement. *California School Library Association Journal, 23*(2), 11–12.

Long, T., & Bonds-Raacke, J. (2012). Accelerated Reader: The relation to age of entry into formal education. *Reading Improvement, 49*(4), 168–188.

McGlinn, J., & Parrish, A. (2002). Accelerating ESL students' reading progress with Accelerated Reader. *Reading Horizons, 42*(3), 175–189. http://scholarworks.wmich.edu/cgi/viewcontent.cgi?article=1186&context=reading_horizons

Mallette, M. H., Henk, W. A., & Melnick, S. A. (2004). The influence of Accelerated Reader on the affective literacy orientations of intermediate grade students. *Journal of Literacy Research, 36*(1), 73–84. DOI:10.1207/s15548430jlr3601_4

Moyer, M. (2006). Accelerated Reader sparks high school reading excitement. *Knowledge Quest, 35*(1), 34–39.

Moyer, M., & Williams, M. (2011). Personal programming: Customizing Accelerated Reader helps Delsea regional high school encourage student reading. *Knowledge Quest, 39*(4), 68–73.

Nunnery, J. A., & Ross, S. M. (2007). The effects of the School Renaissance program on student achievement in reading and mathematics. *Research in the Schools, 14*(1), 40–59. https://search.proquest.com/docview/211015676

Nunnery, J. A., Ross, S. M., & McDonald, A. (2006). A randomized experimental evaluation of the impact of Accelerated Reader/Reading Renaissance implementation on reading achievement in grades 3 to 6. *Journal of Education for Students Placed at Risk, 11*(1), 1–18. https://www.researchgate.net/publication/233069439_A_Randomized_Experimental_EvaluationoftheImpact_of_Accelerated_Reader/Reading_Renaissance_Implementation_on_Reading_Achievement_in_Grades_3_to_6

Pappas, D. N., Skinner, C. H., & Skinner, A. L. (2010). Supplementing accelerated reading with classwide interdependent group-oriented contingencies. *Psychology in the Schools, 47*(9), 887–902. DOI:10.1002/pits.20512

Pavonetti, L. M., Brimmer, K. M., & Cipielewski, J. F. (2002–3). Accelerated Reader: What are the lasting effects on the reading habits of middle school students exposed to Accelerated Reader in elementary grades? *Journal of Adolescent & Adult Literacy, 46*(4), 300–311. https://www.jstor.org/stable/40013588

Peak, J. P., & Dewalt, M. W. (1994). Reading achievement: Effects of computerized reading management and enrichment. *ERS Spectrum, 12*(1), 31–35.

Penuel, B. (1997). *Program evaluation summary: Accelerated Reader*. Nashville: Metropolitan Nashville Public Schools.

Pfeiffer, C. (2011). Achieving a standard of reading excellence in Kansas. *Knowledge Quest, 39*(4), 60–67.

Proctor, C. P., Daley, S., Louick, R., Leider, C. M., & Gardner, G. L. (2014). How motivation and engagement predict reading comprehension among native English-speaking and English-learning middle school students with disabilities in a remedial reading curriculum. *Learning and Individual Differences, 36*, 76–83. DOI:10.1016/j.lindif.2014.10.014

Rejholec, T. (2002). *An action research on the effects of extrinsic rewards on motivation of eighth grade language arts students.* ERIC Document Number: ED473051. https://files.eric.ed.gov/fulltext/ED473051.pdf

Rodriguez, S. (2007). The Accelerated Reader program's relationship to student achievement on the English/Language Arts California Standards Test. *The Reading Matrix, 7*(3), 191–205. http://www.readingmatrix.com/articles/rodriguez/article.pdf

Rosenheck, D., Caldwell, D., Calkins, J., & Perez, D. A. (1996). *Accelerated Reader impact on feelings about reading and library use: A survey of fifth grade students in Lee County, Florida, to determine how a computerized reading management program affects attitudes toward reading and the media center and frequency of library use.* Tampa, FL: University of Southern Florida. https://files.eric.ed.gov/fulltext/ED399508.pdf

Ross, S. M., Nunnery, J., & Goldfeder, E. (2004). *A randomized experiment on the effects of Accelerated Reader/Reading Renaissance in an urban school district: Final evaluation report.* Memphis, TN: Center for Research in Educational Policy, The University of Memphis.

Rudd, P., & Wade, P. (2006). *Evaluation of Renaissance Learning mathematics and reading programs in UK Specialist and feeder schools.* Slough: National Foundation for Educational Research. https://www.nfer.ac.uk/publications/SRY01/SRY01.pdf

Samuels, S. J., & Wu, Y. C. (2003). *The effects of immediate feedback on reading achievement.* Minneapolis, MN: University of Minnesota. https://web.archive.org/web/20060423031356/http://www.tc.umn.edu/~samue001/web%20pdf/immediate_feedback.pdf

Samuels, S. J., Lewis, M., Wu, Y. C., Reininger, J., & Murphy, A. (2003). *Accelerated Reader vs. Non-Accelerated Reader: How students using the Accelerated Reader outperformed the control condition in a tightly controlled experimental study.* Minneapolis: University of Minnesota. https://web.archive.org/web/20040902144751/http://www.tc.umn.edu/~samue001/web%20pdf/Final%20Report--Accelerated%20Reader%20vs%20Non-Accelerated%20Reader.pdf

See, B. H., & Gorard, S. (2020). Effective classroom instructions for primary literacy: A critical review of the causal evidence. *International Journal of Educational Research, 102,* 101577. DOI:10.1016/j.ijer.2020.101577

Shannon, L. C., Styers, M. K., & Siceloff, E. R. (2010). *A final report for the evaluation of Renaissance Learning's Accelerated Reader Program.* Charlottesville, VA: Magnolia Consulting.

Shannon, L. C., Styers, M. K., Wilkerson, S. B., & Peery, E. (2015). Computer-assisted learning in elementary reading: A randomized control trial. *Computers in the Schools, 32*(1), 20–34.

Siddiqui, N., Gorard, S., & See, B. H. (2016). Accelerated Reader as a literacy catch-up intervention during primary to secondary school transition phase. *Educational Review, 68*(2), 139–154. DOI:10.1080/00131911.2015.1067883. http://dro.dur.ac.uk/16393/1/16393.pdf

Slavin, R. E., Cheung, A., Groff, C., & Lake, C. (2008). Effective reading programs for middle and high schools: A best-evidence synthesis. *Reading Research Quarterly, 43*(3), 290–322.

Slavin, R. E., Lake, C., Chambers, B., Cheung, A., & Davis, S. (2009). Effective reading programs for the elementary grades: A best-evidence synthesis. *Review of Educational Research, 79*(4), 1391–1466.

Slavin, R. E., & Madden, N. A. (2008). *Understanding bias due to measures inherent to treatments in systematic reviews in education.* Paper presented at the Society for Research on Effective Education, Virginia. http://www.bestevidence.org/methods/understand_bias_Mar_2008.pdf

Smith, A. F., & Westberg, K. L. (2011). Student attitudes toward Accelerated Reader: "Thanks for asking!" *Current Issues in Education, 14*(2). http://cie.asu.edu/ojs/index.php/cieatasu/article/view/632

Smith, A. F., Westberg, K., & Hejny, A. (2017). Accelerated Reader program: What do teachers really think? *International Journal of Higher Education, 6*(3), 138–146.

Solley, K. (2011). Accelerated Reader can be an effective tool to encourage and bolster student reading. *Knowledge Quest, 39*(4), 46–49.

Stiegemeier, L. (1999). *Language Integrated Technology Project final evaluation report.* Olympia, WA: Washington Office of the State Superintendent of Public Instruction, Olympia. https://files.eric.ed.gov/fulltext/ED462965.pdf

Stringfield, S. G., Luscre, D., & Gast, D. L. (2011). Effects of a story map on Accelerated Reader postreading test scores in students with high-functioning autism. *Focus on Autism and Other Developmental Disabilities, 26*(4), 218–229. DOI:10.1177/1088357611423543

Topping, K. J. (1999). Formative assessment of reading comprehension by computer: Advantages and disadvantages of the Accelerated Reader software. *Reading OnLine* (I.R.A.) [Online]. www.readingonline.org/critical/topping/ [November 4]. (hypermedia).

Topping, K. J., & Fisher, A. M. (2003). Computerised formative assessment of reading comprehension: Field trials in the UK. *Journal of Research in Reading*, *26*(3), 267–279.

Topping, K. J., & Paul, T. (1999). Computer-assisted assessment of practice at reading: A large scale survey using Accelerated Reader data. *Quarterly*, *15*(3), 213–231.

Topping, K. J., Samuels, J., & Paul, T. (2007a). Does practice make perfect? Independent reading quantity, quality and student achievement. *Learning and Instruction*, *17*(3), 253–264.

Topping, K. J., Samuels, J., & Paul, T. (2007b). Computerized assessment of independent reading: Effects of implementation quality on achievement gain. *School Effectiveness and School Improvement*, *18*(2), 191–208.

Topping, K. J., Samuels, J., & Paul, T. (2008). Independent reading: The relationship of challenge, non-fiction and gender to achievement. *British Educational Research Journal*, *34*(4), 505–524.

Topping, K. J., & Sanders, W. L. (2000). Teacher effectiveness and computer assessment of reading: Relating value added and learning information system data. *School Effectiveness and School Improvement*, *11*(3), 305–337.

Vollands, S. R., Topping, K. J., & Evans, H. M. (1999). Computerized self-assessment of reading comprehension with the Accelerated Reader: Action research. *Reading and Writing Quarterly*, *15*(3), 197–211 (themed issue on Electronic Literacy).

What Works Clearinghouse. (2008). *Accelerated Reader. WWC Intervention Report*. Washington, DC: U.S. Department of Education. https://ies.ed.gov/ncee/wwc/Docs/InterventionReports/wwc_accelreader_101408.pdf

What Works Clearinghouse. (2010). *Read 180: Students with learning disabilities. WWC intervention report*. Washington, DC: U.S. Department of Education. https://ies.ed.gov/ncee/wwc/Docs/InterventionReports/wwc_read180_071310.pdf

What Works Clearinghouse. (2016). *Accelerated Reader. A summary of findings from a systematic review of the evidence.* Washington, DC: U.S. Department of Education. https://ies.ed.gov/ncee/wwc/Docs/InterventionReports/wwc_acceleratedreader_061416.pdf

Yeh, S. S. (2010). The cost-effectiveness of 22 approaches for raising student achievement. *Journal of Education Finance, 36*(1), 38–75. https://www.jstor.org/stable/40704405

5

How to Implement for Increased Student Success

This chapter describes how these programs *should* be implemented, outlining best implementation practices in schools – allowing book reading time and helping manage engagement, motivation, and goal orientation (although, of course, many students do much of this for themselves). Poock (1998) and Persinger (2001) described some of these requirements. Electronic reading can be encouraged also (e.g., with the myON software, which provides screen versions of books and allows online quizzing; see Chapter 12). Much of the research literature on implementation will be discussed in the next chapter (Chapter 6: How Have Schools Done with Implementation?). There will be very little research literature in this chapter.

Research Literature on Accelerated Reader

However, here we can report a research study which links to both Accelerated Reader (AR) and Reading Counts (RC), showing that more time spent on reading was associated with higher reading achievement (Wu & Samuels, 2004). This experimental study tested the effects of allowing more versus less time for independent reading for students who differed in reading ability. The participants were in grades 3 and 5 and the study lasted

DOI: 10.4324/9781003215882-5

six months. The control group spent 15 minutes per day reading books, and the experimental group spent 40 minutes per day reading books. Both third- and fifth-grade experimental students who were average or above readers showed significantly greater gains on a variety of reading and vocabulary tests compared with control (alternative treatment) students, the third grade showing a greater gain than fifth grade. However, average or below readers did not show such a gain, and it was speculated that 40 minutes might have been too long for these poorer readers.

Before starting AR, the teacher has to be clear that a minimum amount of time has to be allocated to independent reading every day. This should be a minimum of 20 minutes and a maximum of about 45 minutes. Of course, this means that something else has to give way, and teachers find it very difficult to stop doing something they have done for a long time, especially when under pressure from the school administration to continue as before. Students can, of course, read outside of class time while still in school or indeed at home or in the community if they are allowed to take books home. Some schools do not allow this for fear of losing the books, but remember that these books are of high interest and highly motivating and the students actually want to read them – all of which is likely to militate against the books being lost.

After this, AR usually commences with the student taking a placement test using the Star Reading test. This gives an idea of the difficulty level of book the student should be working with. However, evidence shows that students can read books with good comprehension that are supposed to be much too difficult for them provided they are very interested in them, so this should be taken as only a very rough guide. Students should never be told "that book is too hard for you" – although they certainly can be told "that book is too easy for you".

Of course, book difficulty is levelled using either the Lexile framework or the ATOS (Advantage/TASA Open Standard for Readability) system, and this information is available to both student and teacher online, even if it not marked on the book itself. However, book difficulty is by no means the only criterion, and interest level and the suitability of the text for the maturity of the reader should be taken into account. Beyond this, search criteria might include favorite title stems, favorite authors, specific subjects, award winners and so forth. The AR Book Guide is an indispensable tool for supporting this searching. With this, one can quickly access details about every book in the AR quiz library, identify and sort new titles, develop custom reading lists, see detailed profiles on each book, import ATOS book levels and point values, and print book labels.

AR is a student-driven but teacher-guided system to help students access interesting books. Teachers should help students find books of interest to them. Discussing a student's interests to see what kind of book (non-fiction or fiction) would stimulate their motivation is an essential part of AR, but, of course, this kind of counseling is very time-consuming, so teachers may have students work in pairs or small groups to identify each other's interests. Teachers should set personalized goals to help students stay focused on the factors that matter most for reading growth. These could be about comprehension quality, engaged reading time, or students' reading levels. Teachers should monitor student progress using some of the many different kinds of reports (and especially the At-Risk Report) and provide face-to-face feedback to keep learners on track. Teachers should especially respond to alerts which indicate that students are having problems, either through failing to keep to the AR system or by deliberate cheating. Through AR, teachers and librarians are given many opportunities to praise students for their successes and to discuss with them what they have been reading. Finally, teachers should encourage students to recommend favorite books to each other.

This leads to a list of essential behaviors that students and teachers must pursue, and it is evident that there is as much work for the teacher as for the student (see below). This list is cross-referred with the observation checklist of Holmes and Brown (2003), although their list was to measure implementation quality, while this list is intended to promote implementation quality. There are 28 items in this list, and only seven of them are intended to be initiated by the student (* marks these) – the remaining 21 are for teacher action. This emphasizes the amount of work the teacher (or librarian or teaching assistant or other relevant staff) needs to put in. While AR might save a good deal of teacher time, it also requires that teacher time be redirected into other (more effective and efficient) activities.

1. Assign reading time in class
2. Ensure ease of access to class and school library or other sources
3. *Student selects books of high interest (teacher helps if needed), *and*
4. *Student selects books of appropriate difficulty (teacher helps if needed)
5. *Use AR Book Guide as needed
6. Allow books to be taken home
7. STAR placement test – obtain broad band of target difficulty
8. Counsel students about interests and/or have class or peer discussion
9. Assess appropriateness of interest level of book to student maturity
10. Include non-fiction as well as fiction
11. *Students read independently
12. *Students use computer to take quizzes on books
13. *Students create own reading lists (teacher helps if needed)
14. *Student sets personalized goals for relevant variable (teacher helps if needed)
15. Teachers talk to students about books they are reading
16. Counsel students as to what feedback means
17. Teachers can write their own quizzes
18. Monitor reports (especially At-Risk) to identify student progress/problems
19. Teacher intervenes with struggling students
20. Respond to alerts about student struggling or cheating
21. Praise where merited and modify system where not

22. Encourage students to recommend favorite books to each other
23. Reading progress reports sent home to parents
24. Teacher reviews progress of individual student and whole class regularly
25. Teacher gives feedback to class on progress of individuals and whole class
26. Teacher encourages student to read a harder book
27. Consider use of electronic readers if available
28. STAR test at end of semester or year to evaluate progress.

Research Literature on Reading Counts

We learned in Chapter 4 on What Works that there was little independent peer-reviewed literature on RC and indeed this certainly applies to the issue of implementation quality, where none was evident.

RC differs somewhat from AR, mainly in terms of additional features to AR. Here is the list of AR implementation items with the RC additional items added (RC only).

1. Assign reading time in class
2. Ensure ease of access to class and school library or other sources
3. *Student selects books of high interest (teacher helps if needed), *and*
4. *Student selects books of appropriate difficulty (teacher helps if needed)
5. *Use AR Book Guide as needed
6. Allow books to be taken home
7. STAR placement test or RC Reading Inventory
8. Counsel students about interests and/or have class or peer discussion
9. Targeted book recommendations given (RC only)
10. Assess appropriateness of interest level of book to student maturity
11. Include non-fiction as well as fiction

12. *Students read independently
13. Use varied quiz question formats (embedded cloze, modified cloze, direct questions and complete-the-stem questions) (RC only)
14. *Students use computer to take quizzes on books
15. *View personalized and printable Congratulations Screen (RC only)
16. Retake a different version of the quiz if score is below 70% (RC only)
17. Teacher modifies the number of questions per quiz (5–30; default is 10) (RC only)
18. Teacher modifies passing rate for the quiz (0%–100%; default is 70%) (RC only)
19. Teacher decides number of quiz attempts allowed (1–6 times; default is 3) (RC only)
20. *Students create own reading lists (teacher helps if needed)
21. *Student sets personalized goals for relevant variable (teacher helps if needed)
22. Teachers talk to students about books they are reading
23. Counsel students as to what feedback means
24. Teachers can write their own quizzes
25. Monitor reports (especially At-Risk) to identify student progress/problems
26. Teacher intervenes with struggling students
27. Respond to alerts about student struggling or cheating
28. Praise where merited and modify system where not
29. Encourage students to recommend favorite books to each other
30. Reading progress reports sent home to parents
31. Teacher reviews progress of individual student and whole class regularly
32. Teacher gives feedback to class on progress of individuals and whole class
33. Teacher encourages student to read a harder book
34. Consider use of electronic readers if available (AR only)
35. STAR test at end of semester or year to evaluate progress (AR only).

Chapter Summary

Thus, in terms of items important for implementation, RC has seven extra which are for RC only (mainly to do with teachers' ability to customize the RC program), while AR has two extra which are for AR only, and the remaining 26 items are common to AR and RC. RC seems to be somewhat more complex than AR and has more features that are customizable by teacher users. However, while this ability to customize might appear intuitively appealing to teachers, the amount of teacher time this would involve is likely to prove prohibitive. Indeed, the number of teachers using these extra features is very small, as we will see in Chapter 6.

References

Holmes, C. T., & Brown, C. L. (2003, February 7). *A controlled evaluation of a total school improvement process, School Renaissance.* Paper presented at the National Renaissance Conference, Nashville, TN. https://files.eric.ed.gov/fulltext/ED474261.pdf

Persinger, J. M. (2001). What are the characteristics of a successful implementation of Accelerated Reader? *Knowledge Quest, 29*(5), 30.

Poock, M. M. (1998). The Accelerated Reader: An analysis of the software's strengths and weaknesses and how it can be used to its best potential. *School Library Media Activities Monthly, 14*(9), 32–35.

Wu, Y. C., & Samuels, S. J. (2004). *How the amount of time spent on independent reading affects reading achievement: A response to the National Reading Panel.* Minneapolis, MN: University of Minnesota. https://web.archive.org/web/20070315152118/http://www.tc.umn.edu/~samue001/web%20pdf/time_spent_on_reading.pdf

6

How Have Schools Done with Implementation?

This chapter considers how well the program actually *is* implemented. It notes that implementation quality is very diverse across schools (and times) and shows that the more best implementation practices are followed, the higher is student attainment. This issue of implementation integrity is an important one for practicing teachers, who must be aware that the degree of student gains will relate to how well they deliver the program.

Research Literature on Accelerated Reader

Topping (2018) showed that higher implementation fidelity was related to higher achievement (implementation fidelity or implementation integrity are somewhat technical terms for implementation quality). Neither implementation fidelity nor reading achievement related to socioeconomic status. Other findings in the research literature fall into natural categories and so are reported in those categories.

Reading Volume
Reading Volume was found to be significantly related to teacher effectiveness in almost all cases in grades 3 to 6 by Topping and

Sanders (2000), who investigated 62,739 students. The relationship appeared particularly strong in third and fourth grade. In other words, teachers whose students read at high volume added most value.

Number of Books

Following on from the above, Topping and Sanders (2000) found that in the third and fourth grade, a consistent trend of rising value added with increased number of books read was evident. Fifth and sixth grade showed some similarity, except for the additional striking negative impact of very large numbers of books. Perhaps reading a large number of very easy books has positive effects in grade 3 but negative effects if continued into grade 5 and beyond.

Book Difficulty

Topping and Sanders (2000) found that the mean difficulty level of books read showed a significant effect on value added in all grades except the sixth. In addition, they reported that, beyond the third grade, students increasingly tended to read books below their actual grade level. Yeh (2007) found that if teachers were inflexible about allowing students to read books outside their established reading levels, the students could become frustrated. Topping (2017) reported that elementary school students did far better than secondary school students on a measure of book difficulty or challenge in terms of the relationship between book difficulty and actual age.

Reading Ability of Students

Topping and Sanders (2000) divided students into six groups of ascending prior reading achievement. In all grades (3 through 6), the lowest-ability group had the lowest Average Percent Correct (APC) (72–74) and the highest-ability group the highest (89–92). Topping, Samuels and Paul (2007) found that when minimum implementation quality criteria were met, the positive effect of Accelerated Reader (AR) was higher for lower-achievement students. With higher implementation quality, reading achievement gains were higher for students of all levels of achievement and across all grades but especially in the higher grades. Very high gains and effect sizes (ESs) were evident with very high implementation quality, particularly in grades 1 through 4. On the other hand, Topping (2018) had a contradictory finding: students of higher reading ability implemented AR at a higher level but did not gain in reading at a higher level.

Teacher Monitoring of Students

Yeh (2007) reported that if teachers did not monitor their students, it was possible that some of them would share their answers to the reading quizzes with other students (although, of course, teacher monitoring should not just be about preventing cheating.) He also cautioned that students might choose to read books full of illustrations to rack up points.

Accuracy of Comprehension (APC)

Topping and Sanders (2000) found a positive relationship between APC on AR quizzes and value added, which was consistent across all grades. APC was significantly related to teacher effectiveness in almost all cases in grades 3 through 6 (the grades being studied). Increased APC was associated with increased teacher effectiveness at all levels of volume of reading. The relationship appeared particularly strong in the third and fourth grade. More-effective teachers tended to show a higher APC across all grades and ability levels. As noted above, the authors divided students into six groups of ascending prior reading achievement. In all grades (3 through 6), the lowest-ability group had the lowest APC (72–74) and the highest-ability group the highest (89–92). In 2017, Topping found that elementary school students did far better on APC than secondary school students.

Average Percent Correct above 85%

Topping and Sanders (2000) noted that the recommendation given in implementation training was to sustain APC above 85%. Their data strongly supported this recommendation in all grades, as this was clearly the point at which positive value added emerged. Alarmingly, however, more than half of the students in the study were operating below this level.

Variation in Implementation Quality across Grades

Three separate studies found that implementation quality was higher in the earlier grades and declined in the higher grades. Topping, Samuels and Paul (2007) found that when minimum implementation quality criteria were met, the positive effect of AR was higher in the earlier grades. Implementation quality tended to decline at higher grade levels. Topping (2017) reported that elementary school students did far better than secondary school students on implementation variables such as APC and ABL-MidGP (a measure of book difficulty or challenge) and on Star Reading test outcomes. Topping (2018) found that elementary schools had higher implementation fidelity and achievement than secondary schools. It appears that the decline in book difficulty levels in the secondary grades is due not just to student preference but also to poorer implementation in secondary schools.

Variation in Implementation Quality Across Gender

Topping (2017) found marked differences between genders on both outcome measures and implementation fidelity measures, males being significantly worse on both. Similarly, Topping (2018) reported that females showed higher implementation fidelity and achievement than males.

Research Literature on Reading Counts

There is no research literature on implementation quality of Reading Counts (RC).

New Data on Accelerated Reader

Data were available for 8,745,130 students for the academic year 2018–2019, which was the year before the covid pandemic disrupted schools.

Quizzes Taken and Quizzes Passed (QP)

The average number of quizzes taken during the year over all grades was 37.83 (standard deviation [s.d.] 49.37). This large s.d. indicates considerable variance over the grades, which is not surprising. The average number of Quizzes Passed (QP) (scoring 60% or 70%) during the year over all grades was 32.77 (s.d. 44.84). This s.d. is still large and again indicates considerable variance over the grades.

QP was positively correlated with APC, Average Book Level (ABL), Engaged Reading Time (ERT) and Star Reading, and all the correlations were statistically significant, but again this was partly due to the large size of the sample. The correlation between ERT and QP was particularly high ($r = 0.61$), as might be expected.

If we compare QP for the High (n = 768,697) and Low (n = 1,242,676) quartiles of student English reading ability on the Star test, we find that the High mean was 45.22 (s.d. 53.75) and the Low mean was 34.13 (s.d. 42.52). The ES for this difference was 0.24, which is small (reduced because of the large variance within the sub-samples). Thus, lower-ability students passed many fewer quizzes.

If we subtract Grade Level from ABL, we get an indication of the relationship between book difficulty and chronological age. The correlation between ABL - Grade with QP is +0.25, quite a high positive relationship. This suggests that the harder the books, the more likely the quizzes were to be passed. This is interesting as it suggests that books with a greater challenge cause students to read them more carefully and be more likely to pass the quiz.

Engaged Reading Time

The average ERT was 21.91 minutes per day (s.d. = 27.40), slightly above the recommended minimum of 20 minutes per day, but this was calculable only for 6,265,478 students (71.65% of the total). The high s.d. indicates a good deal of variance about this mean. The correlation between ERT and QP was particularly high ($r = 0.61$), as might be expected.

If we compare ERT for the High (n = 768,697) and Low (n = 1,242,676) quartiles of student English reading ability, we find that the High mean was 34.64 (s.d. 39.92) and the Low mean was 18.23 (s.d. 20.43). This difference was significant at far beyond p = 0.001 (t = 383.99), and the ES was 0.56, which is moderate.

The correlation of book difficulty – chronological age with ERT was r = 0.15, a positive but small relationship. This suggests that the more ERT is available, the more students tend to read harder books. This is understanable as it would take a longer time for students to become immersed in a harder book, and they would be less likely to want to leave it when time was up.

Average Percent Correct

The APC was 0.79 (or 79%) (s.d. 0.17), well above the quiz pass score but lower than the 85% recommended by the manufacturers for maximum effect. However, if quizzes which were not passed were excluded, the APC rose to 85%. If we compare APC for the high (n = 768,620) and low (n = 1,241,891) quartiles of student reading ability, we find that the High mean was 0.88 (88%) (s.d. 0.10) and the Low mean was 0.73 (73%) (s.d. 0.17). This difference is significant at far beyond p = 0.001 (t = 704.17), and the ES is 1.02, which is very large.

The correlation between ERT and APC was quite high at r = 0.31, suggesting that the more time was spent reading, the higher was the comprehension quality. Conversely, this suggests that low ERT is associated with low comprehension quality. The correlation of book difficulty – chronological age with APC was r = 0.07 (i.e., small). This suggests also that the quality of reading comprehension is relatively independent of how difficult the book is for the student. This is surprising since one would expect that harder books would result in lower APC, but this is not so. It seems that students rise to the challenge of harder books.

Average Book Level

The overall ABL was 3.61 (s.d. 1.34; n = 8,728,995). If we compare ABL for the High (n = 768,620) and Low (n = 1,241,891) quartiles of student reading ability, we find that the High mean was 4.20 (s.d. 1.41) and the Low mean was 3.24 (s.d. 1.15). The ES was 0.76, which is large.

The relationship between ABL and ABL – grade (book difficulty – chronological age) is quite large and negative ($r = -0.30$); in other words, the higher the book difficulty, the lower is the difference between book difficulty and grade level. This reflects the tailing off of book difficulty in the secondary grades.

Star Reading Student Growth Percentile (SGP)

Star Student Growth Percentile was 49.41 (s.d. 29.30), almost an average score for all students, but this was available only for 3,775,548 students.

New Data on Reading Counts

We noted in Chapter 4 that overall RC resulted in gains in reading achievement. Now we can look at this by grade (see Table 6.1).

Grade 0 and grades 10–12 have too few numbers to allow any confidence to be placed in the data. The variation for each data point is high, which is a factor in the relatively low ESs. In the remaining grades, the ESs vary from 0.22 to 0.30, which is a relatively small degree of impact. However, what is surprising is that the Lexile range in each grade is rather similar, when the Lexile range would be expected to rise in relation to grade/age. This appears to be evidence of a failure to implement RC appropriately.

Looking at Average Reading Level of Books by grade (Table 6.2), a rather disturbing picture emerges with respect to implementation integrity. Grades 0 and 10–12 can be disregarded. From grades 1 through 3, the Average Reading Level of Books does not rise at all. In grades 4 and 5, it suddenly rises sharply. However, it then plateaus from grade 5 and indeed in grades 10 to 12 it goes down. This suggests that, in general, students are not choosing books appropriate to their actual reading level and

TABLE 6.1 Difference Between Initial and Final Lexile: Reading Counts–Only Students

Grade	n	Initial Lexile average (s.d.)	Final Lexile average (s.d.)	Difference	t (d.f.)	Significance	ES
0	78	−78.38 (283.15)	−24.87 (282.52)	53.51	3.62 (77)	0.001	0.19
1	512	628.83 (432.54)	723.46 (397.86)	94.63	12.76 (511)	<0.001	0.23
2	1,245	644.94 (413.62)	736.32 (382.54)	91.38	19.81 (1244)	<0.001	0.30
3	2,436	643.22 (427.87)	733.60 (398.16)	90.38	28.98 (2435)	<0.001	0.22
4	1,833	639.71 (425.28)	738.94 (390.67)	99.23	26.36 (1832)	<0.001	0.24
5	1,586	630.73 (342.84)	730.65 (380.41)	99.92	23.51 (1585)	<0.001	0.28
6	2,010	621.55 (428.04)	721.27 (395.54)	99.72	27.30 (2009)	<0.001	0.24
7	1,852	617.16 (417.19)	714.77 (391.41)	97.61	25.76 (1851)	<0.001	0.24
8	1,320	610.44 (430.02)	705.97 (406.40)	95.53	20.34 (1319)	<0.001	0.23
9	425	589.31 (444.71)	698.91 (402.18)	109.60	12.73 (424)	<0.001	0.26
10	172	691.85 (398.53)	777.49 (365.70)	85.64	8.25 (171)	<0.001	0.22
11	101	621.14 (435.21)	724.71 (382.70)	103.57	5.44 (100)	<0.001	0.25
12	38	603.53 (397.67)	741.34 (325.27)	137.81	3.92 (37)	<0.001	0.38
Total	13,602	629.72 (424.41)	726.34 (392.45)	96.63 (163.43)	68.96 (13601)	<0.001	0.24

that teachers are not guiding them in this respect. Furthermore, the difficulty of books is not rising at all in high school, and in each grade, students are continuing to read books appropriate for elementary age students.

In regard to Average Lexile of Books by Grade (Table 6.3), the rather disturbing picture is confirmed with respect to implementation integrity. Grades 0 and 10–12 can be disregarded. From grades 1 through 3, the Average Lexile of Books does not rise at all. In grades 4 and 5, it suddenly rises sharply. However, it

TABLE 6.2 Average Reading Level of Books by Grade

Grade	N	Minimum	Maximum	Average	Std. deviation
0	74	1	4	1.80	0.45
1	514	1	6	1.82	0.49
2	1,233	1	7	1.83	0.46
3	2,428	0	6	1.81	0.45
4	1,788	0	22	2.90	1.46
5	1,536	0	53	3.39	1.89
6	1,956	0	11	3.36	1.35
7	1,813	0	10	3.38	1.40
8	1,308	0	10	3.34	1.42
9	423	0	37	3.39	2.18
10	176	0	8	3.11	1.50
11	93	0	7	3.26	1.35
12	33	0	9	3.36	1.66

TABLE 6.3 Average Lexile of Books Read by Grade

Grade	N	Minimum	Maximum	Average	Std. deviation
0	74	115	753	237.55	87.19
1	514	63	787	241.85	81.03
2	1,233	0	700	241.48	72.04
3	2,428	0	920	238.62	76.99
4	1,785	0	1,100	452.53	215.64
5	1,534	30	1,120	552.89	186.46
6	1,951	84	1,140	546.16	189.17
7	1,810	79	1,170	550.83	185.28
8	1,306	0	1,100	548.85	192.00
9	423	133	1,140	550.55	192.92
10	176	207	1,010	541.74	190.05
11	93	187	860	539.81	175.38
12	32	282	960	609.51	186.72

then plateaus from grade 5. This again suggests that, in general, students are not choosing books appropriate to their actual reading level and that teachers are not guiding them in this respect. Furthermore, the difficulty of books is not rising at all in high school, and in each grade, students are continuing to read books appropriate for elementary age students.

Chapter Summary

There is evidence of variability in implementation in both AR and RC, and there are special concerns about RC. This variability may occur at the school level (with many teachers misunderstanding how AR and RC work), at the class level (with particular teachers failing to understand) or at the individual student level (where the progress of individual students is not carefully monitored). Secondary schools showed the worst implementation.

We can now look at the list of 35 implementation quality variables listed in Chapter 5 and see if we should add to them in the light of the findings of Chapter 6 (below). The new items are inserted in UPPERCASE text. Where a new entry echoes an existing entry, it is placed next to that entry, again in UPPERCASE text.

1. Assign reading time in class
2. Ensure ease of access to class and school library or other sources of books
3. *Student selects books of high interest (teacher helps if needed), *and*
4. *Student selects books of appropriate difficulty (teacher helps if needed)
5. *Use AR Book Guide as needed
6. Allow books to be taken home
7. Star placement test or RC Reading Inventory
8. SUSTAIN HIGH READING VOLUME IN AND OUT OF SCHOOL
9. SUSTAIN HIGH NUMBER OF BOOKS IN LOWER GRADES BUT NOT IN HIGHER GRADES
10. Counsel students about interests and/or have class or peer discussion
11. Targeted book recommendations given (RC only)
12. Assess appropriateness of interest level of book to student maturity
13. Include non-fiction as well as fiction
14. *Students read independently

15. Use varied quiz question formats (embedded cloze, modified cloze, direct questions, and complete-the-stem questions) (RC only)
16. SUSTAIN DIFFICULTY OF BOOKS IN RELATION TO STUDENT ABILITY, PARTICULARLY IN SECONDARY GRADES
17. ALLOW STUDENTS TO READ ABOVE NOTIONAL READING LEVEL IF HIGHLY MOTIVATED
18. *Students use computer to take quizzes on books
19. *View personalized and printable Congratulations Screen (RC only)
20. Retake a different version of the quiz if score is below 70% (RC only)
21. Teacher modifies the number of questions per quiz (5–30; default is 10) (RC only)
22. Teacher modifies passing rate for the quiz (0%–100%; default is 70%) (RC only)
23. Teacher decides number of quiz attempts allowed (1–6 times; default is 3) (RC only)
24. *Students create own reading lists (teacher helps if needed)
25. *Student sets personalized goals for relevant variable (teacher helps if needed)
26. Teachers talk to students about books they are reading
27. Counsel students as to what feedback means
28. SUSTAIN HIGH AVERAGE PERCENT CORRECT (AR) OR AVERAGE TEST SCORE (ATS)
29. SUSTAIN APC OR ATS AT OR ABOVE 85%
30. Teachers can write their own quizzes
31. Monitor student reports (especially At-Risk) CAREFULLY AND REGULARLY
32. MONITOR MALES MORE CLOSELY THAN FEMALES
33. Teacher intervenes with struggling students
34. Respond to alerts about student struggling or cheating
35. Praise where merited and modify system where not
36. Encourage students to recommend favorite books to each other

37. Reading progress reports sent home to parents
38. Teacher reviews progress of individual student and whole class regularly
39. Teacher gives feedback to class on progress of individuals and whole class
40. Teacher encourages student to read a harder book
41. Consider use of electronic readers if available (AR only)
42. Star test at end of semester or year to evaluate progress (AR only)
43. SUSTAIN HIGH IMPLEMENTATION QUALITY, PARTICULARLY IN SECONDARY GRADES
44. SUSTAIN HIGH IMPLEMENTATION QUALITY FOR LESS-ABLE STUDENTS (LOWEST QUARTILE)
45. SUSTAIN HIGH IMPLEMENTATION QUALITY FOR MORE-ABLE STUDENTS (HIGHEST QUARTILE).

Thus, our list of implementation quality variables has grown to 45. These 45 variables can be made into a checklist for teachers to refer to from time to time as a check on their own behavior (or, in the case of headteachers and school administrators, as a check to make sure somebody somewhere in the school is taking care of all these issues). Such a checklist has been produced and you will find it in the Appendices under the title Implementation Quality Checklist.

References

Topping, K. J. (2017). Implementation fidelity in computerised assessment of book reading. *Computers and Education*, *116*, 176–190. DOI:10.1016/j.compedu.2017.09.009.

Topping, K. J. (2018). Implementation fidelity and pupil achievement in book reading: Variation between regions, local authorities and schools. *Research Papers in Education*, *33*(5), 620–641. DOI:10.1080/02671522.2017.1329340.

Topping, K. J., Samuels, J., & Paul, T. (2007). Computerized assessment of independent reading: Effects of implementation quality on achievement gain. *School Effectiveness and School Improvement*, *18*(2), 191–208.

Topping, K. J. & Sanders, W. L. (2000). Teacher effectiveness and computer assessment of reading: Relating value added and learning information system data. *School Effectiveness and School Improvement*, *11*(3), 305–337.

Yeh, S. S. (2007). The cost-effectiveness of five policies for improving student achievement. *American Journal of Evaluation*, *28*(4), 416–436. DOI:10.1177/1098214007307928.

7

Increasing Student Achievement in Elementary and High School

This chapter asks whether there are differences in performance between elementary and secondary or high schools. The answer is yes, there are, and elementary school students generally do much better than high school students. This may reflect differences in implementation between the types of school, particularly in Engaged Reading Time [ERT] and/or differences in reading habits as students grow older. The chapter reviews the existing published independent literature and offers a new analysis of fresh data.

Research Literature on Accelerated Reader

We have already seen in previous chapters that there tends to be a considerable difference between elementary and secondary schools in how Accelerated Reader (AR) operates. However, the majority of studies of AR have been in elementary schools.

In Chapter 4, we saw that Topping and Paul (1999) reported that the time allocated in school to independent reading practice on self-selected materials declined after grade 6. Nunnery and Ross (2007) studied nine elementary schools and two middle schools, finding that whereas the elementary schools showed significant gains, the middle schools did not. Rudd and Wade

(2006) found elementary schools were more successful with AR than secondary schools.

Nonetheless, there have been some positive results from middle and secondary schools. Peak and Dewalt (1994) found positive results in secondary school. Goodman (1999) evaluated AR use in a middle school, finding statistically significant improvement in vocabulary and comprehension. Rodriguez (2007) investigated AR in a middle school, finding that AR had a significant effect on reading tests scores for both Reading Comprehension and Literary Analysis, and higher AR participation increased these scores. Middle school students were studied by Huang (2012) in what appears to be a poor implementation, but pre-post test differences were negative (i.e., scores went down). Foster and Foster (2014) collected data over three years from about 100 students each year in grades 2 through 8 in a school the USA, and there was no evidence of a plateau at the secondary level, but, of course, only the first two years of secondary education were examined. Siddiqui et al. (2016) evaluated AR in the first year of secondary school in England and found the AR group did better than the control group (effect size [ES] 0.24), while the ES for Free School Meals students was 0.38. Gorard et al. (2017) evaluated seven literacy interventions for students transitioning to secondary school in England and found that two were promising, including AR. However, a lot of these positive results (and one negative result) came from middle schools or the early years of secondary school rather than the full age range of secondary schools.

In Chapter 6, we saw that Topping and Sanders (2000) reported that, beyond the third grade, students increasingly tended to read books below their actual grade level. Topping, Samuels and Paul (2007) found that when minimum implementation quality criteria were met, the positive effect of AR was higher in the earlier grades, but implementation quality tended to decline at higher grade levels. Topping (2017) found that elementary school students did far better than secondary school students on a measure of book difficulty or challenge and on Average Percent Correct (APC) and Star Reading test outcomes. Topping (2018) reported that elementary schools had higher implementation fidelity and achievement than secondary schools. It appears that the decline in book difficulty levels in the secondary grades is due not just to student preference but also to poor implementation in secondary schools.

Research Literature on Reading Counts

There is no research literature on the comparison of elementary and secondary education for Reading Counts (RC).

New Data on Accelerated Reader

The USA system of grades translates into Years in the UK (and into P and S levels in Scotland) and New Zealand. To synthesize these requires adding one to the grade indicator in the UK and New Zealand. Table 7.1 shows the number of students participating in AR in each grade. However, the number of students for which data were available on all the following measures was

TABLE 7.1 AR Students by Grade

Grade	Number of students	Percentage of students	Number of students with data	Percent of total students
0	241,139	2.76		
1	820,069	9.38	553,457	49.2%
2	1,124,775	12.86	638,454	50.5%
3	1,263,829	14.45	622,781	48.3%
4	1,289,414	14.74	585,918	45.7%
5	1,281,168	14.65	367,723	41.3%
6	891,360	10.19	350,832	44.5%
7	787,963	9.01	278,371	41.3%
8	674,149	7.71	69,051	38.7%
9	178,591	2.04	23,074	26.4%
10	87,285	1.00	15,404	25.1%
11	61,324	0.70	8,462	19.8%
12	42,778	0.49	258,304	31.5%
13	1,286	0.01		
Total	8,745,130	100.00	3,771,831	

considerably smaller than this, and columns 4 and 5 show the numbers and the percentage of total student numbers with data available for each grade. While we have to bear in mind that these data are from a sub-sample of each grade, ranging from 51% to 20%, the numbers are quite large and we have no reason to suppose that schools/classes/students who omitted to tell us their grade are any worse or better than those who did tell us. Approaching four million students yielded data, which might be considered sufficient for the analyses that follow.

The grades in which usage of AR was heaviest (bearing in mind that the data are dominated by the large quantity from the USA) were the elementary/primary grades 3 through 5, although there was quite high usage in grades 1 and 2. Secondary school usually commences with grade 7, and usage of AR is still fairly high in the first two years of secondary school but declines after that.

We can now relate grades to AR and STAR outcomes. First, we will look at Average Book Level (ABL) or book difficulty (Table 7.2).

ABL ranged from 1.80 in grade 1 to 4.52 in grade 6 through elementary school (2.72 in six grades), increasing steadily. In secondary school, however, the rate of increase was much slower, from 4.63 in grade 7 to 5.34 in grade 10 and 5.71 in grade 12 (1.08 in six grades). The variance (standard deviation [s.d.]) increased

TABLE 7.2 Average Book Level (ABL) by Grade

Grade	ABL average	ABL s.d.
1	1.80	0.59
2	2.55	0.64
3	3.19	0.71
4	3.73	0.80
5	4.14	0.85
6	4.52	0.85
7	4.63	0.88
8	4.82	0.91
9	4.92	1.01
10	5.34	1.16
11	5.53	1.22
12	5.71	1.40

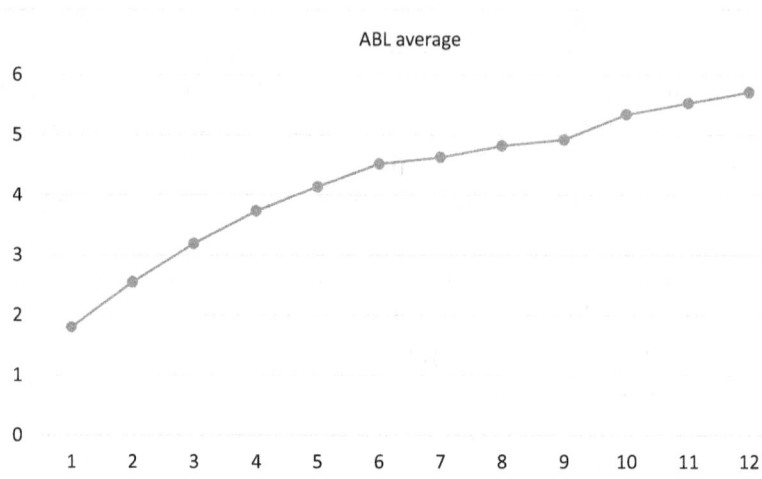

FIGURE 7.1 Average Book Difficulty (ABL) by Grade

steadily throughout elementary school but even more so in secondary school. It seems that only up to grade 4 are students reading books which are at the appropriate level of difficulty. Once secondary school begins, students are still tending to read books which arguably should be read by elementary school students in terms of difficulty (although perhaps not interest level). Figure 7.1 graphs these data and shows that ABL rises quite steeply up to the end of elementary school but after that rises much more slowly.

Then, we look at Average Percent Correct (APC) by grade (Table 7.3).

APC remained above 0.80 right through the elementary grades but declined sharply immediately on entry to secondary school (to 0.75). Comparing the high (first grade 0.82) and low (ninth grade 0.75) scores yielded an effect size of 0.46, which was moderate. The variance (s.d.) in scores also increased in secondary school. Thus, APC (quality of reading comprehension) is relatively flat in the elementary grades but declines sharply on entry to secondary and remains low apart from a small rise with small numbers in the later grades (see Figure 7.2).

When the ABL finding is put next to this finding, the overall picture is worrying – secondary school students are not reading

TABLE 7.3 Average Percent Correct (APC) by Grade

Grade	APC average	APC s.d.
1	0.82	0.15
2	0.80	0.15
3	0.80	0.14
4	0.81	0.14
5	0.81	0.14
6	0.81	0.15
7	0.77	0.17
8	0.77	0.18
9	0.75	0.19
10	0.77	0.19
11	0.78	0.19
12	0.77	0.20

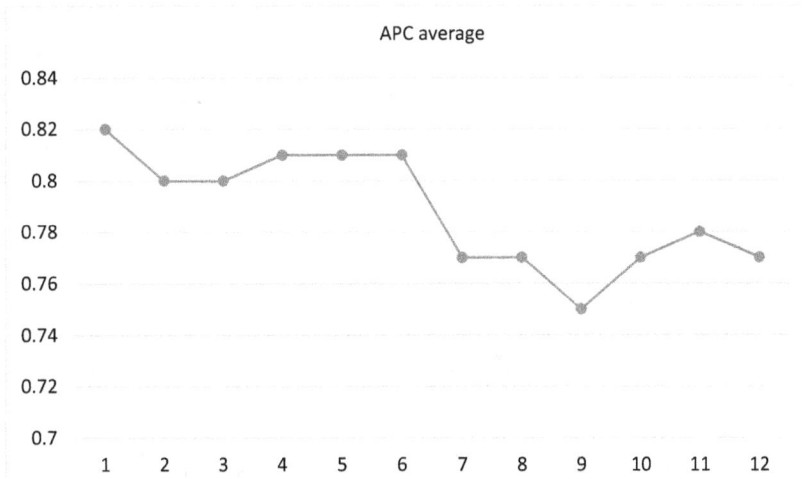

FIGURE 7.2 Average Percent Correct (APC) by Grade

books hard enough for their chronological age but nonetheless are reading them with poorer comprehension.

Next, we inspect Engaged Reading Time ERT (Table 7.4).

Why might this be? The ERT data give one possible clue. ERT in minutes per day ranges from 27.02 in grade 5 to 23.93 in grade 6 in the elementary school but from only 18.40 in grade 7 to 13.16 in grade 9 in the secondary school. Secondary school students

TABLE 7.4 Average Engaged Reading Time (ERT) by Grade

Grade	ERT average	ERT s.d.
1	24.38	26.40
2	26.35	25.30
3	26.22	25.82
4	26.67	28.20
5	27.02	30.58
6	23.93	29.49
7	18.40	25.12
8	15.92	22.06
9	13.16	21.36
10	16.90	28.53
11	15.08	21.50
12	15.45	22.72

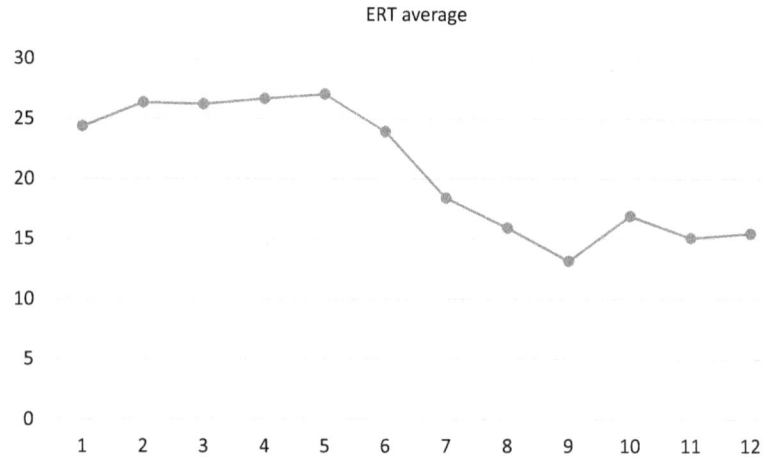

FIGURE 7.3 Average Engaged Reading Time (ERT) by Grade

are given less time to read independently in school than elementary school students (see Figure 7.3). This is, of course, just one factor in poorer implementation in secondary schools.

Quizzes Passed (QP) is the next variable to be studied by grade (Table 7.5).

QP ranges from 68.09 in grade 2 to 6.55 in grade 11, declining steadily through the grades, as one would expect as older students

TABLE 7.5 Average Quizzes Passed (QP) by Grade

Grade	QP average	QP s.d.
1	61.15	67.35
2	68.09	64.70
3	56.70	52.53
4	41.48	40.20
5	31.52	33.23
6	19.60	21.69
7	12.87	14.46
8	10.33	12.05
9	7.79	9.48
10	7.00	9.10
11	6.55	10.48
12	6.80	11.11

TABLE 7.6 Average Star Reading Test Scores by Grade

Grade	STAR average	STAR s.d.
1	51.73	29.41
2	50.46	29.54
3	50.07	29.24
4	49.11	29.15
5	48.10	29.23
6	48.73	29.26
7	48.98	29.25
8	48.69	29.32
9	49.50	29.10
10	49.04	28.75
11	48.23	28.88
12	48.28	28.85

read fewer (and longer and harder) books. As would be expected, the effect size between these extremes is very large (0.96), but it does not tell us anything we do not already know.

Finally, we consider Star Reading test results by grade (Table 7.6).

Star Reading Student Growth Percentile (SGP) scores range from 52 to 48, highest in grade 1 and declining steadily thereafter (with a slight upturn where sample numbers are smaller). Only in the first three grades were the Star Reading scores above average. However, comparing grade 1 with grade 5 gives an effect size of 0.12, which is small.

New Data on Reading Counts

In Chapter 6, we saw that from grades 1 through 3 the Average Reading Level of books did not rise at all. In grades 4 and 5, it suddenly rose sharply. However, it then plateaued from grade 5 and indeed in grades 10 to 12 it went down. The Average Lexile of Books by grade confirms this picture. From grades 1 through 3, the Average Lexile of Books did not rise at all. In grades 4 and 5, it suddenly rose sharply. However, it then plateaued from grade 5. Correspondingly, the Lexile range in each grade is rather similar, when the Lexile range would be expected to rise in relation to grade/age. This suggests that, in general, students are not choosing books appropriate to their actual reading level and that teachers are not guiding them in this respect. The difficulty of books is not rising at all in high school, and students are continuing to read books appropriate for elementary age students. This is the same plateau issue as with AR.

Chapter Summary

Many studies of AR have focused on the elementary grades, which seem to perform considerably better than secondary schools, as seven studies testify. This may be due to differences between sectors in implementation quality, or to changes in the preferences of students as they grow older, or to some other factor, or to all of these. However, six of seven other studies did find gains in secondary schools. New data on AR indicated that maximum use occurred in grades 3 through 5, and some use extended into the first two grades of secondary but much less after this. Book difficulty (ABL) rose steadily through elementary school but much less in secondary school. Quality of comprehension (APC) remained above 0.80 through elementary school but declined and remained low in secondary. ERT in minutes per day was much higher in elementary schools than secondary schools. The new data on RC showed a similar but even more erratic picture. Book difficulty and Average Lexile plateaued in the early grades, rose sharply in the later elementary years, then plateaued again in secondary. This again indicated problems with implementation, not only at secondary but also in the early elementary years.

References

Foster, D. K., & Foster, D. P. (2014). Estimating reading growth attributable to Accelerated Reader at one American School in the Caribbean. *Reading Psychology*, *35*(6), 529–547. DOI:10.1080/02702711.2013.789764

Goodman, G. (1999). *The Reading Renaissance/Accelerated Reader program. Pinal county school-to-work evaluation report.* Tucson, AZ: Creative Research Associates, Inc. https://files.eric.ed.gov/fulltext/ED427299.pdf

Gorard, S., Siddiqui, N., & See, B. H. (2017). What works and what fails? Evidence from seven popular literacy 'catch-up' schemes for the transition to secondary school in England. *Research Papers in Education*, *32*(5), 626–648.

Huang, S. (2012). A mixed method study of the effectiveness of the Accelerated Reader program on middle school students' reading achievement and motivation. *Reading Horizons: A Journal of Literacy and Language Arts*, *51*(3), 5.

Nunnery, J. A., & Ross, S. M. (2007). The effects of the School Renaissance program on student achievement in reading and mathematics. *Research in the Schools*, *14*(1), 40–59. https://search.proquest.com/docview/211015676

Peak, J. P., & Dewalt, M. W. (1994). Reading achievement: Effects of computerized reading management and enrichment. *ERS Spectrum*, *12*(1), 31–35.

Rodriguez, S. (2007). The Accelerated Reader program's relationship to student achievement on the English/Language Arts California Standards Test. *The Reading Matrix*, *7*(3), 191–205. http://www.readingmatrix.com/articles/rodriguez/article.pdf

Rudd, P., & Wade, P. (2006). *Evaluation of Renaissance Learning mathematics and reading programs in UK Specialist and feeder schools.* Slough: National Foundation for Educational Research. https://www.nfer.ac.uk/publications/SRY01/SRY01.pdf

Siddiqui, N., Gorard, S., & See, B. H. (2016). Accelerated Reader as a literacy catch-up intervention during primary to secondary school transition phase. *Educational Review*, *68*(2), 139–154. DOI:10.1080/00131911.2015.1067883. http://dro.dur.ac.uk/16393/1/16393.pdf

Topping, K. J. (2017). Implementation fidelity in computerised assessment of book reading. *Computers and Education*, *116*, 176–190. DOI:10.1016/j.compedu.2017.09.009.

Topping, K. J. (2018). Implementation fidelity and pupil achievement in book reading: Variation between regions, local authorities and schools. *Research Papers in Education*, *33*(5), 620–641. DOI:10.1080/02671522.2017.1329340.

Topping, K. J., & Paul, T. (1999). Computer-assisted assessment of practice at reading: A large scale survey using Accelerated Reader data. *Reading and Writing Quarterly*, *15*(3), 213–231.

Topping, K. J., Samuels, J., & Paul, T. (2007). Computerized assessment of independent reading: Effects of implementation quality on achievement gain. *School Effectiveness and School Improvement*, *18*(2), 191–208.

Topping, K. J., & Sanders, W. L. (2000). Teacher effectiveness and computer assessment of reading: Relating value added and learning information system data. *School Effectiveness and School Improvement*, *11*(3), 305–337.

8

Improving Outcomes for Low- and High-Ability Readers

We need to know whether the program is effective in impacting the weakest readers (which can be defined as the lowest quartile of readers), since they are the most difficult to encourage to read more books and more difficult books. However, in general, it seems that weaker readers respond well and show the same or better attainment gains than all other readers, which is highly encouraging (although it should not lead teachers to assume that the program is a remedial program). An equally valid question is whether the program impacts high-ability readers (defined here as the highest quartile of readers), since it might be argued that more-able readers neither need nor want this kind of structured approach to managing their reading. However, it seems that, in general, the program works equally well with able readers, and their reading attainment also increases.

Research Literature on Accelerated Reader

In Chapter 4, we saw that Stiegemeier (1999) found that in 23 schools, Accelerated Reader (AR) was most beneficial for students in the lowest two quartiles – those with the greatest need to improve their reading skills. However, Topping and Paul (1999) reported that the difference in AR points acquired between high-performing quartile and low-performing quartile students at each grade level was at a factor of between three and four times. When the top 5% of readers were compared with the bottom 5%, the difference was even greater – the difference in AR points was 144 times more than the bottom readers, suggesting the top 5% had vastly more reading practice.

In 2000, Topping and Sanders (2000) divided students into six groups of ascending prior achievement on a reading test. They found a positive relationship between Average Percent Correct (APC) and value added (teacher effectiveness), which was consistent across all grades 3 to 7. In all grades (3 through 8), the lowest-ability group had the lowest percentage correct (72–74) and the highest-ability group the highest (89–92). There was some evidence that operation at low percent correct was particularly likely to be true of students of low overall ability, and this implied that teachers were not generating or not responding to AR At-Risk Reports. Samuels and Wu (2003) established three groups of varying reading ability (low, moderate and high) in a highly disadvantaged elementary school with a high proportion of ethnic minorities. The low-ability group had significantly higher gain scores than the other two groups on sentence reading and composite comprehension. However, the moderate group had the greatest gain score in speed of reading. In a middle school, Rodriguez (2007) found that subgroups with higher AR participation out-performed groups with higher reading levels but lower AR participation rates.

In Chapter 6, we saw that Topping (2017) found that elementary school students did far better on APC than secondary school students did. However, Topping et al. (2007) found that with higher implementation quality, reading achievement gains were higher for students of all levels of achievement and across all grades but especially in the higher grades. On the other hand, Topping (2018) had a contradictory finding: students of higher reading ability implemented AR at a higher level but did not gain in reading at a higher level.

Research Literature on Reading Counts

There is no research literature on low and high achievers for Reading Counts.

New Data on Accelerated Reader

Not all AR users had taken the Star Reading test at the beginning and end of the academic year (some had taken only the pre-test or the post-test but not both), so numbers for this analysis are smaller than for the whole analysis. Nonetheless, the total number of students available with full data was 3,833,170, which might be taken as sufficient for this analysis.

AR users who had taken both pre- and post-Star Reading tests were divided into quartiles: Low Reading Ability (bottom quartile), High Reading Ability (top quartile) and Average Reading Ability (middle two quartiles). These three were then compared on Average Book Level (ABL), Average Percent Correct (APC), Engaged Reading Time (ERT), Quizzes Passed (QP) and Star Reading student growth percentiles (SGPs) (Table 8.1).

The Average Book Level rose steadily from Low to Average to High (see Figure 8.1). The reader might think that this is natural, as more-able readers will read harder books. Or is it because students who read harder books become more-able readers?

TABLE 8.1 Implementation Variables by High, Low and Average Reading Ability

Reading ability	n	ABL	APC	ERT	QP	Star SGP
Low	1,227,989	3.23 (1.15)	0.73 (0.17)	18.24 (20.43)	34.38 (42.68)	48.62 (29.51)
Average	1,841,974	3.78 (1.16)	0.81 (0.13)	40.47 (48.63)	24.45 (25.54)	49.41 (29.27)
High	763,207	4.19 (1.14)	0.88 (0.10)	34.67 (39.48)	45.64 (54.11)	50.55 (28.98)

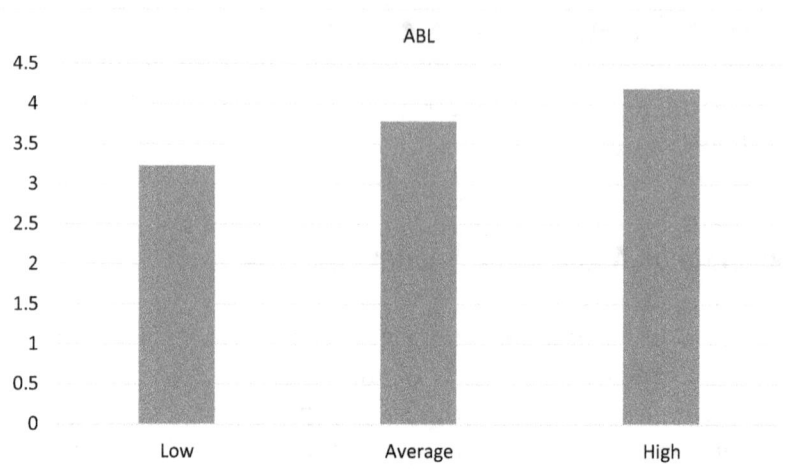

FIGURE 8.1 Average Book Level for Low, Average and High Reading Ability

The APC also rose steadily from Low to Average to High, as shown in Figure 8.2. Clearly, more-able readers have a higher quality of comprehension, even though they are reading harder books. The APC for high-ability readers is well above the 85% recommended by Renaissance Learning.

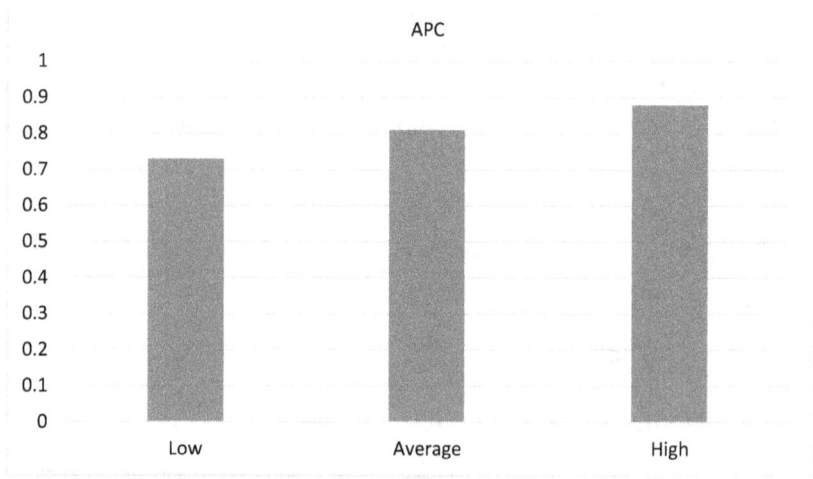

FIGURE 8.2 Average Percent Correct for Low, Average and High Reading Ability

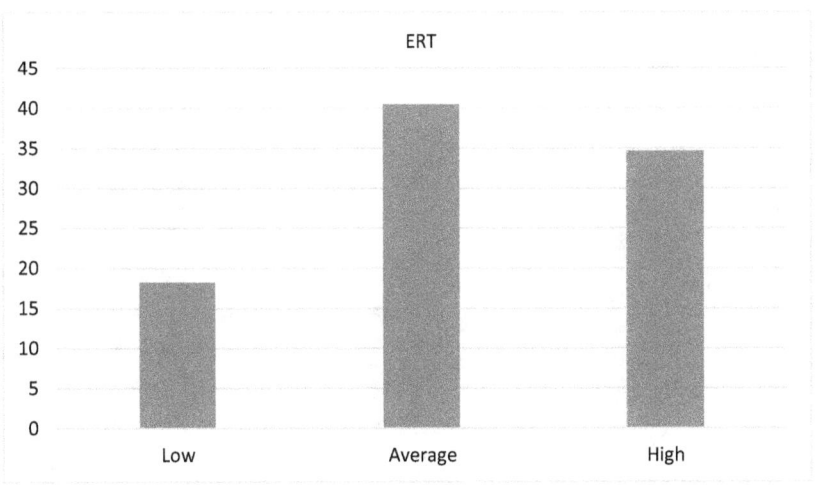

FIGURE 8.3 Average Engaged Reading Time for Low, Average and High Reading Ability

ERT rose sharply from Low to Average but declined somewhat for the High reading ability group, as shown in Figure 8.3. This indicates that although the High group was showing higher ABL and APC than the other groups, they were not actually reading for as long a time as the Average group. It is interesting that the Average group appeared to be reading for a full 40 minutes per day, the amount of time recommended by Renaissance Learning.

QP was high for students of Low ability, who were undoubtedly reading many easy books and quizzing on them (see Figure 8.4). This reduced for Average readers, who could be expected to be reading longer and harder books and therefore taking fewer quizzes. Remarkable, however, was the very high rate of QP by the High reading ability group, which was reading hard books with a high level of comprehension in less time than the Average group but nevertheless reading more books than the Average group.

Finally, we come to Star Reading SGPs and see that reading ability and potential rose steadily from Low to Average to High, as one might expect (Figure 8.5). This is an interesting demonstration of the Matthew Effect in reading, which essentially states

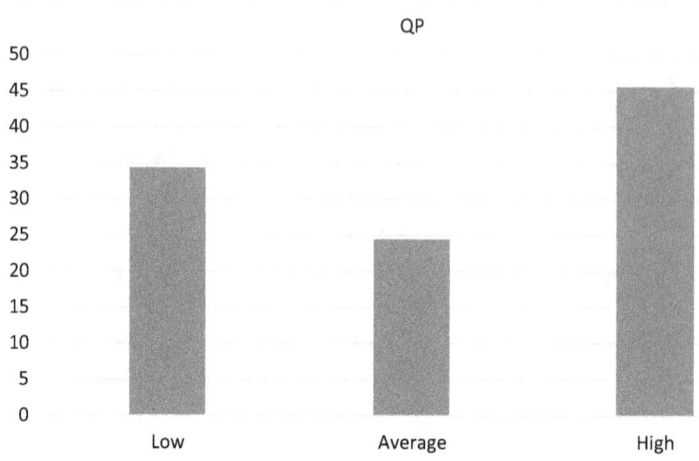

FIGURE 8.4 Quizzes Passed for Low, Average and High Reading Ability

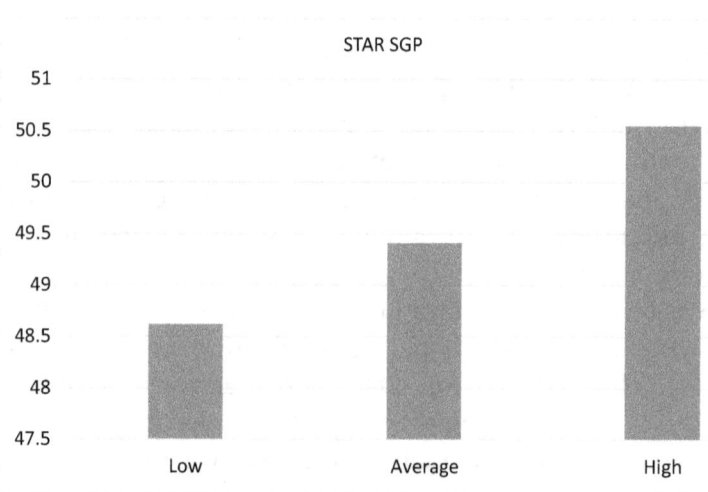

FIGURE 8.5 Star Reading SGPs for Low, Average and High Reading Ability

that children who learn to read early become fluent readers more quickly, read more with less effort and learn more vocabulary, which then enables them to comprehend more advanced texts – so they advance further. The students who are slow readers read less, are less fluent, have a poorer vocabulary and comprehend less – and the gap between the able and the unable keeps growing wider. It is the principle of 'the rich get richer and the poor get poorer' (Stanovich, 2017). In order to slow down or reverse this tendency, better-quality implementation of AR with low-ability readers is needed.

New Data on Reading Counts

There were no new data on Reading Counts which related to the issue of low and high achievers.

Chapter Summary

With AR, two studies found that low-ability students made the largest gains, while two studies noted major differences between low and high groups (with high groups doing better). A further two studies found that performance depended very much on participation and quality of implementation. According to new data, the highest quartile of reading ability had the highest book difficulty (ABL), APC (quality of comprehension) and Star Reading test SGP scores. However, ERT was highest for the middle-ability group and lowest for the low-ability group, while QP was high for both low- and high-ability groups. The general picture is that high-ability readers do better on AR than middle-ability or low-ability readers. Low-ability readers can make large gains but probably only if participation and implementation quality are high.

References

Rodriguez, S. (2007). The Accelerated Reader program's relationship to student achievement on the English/Language Arts California Standards Test. *The Reading Matrix, 7*(3), 191–205. http://www.readingmatrix.com/articles/rodriguez/article.pdf

Samuels, S. J., & Wu, Y. C. (2003). *The effects of immediate feedback on reading achievement.* Minneapolis, MN: University of Minnesota.

https://web.archive.org/web/20060423031356/http://www.tc.umn.edu/~samue001/web%20pdf/immediate_feedback.pdf

Stanovich, K. E. (2017). Matthew Effects in reading: Some consequences of individual differences in the acquisition of literacy. *Journal of Education*, *189*(12), 23–55. DOI:10.1177/0022057409189001-204

Stiegemeier, L. (1999). *Language integrated technology project final evaluation report*. Olympia, WA: Washington Office of the State Superintendent of Public Instruction, Olympia. https://files.eric.ed.gov/fulltext/ED462965.pdf

Topping, K. J. (2017). Implementation fidelity in computerised assessment of book reading. *Computers and Education*, *116*, 176–190. DOI:10.1016/j.compedu.2017.09.009.

Topping, K. J. (2018). Implementation fidelity and pupil achievement in book reading: Variation between regions, local authorities and schools. *Research Papers in Education*, *33*(5), 620–641. DOI:10.1080/02671522.2017.1329340.

Topping, K. J., & Paul, T. (1999). Computer-assisted assessment of practice at reading: A large scale survey using Accelerated Reader data. *Reading and Writing Quarterly*, *15*(3), 213–231.

Topping, K. J., Samuels, J., & Paul, T. (2007). Computerized assessment of independent reading: Effects of implementation quality on achievement gain. *School Effectiveness and School Improvement*, *18*(2), 191–208.

Topping, K. J. & Sanders, W. L. (2000). Teacher effectiveness and computer assessment of reading: Relating value added and learning information system data. *School Effectiveness and School Improvement*, *11*(3), 305–337.

9

Using Favorite Books as a Major Motivator

Readers can also vote for their Favorite Books after completing a reading, and this chapter analyzes whether these Favorite Books generate a different kind of performance from students. In fact, they do, and especially in the elementary grades, Favorite Books tend to be much harder than ordinarily quizzed books but are nonetheless read with a high level of comprehension.

So, students complete quizzes on books to assess their understanding but can also vote for books in terms of whether they enjoyed the book or not. Of course, degree of understanding is not the same as personal preference, and the two measures should not be confused. The Accelerated Reader (AR) voting system enables students to select one of four ratings of a book: "One of the best books I have ever read", "A very good book", "An OK book" and "Not a good book". These four ratings are used to generate an Average Book Rating, which is then weighted taking into account issues such as a minimum number of votes, the overall number of votes cast for a particular book, and the context of ratings in that particular year. The Reading Counts (RC) voting system uses the Read-0-Meter, which offers a more variable range of options.

The Favorite Books issue is important because if books preferred and most enjoyed by students are at a higher level of

DOI: 10.4324/9781003215882-9

difficulty than other books, by following and publicizing student's recommendations, teachers and librarians could raise the difficulty of books independently read in relation to students' chronological age. This would increase the level of challenge and very likely increase students' reading ability.

Research Literature on Accelerated Reader

It has long been known that students can successfully understand books well above their notional reading level provided they are highly motivated to read the book. For example, in a long-ago study of the Edward Fry Readability Principle (high motivation can overcome high readability, but low motivation demands low readability), Williams (1979) found that students with high interest in the book read more pages than those with low interest, irrespective of the relationship between student reading levels and the readability level of the book.

Topping (2015) specifically studied Favorite Books with 150,220 students in 967 schools in the UK. For grades 1 through 4, students were reading Favorite Books at a difficulty level far above their actual age but still maintaining a high rate of success in terms of high Average Percent Correct (APC). The effect of reading highly motivating books was remarkable. This was especially true of the Harry Potter books, which have high readability but appear to be read and understood by very young children. Some of these Favorite Books were aligned with the regular quiz lists, but many of the authors were not (particularly in the early and late grades). In grades 5 and 6, relative difficulty declined somewhat, but students were still reading above their chronological level. There was a marked difference after grade 6 (the year of secondary school transfer). Beyond this point, the favored books were no longer above chronological age and a rapid decline in difficulty set in.

Why were students in the quiz lists reading books they did not prefer? Possibly because they knew their favorites only after the book had been read. Alternatively, students may be constrained by the books available in school, which will have been chosen by teachers or librarians and may tend to reflect the preferences of those groups rather than the preferences of students.

Research Literature on Reading Counts

There is no research literature on Favorite Books for RC, although the RC system certainly encourages students to rate books after reading using the Read-o-Meter.

New Data on Accelerated Reader

No data were available from the USA on Favorite Books. However, data were available from the UK. In Table 9.1, the UK Year is given with the US Grade in brackets. Then, in the second column, the difficulty of the book is noted, along with the ATOS (Advantage/TASA Open Standard for Readability) in relation to USA grades and in brackets the amended ATOS to be relevant to UK Years. Consequently, readers need to be comparing the first number on column 1 with the last number in column 2. Column 3 gives the expected UK ATOS number to help this comparison. The APC is the same concept for USA and UK readers, as is the number of books falling below the recommended 85% criterion, although these data are from the UK only.

TABLE 9.1 ATOS in UK and USA, Expected ATOS, APC and Books below 85% Criterion

Year (Grade)	ATOS (UK ATOS)	Expected UK ATOS	APC	Books falling below 85% criterion
1 (0)	1.4 (2.4)	1.0	0.92	1
2 (1)	3.9 (4.9)	2.0	0.90	4
3 (2)	5.6 (6.6)	3.0	0.91	0
4 (3)	5.7 (6.7)	4.0	0.91	0
5 (4)	5.6 (6.6)	5.0	0.94	0
6 (5)	5.8 (6.8)	6.0	0.94	0
7 (6)	5.9 (6.9)	7.0	0.92	0
8 (7)	5.6 (6.6)	8.0	0.94	0
9–11 (8–10)	5.7 (6.7)	9–11	0.94	0

140 ◆ Using Favorite Books as a Major Motivator

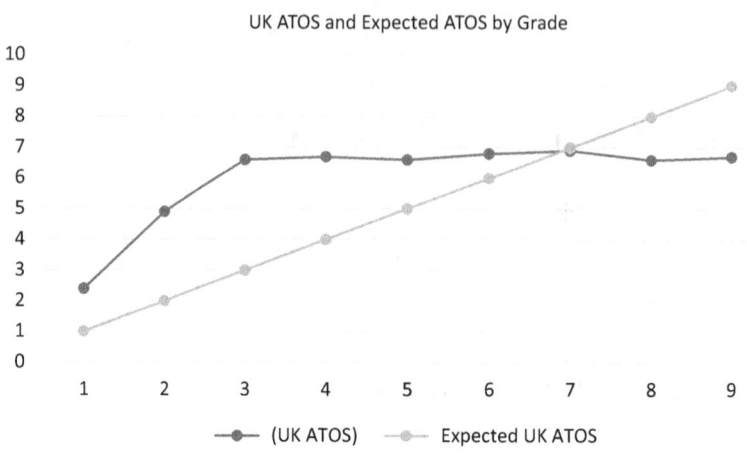

FIGURE 9.1 UK ATOS and Expected ATOS by Grade

For simplicity, we can graph the UK ATOS UK and expected UK ATOS data by grade (Figure 9.1).

In the elementary years, students were reading Favorite very difficult books with a high degree of success. In Years 1 through 3, the difficulty of books rose steeply to peak in terms of difference from expectations in Year 3. From Years 4 through 6, however, the difficult of books hardly rose at all, and the expected level of ATOS rose to almost match the existing rate. Once beyond the age of secondary transfer, the UK ATOS continued to plateau (and indeed eventually decline), so in each ensuing year the Favorite Books fell further and further behind the UK ATOS expectation. Quality of comprehension (APC) was a little lower in the early years, which was hardly surprising given the difficulty of these books, but it was still well above the 85% recommended criterion. It rose to 0.94 in grade 5 and did not decline after this, although the difficulty of books in relation to student Year did decline.

We should also consider the extent to which voting for Favorite Books was common in the elementary and secondary grades. The top 10 books in the primary (elementary) grades amassed 68,574 votes (seven of them were Harry Potter books), while the top 10 books in the secondary grades amassed only

9,050 votes (Rick Riordan, Christopher Paolini and Erin Hunter had two books each). Clearly, voting for Favorite Books was much less common in secondary school than elementary school, which perhaps suggests less student motivation to do this and/or less emphasis in the secondary school on recommending books to other students.

New Data on Reading Counts

There are no new data on Favorite Books for RC.

Chapter Summary

In both AR and RC, readers can vote for their Favorite Book after completing a book. One study of AR found that for grades 1 through 4, students were reading Favorite Books at a difficulty level far above their actual age but still maintaining a high rate of success in terms of high APC. In grades 5 and 6, relative difficulty declined somewhat, but there was a marked difference after grade 6 (the year of secondary school transfer), when favored books were no longer above chronological age and a rapid decline in difficulty set in. New data were available only from the UK, which confirmed these findings. Book Difficulty (Average Book Level [ABL]) rose very sharply in grades 1 through 3, then plateaued. At grade 7 (the first year of secondary school), book difficulty became equal to actual grade level, and after that it increasingly slipped below grade level. Quality of comprehension (APC) was a little lower in the early years but still well above the 85% recommended criterion. It rose to 0.94 in grade 5 and did not decline after this, so at least quality of comprehension remained high, albeit on books that were much too easy in relation to the chronological age of the students. Voting for Favorite Books was much less common in secondary school than elementary school, which perhaps suggests less student motivation to do this and/or less emphasis in the secondary school on recommending books to other students.

References

Topping, K. J. (2015). Fiction and non-fiction reading and comprehension in preferred books. *Reading Psychology*, *36*(4), 350–387. DOI:10.1080/02702711.2013.865692.

Williams, L. (1979). *Reading interest in free-choice books, readability, and the readability principle.* Educational Resources Information Center Document Reproduction Service ED166657.

10

Encouraging Careful Reading of Non-Fiction Books

This chapter considers the difference between fiction and non-fiction reading, asking whether performance differs by type of reading and gender. Although many more fiction books are read than non-fiction books, we find that overall non-fiction is read to the same level of comprehension. Interestingly, however, it is read with less understanding by boys than girls. Thus, while boys might prefer non-fiction (as they seem to, especially in high school), they do not seem to read it any more effectively.

Research Literature on Accelerated Reader

Topping and Sanders (2000) found no significant differences between males and females or fiction and non-fiction in their value-added study in Tennessee. Topping et al. (2008) found that girls read proportionately more fiction than boys at all grade levels and that boys read more non-fiction than girls. Moderate (rather than very high or low) levels of challenge were positively associated with achievement gain, but non-fiction reading was generally more challenging than fiction. However, students reading a high proportion of non-fiction gained significantly less in reading achievement than the remainder of students. Non-fiction reading was negatively correlated with reading achievement gain, Average Percent Correct (APC) and Engaged Reading Volume across all grades. Lower APC on non-fiction books was particularly pronounced for boys, consistently falling below the 85% criterion for reading achievement gain. The 85% criterion was found across four quintiles for fiction, but only in the highest quintile for non-fiction, and this latter was associated with particularly high reading achievement gains. Thus, boys generally appeared to read less than girls, but proportionately more non-fiction, but this less carefully – especially in the higher grades – and had lower reading achievement. Classrooms characterized by particularly successful comprehension were almost equally good at achieving this with fiction and non-fiction. Classrooms not characterized by successful comprehension were particularly poor with comprehension of non-fiction.

Topping (2015) specifically studied the fiction vs. non-fiction issue with 150,220 students in 967 schools in the UK. Boys are thought to like non-fiction reading more than girls do. If non-fiction can be read successfully at a higher level than fiction, especially for boys, there is a strong case for much wider use of non-fiction. In the lower grades, non-fiction difficulty was above the actual age of the students. However, once beyond grade 5, it began to decline, just as with average fiction books. There was thus no evidence that students read harder non-fiction books than fiction. Additionally, APC tended to be lower than was the case for fiction – it seemed that the non-fiction books were not read or understood as carefully as the fiction books. From grade 5 on, it seemed that students began to develop preferences for particular non-fiction authors – and so the same author names were repeated grade after grade. A male orientation was more frequently found than a female orientation in book preferences up to grade 6. From grade 7 (the first year of high school), the male orientation became very strong, far outweighing any female preference. So, boys do like non-fiction more than girls do. Unfortunately, the difficulty of the books read from grade 7 declined substantially and in an erratic way. Thus, there was evidence of a male orientation to non-fiction, which became much more extreme once the students transferred to high school. However, there was no evidence that students read more difficult non-fiction than fiction, and this was true of both boys and girls. Additionally, APC for non-fiction tended to be lower than was the case for fiction – it seemed that the non-fiction books were not read and understood as carefully as fiction books.

So, why was it that so many fiction books were chosen? Is it something to do with the reading preferences of school teachers, who might tend to encourage students to read fiction but not non-fiction? This is likely to result in higher performance by girls, who are known to favor fiction. Is this a gendered preference, so that predominantly female elementary school teachers and the half of high school teachers who are female prefer fiction and are unconsciously promoting fiction at the expense of non-fiction and thereby disadvantaging boys?

What can be done to raise student performance in reading non-fiction? Various authors have evaluated different methods, such as the following: suggesting a pair of books on same subject, one fiction and one non-fiction; using reciprocal teaching (predicting, questioning, clarifying and summarizing where the teacher leads and then the students lead the dialogue); extension reading and writing activities seeking to synthesize informational texts; engaging students in interactive read-alouds of non-fiction texts; and providing students with strategy instruction regarding the text structure of non-fiction books.

Research Literature on Reading Counts

There is no research literature on fiction and non-fiction for Reading Counts (RC).

New Data on Accelerated Reader

New data are available which give the Quizzes Passed (QP), Average Book Level (ABL) and APC for fiction and non-fiction in 6,033,429 cases (69% of the total) (Table 10.1). Unfortunately, Engaged Reading Time was not available.

Overall, almost three times more fiction books than non-fiction books were read and the quizzes passed. This difference had an effect size (ES) of 0.72, which is large, although the variance for both was also large. Non-fiction books tended to be harder than fiction books – this ES was 0.26, which is small but nonetheless substantial. Perhaps if students in secondary schools read more non-fiction books, the difficulty plateau effect would not be so severe, but, of course, this would also require a relatively high level of success on QP and APC. In fact, the APC for non-fiction was much less than the APC for fiction, the ES being 0.39, so at the moment reading more non-fiction would not help, as it is not understood as well as fiction.

Interestingly, there is some evidence that non-fiction reading is slowly rising over the years in the US (see Figure 10.1). This may be because of the greater emphasis placed on non-fiction reading by the US Common Core guidelines and related state-led English Language Arts standards revisions. These suggest that non-fiction reading should be about 40% in elementary school, 55% in middle school and 70% in high school. Clearly, students are a long way from achieving those figures if data are anything to go by.

TABLE 10.1 QP, ABL and APC for Fiction and Non-Fiction

	Fiction	*Non-fiction*
QP	32.56	10.85
	(37.13)	(20.42)
ABL	3.36	3.71
	(1.20)	(1.46)
APC	0.81	0.74
	(0.16)	(0.20)

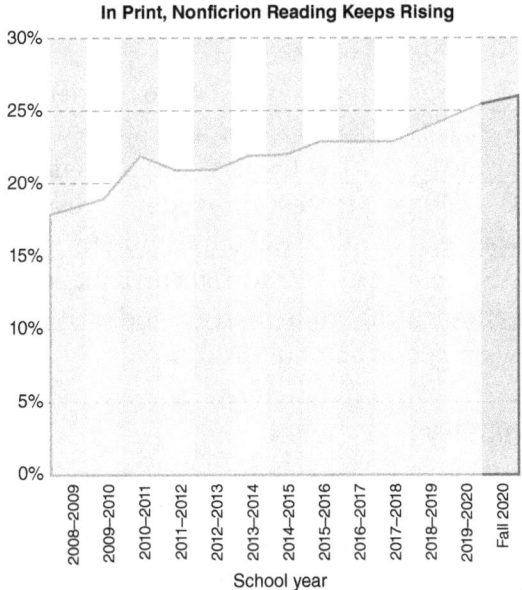

FIGURE 10.1 Trends in Proportion of AR Non-fiction Reading 2008–2020

New Data on Reading Counts

The initial data here are purely for RC used alone. (When RC is used within Read 180, the prescribed reading is half fiction and half non-fiction, which, of course, creates a different situation.) Data were available on Fiction vs. Non-fiction reading (in both cases only when the quiz was passed, on whatever try). Fiction reads were recorded for 12,774 students (62%), and the average number of fiction reads was 13.44 (20.35). By contrast, Non-fiction reads were recorded for 7,702 students (38%), and the average number of fiction reads was 5.88 (10.04). Obviously, Fiction reads were much more frequent than Non-fiction reads, and comparing frequencies of the two yielded $t = 45.34$, $p < 0.001$, $ES = 0.59$, which is above moderate and heading towards large. Thus, there was much more Fiction than Non-fiction reading, at a ratio of 3:2. However, even when RC is used alone, there was much more reading of non-fiction than with AR, and it is interesting to speculate as to why this should be so.

Regarding Read 180 and System 44 (for comparison), data were available on Fiction vs. Non-fiction reading (when the quiz was passed, on whatever try). Fiction reads were recorded for 20,484 students (50%), and the average was 4.73 (6.70). Non-fiction reads were recorded for 20,286 students (50%), and average was 4.78 (5.14). Thus, Fiction equated to Non-fiction reading, at a ratio of 1:1. The ES was 0.01, showing no difference at all. For RC + Other Intervention students, relatively far more non-fiction was read than for RC-only students. This reflects the nature of the System 44 and Read 180 curricula, which are more prescriptive about what students read and strive to establish a balance between fiction and non-fiction.

Chapter Summary

There were three studies of fiction and non-fiction reading with AR. One found no differences between boys and girls, but the other two found marked differences. In these, girls preferred fiction and boys preferred non-fiction, and this was especially marked at secondary school. However, boys' reading of non-fiction showed a lower quality of comprehension (APC) than girls' reading. New data on AR showed that three times more fiction books than non-fiction books were read. The book difficulty for non-fiction was markedly higher than for fiction, and it was confirmed that the APC for non-fiction was much lower than the APC for fiction. New data on RC showed that there was much more fiction than non-fiction reading, at a ratio of 3:2, but clearly there was more non-fiction reading in RC than AR.

References

Topping, K. J. (2015). Fiction and non-fiction reading and comprehension in preferred books. *Reading Psychology*, *36*(4), 350–387. DOI: 10.1080/02702711.2013.865692.

Topping, K. J., Samuels, J., & Paul, T. (2008). Independent reading: The relationship of challenge, non-fiction and gender to achievement. *British Educational Research Journal*, *34*(4), 505–524.

Topping, K. J., & Sanders, W. L. (2000). Teacher effectiveness and computer assessment of reading: Relating value added and learning information system data. *School Effectiveness and School Improvement*, *11*(3), 305–337.

11

Working Effectively with Spanish-Speaking, Disadvantaged, Disabled or EFL Students

Many studies have found that students who are socioeconomically disadvantaged do markedly worse at reading. Consequently, here we explore whether this is the case with Accelerated Reader (AR) and Reading Counts (RC), defining disadvantage in terms of proportion of Free or Reduced-Price Lunch (USA) or Free School Meals (UK), although these indices are not the same. Generally, it seems that disadvantaged students can do well on AR (although this might need high quality of implementation), a most encouraging finding. There is also some evidence on the effectiveness of AR with students with certain kinds of disability, although again high quality of implementation might be needed. Only two studies specifically investigated AR with English as a Foreign Language (EFL) students and both reported positive effects. For students reading Spanish books and taking Spanish quizzes, performance was much worse than for students reading English books and taking English quizzes.

DOI: 10.4324/9781003215882-11

Research Literature on Accelerated Reader

Disadvantaged
Ten studies have reported the use of AR in schools which had a higher-than-average proportion of students with some degree of social disadvantage, whether indicated by free/reduced-price lunch, free school meals or some other indicator, both in the USA and in the UK (Goodman, 1999; Gorard et al., 2017; Holmes & Brown, 2003; Johnson & Howard, 2003; Pappas et al., 2010; Ross et al., 2004; Samuels et al., 2003; Samuels & Wu, 2003; Topping & Fisher, 2003; Vollands et al., 1999). However, none of these studies compared notionally disadvantaged students against advantaged students in the same school. Given the doubtful reliability of free/reduced-price lunch as an indicator, this is perhaps understandable. Nonetheless, it seems clear that AR can certainly be effective in schools with a high proportion of disadvantaged students.

Disability
Only three studies specifically mentioned disability. In the second study by Ross et al. (2004), 3.3% of the student population had a specified learning disability. "High" implementation classrooms significantly reduced the negative impact of learning disability status on growth in reading when compared with control classrooms or "low" implementation classrooms. Moyer and Williams (2011) described how a school customized AR to the needs of disabled students. Stringfield et al. (2011) reported a study with three students with autism and found that story maps had a positive effect on AR scores. As with disadvantage, although the number of studies is small, it appears that AR can impact students with a disability, but high implementation quality might be needed.

English as a Foreign Language
Hamilton (1997) reported the use of AR with high school English as a Second Language (ESL) students. There were changes in the students' reading habits. McGlinn and Parrish

(2002) examined the AR program over three months with ten ESL students in the fourth and fifth grade in one school in rural North Carolina. The quantity of reading greatly increased, attitudes towards reading improved, and there was a moderate overall increase in student reading level. Thus, only two studies specifically of AR with EFL/ESL students could be identified, and although outcomes were positive, the quality of evidence was weaker.

Race/Ethnicity
In the second study by Ross et al. (2004), involving 978 students in grades 3 through 6, 90% were African-American. Topping et al. (2007) investigated 50,823 students in 139 schools in grades 1 through 12 in 24 states in the USA, and analysis by ethnicity showed that Caucasians had the highest scores, followed by Asians, and Hispanics, African-Americans and Native Americans had the lowest scores. Rodriguez (2007) investigated AR in a middle school (grades 7 and 8) where 75% of students were from a Hispanic background and 15% from a Filipino-American background, but results were not differentiated by ethnicity.

School Location
Very few studies reported on the location of the school or schools used in the research. Two studies each reported on location being in the city, suburban or rural environments, and none reported being in a town.

Research Literature on Reading Counts

There is no research literature on disadvantage, race/ethnicity, disability, EFL or school location for RC.

New Data on Accelerated Reader

Some data were available only from the USA on social disadvantage (free/reduced-price lunch), race/ethnicity, whether the student was an English as a Second or other Language learner (ESL), and the location of the school (city, town, suburban or rural). Unfortunately, no data were available specifically on disabled students.

Disadvantage

Regarding free/reduced-price Lunch, 52% of AR Users were eligible, while 52% of the US national population were eligible, so there was no difference. Unfortunately, outcome or implementation data were not available on this factor, but the large proportion of students being eligible for free/reduced-price lunch means that any comparison would be of limited value. A more precise measure of disadvantage is needed.

Race/Ethnicity

Although ethnicity was not given for a large percentage of the students in the database (60%), comparing the figures given to the proportions of school students in the US population at about the same time (National Center for Educational Statistics, 2021 – most of the data come from the USA) indicates that Asians (especially) and those with Multiple Ethnicities were considerably under-represented, Hispanics were represented in line with their proportion in the population, African-Americans and Caucasians were somewhat over-represented, and Native Americans and especially Pacific Islanders were greatly over-represented (see Table 11.1).

TABLE 11.1 Ethnicity of Participants in Relation to Population

Ethnicity	Number	Overall percentage	Percentage of specified*	Percentage in USA population 2018
Asian	11,786	0.13	0.33	5
African-American	653,782	7.48	18.63	15
Hispanic	962,000	11.00	27.41	27
Multiple	94,546	1.08	2.69	4
Native American	71,634	0.82	2.04	1
Native Hawaiian	131,876	1.51	3.76	0.04
Caucasian	1,576,543	18.03	44.91	47
Other	7,919	0.09	0.23	
Not specified*	5,235,044	59.86		
Total	8,745,130	100	100	99.04

Ethnicity was given for 3,510,089 students (i.e., 40%). Ethnicity was not given for 5,235,044 (60%). Examining Star Reading student growth percentile (SGP) by ethnicity of student, we find that both Ethnicity and Star data were available for only 2,085,960 students (24%), varying by ethnic group from 42% to 60% (see Table 11.2 and Figure 11.1).

The overall average was 50.01 (29.30), almost exactly average for SGPs. Native Hawaiians had the highest average score, followed by Caucasians, then Other, then Asians – all above average. African-Americans came out considerably worse than.

TABLE 11.2 Average Star Reading SGP by Ethnicity

Ethnicity	Number	Percentage of total	SGP average	s.d.
Asian	7,078	60.1%	50.17	28.89
African-American	275,268	42.1%	43.94	28.86
Caucasian	749,200	47.5%	51.54	29.34
Hispanic	494,801	51.4%	46.38	28.93
Multiple	50,259	53.2%	49.98	29.29
Native American	37,178	51.9%	47.68	29.24
Native Hawaiian	72,028	54.6%	52.03	28.87
Other	3,768	47.6%	51.23	28.95

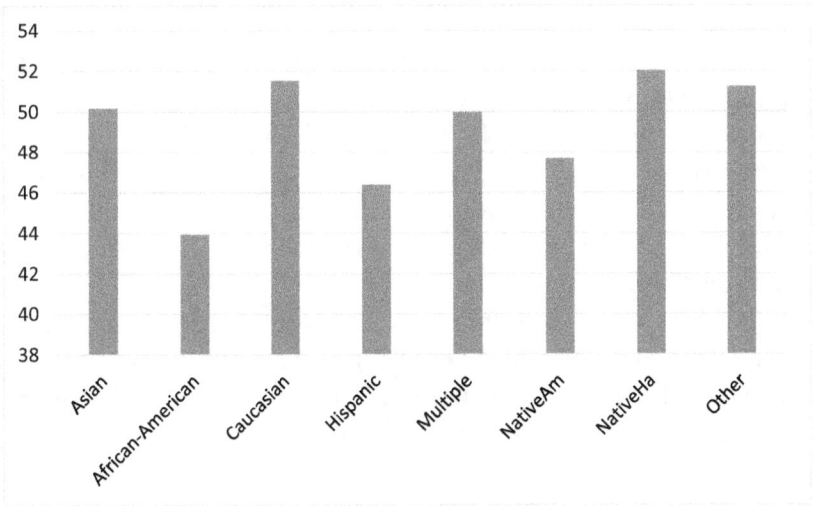

FIGURE 11.1 Average Star Reading SGP by Ethnicity

Data were also available on Quizzes Passed (QP), Average Percent Correct (APC), Engaged Reading Time (ERT) and Average Book Level (ABL) for between 72% and 88% of the ethnic groups (see Table 11.3). QP varied from 25 through 38; Asians showed low numbers, and Hispanics, Caucasians and (particularly) Native Hawaiians had high numbers. For QP, the difference between the lowest and highest ethnic group showed an effect size (ES) of 0.27, which would be considered small but nonetheless indicates a substantial difference. However, QP is always likely to be higher in the early grades and lower in the upper grades since fewer books are read as they become longer and more difficult.

Of course, the number of quizzes passed (QP) reflects the number of books read and quizzed, and reading shorter, easier books leads to a higher number of QP. So, looking at ABL (see Figure 11.2), we find that Asians read the hardest books, so it is fair to assume that for Asians lower QP numbers are strongly associated with higher ABL numbers. However, Native Hawaiians and Caucasians have high QP and high ABL, so they appear to be reading hard books *and* doing relatively well on quizzes. For ABL, the difference between the lowest and highest ethnic group showed an ES of 0.56, which would be considered medium or moderate, indicating a very substantial difference.

For APC, Caucasians, Native Hawaiians and those of Multiple Ethnicities showed the highest numbers, and African-Americans showed the lowest overall, but Asians' numbers were nearly as low (see Figure 11.3). For APC, the difference between the lowest and highest ethnic group showed an ES of 0.31, which would be considered small but nonetheless indicates a substantial difference.

For ERT, large differences were evident (see Figure 11.4). Native Hawaiians had by far the highest numbers, and African-Americans by far the lowest. As ERT in school is not really under the control of the students but under the control of the teacher,

TABLE 11.3 Quizzes Passed, Average Percent Correct, Engaged Reading Time and Average Book Level by Ethnicity

Ethnicity	N	Percent of total	QP average	QP s.d.	APC average	APC s.d.	ERT average	ERT s.d.	ABL average	ABL s.d.
Asian	10,394	88.2%	25.83	32.52	0.77	0.17	20.31	26.43	3.94	1.24
African-American	469,190	71.8%	34.57	45.97	0.76	0.18	16.30	20.66	3.23	1.28
Caucasian	1,150,029	72.9%	37.63	47.36	0.81	0.15	23.08	27.30	3.63	1.32
Hispanic	765,519	79.6%	37.57	46.65	0.78	0.17	21.69	25.45	3.43	1.29
Multiple	74,535	78.8%	34.77	42.47	0.80	0.16	21.25	26.47	3.55	1.28
Native American	57,266	79.9%	35.66	40.69	0.78	0.17	20.22	22.45	3.40	1.26
Native Hawaiian	104,597	79.3%	38.42	47.84	0.81	0.15	28.92	39.51	3.75	1.31
Other	5,866	74.1%	27.34	34.39	0.76	0.18	17.11	22.16	3.61	1.28
Overall	3,623,704	69.2%	32.64	44.19	0.79	0.16	22.18	28.15	3.74	1.28

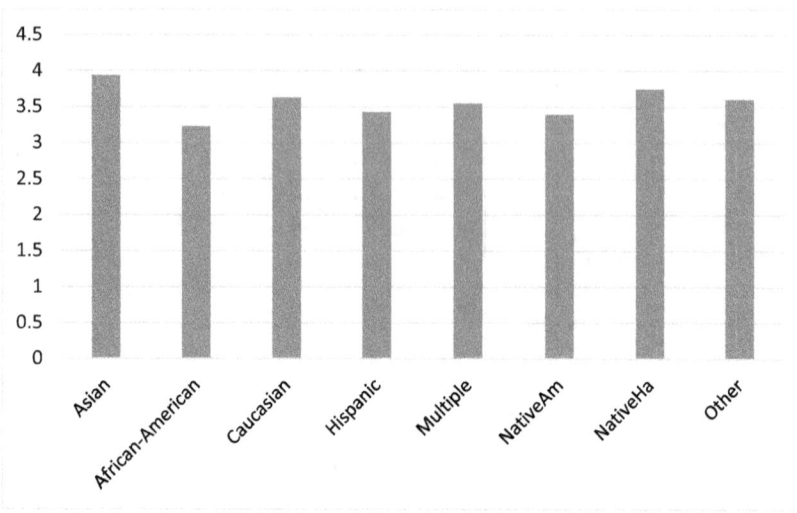

FIGURE 11.2 Average Book Level (ABL) by Ethnicity

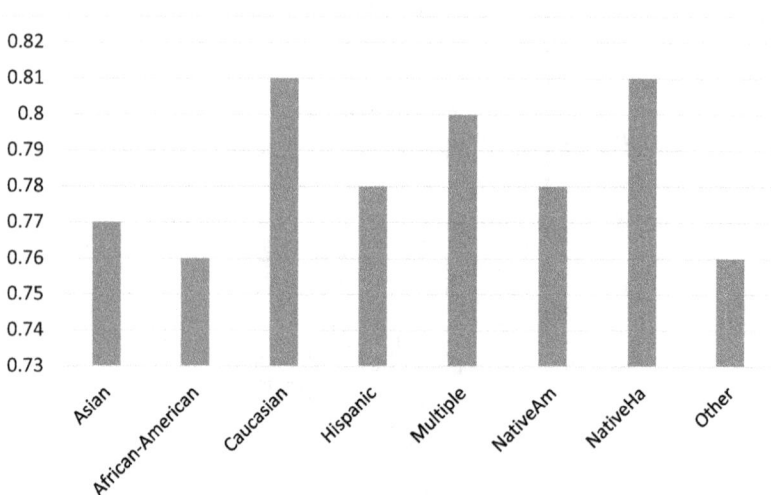

FIGURE 11.3 Average Percent Correct (APC) by Ethnicity

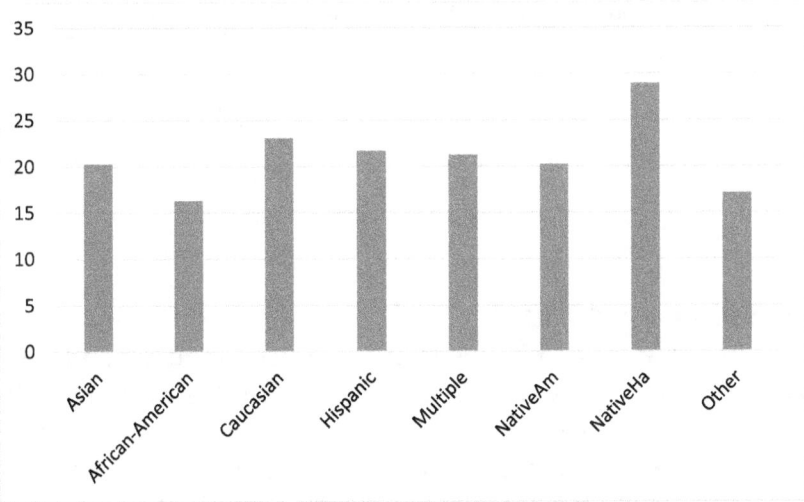

FIGURE 11.4 Engaged Reading Time (ERT) by Ethnicity

one wonders why African-American students are not receiving nearly as much ERT as other ethnic groups. For ERT, the difference between the lowest and highest ethnic group showed an ES of 0.50, which would be considered medium or moderate, indicating a very substantial difference.

English as a Second Language

Turning to the issue of whether AR users were more or less likely to be ESL learners, we find that ESL AR users were 9%, while the ESL US national school population were 10%, so there was very little difference.

School Location

The issue of school location is interesting, and here some differences were found (see Table 11.4).

Compared with the national population, AR users were much more likely to come from rural schools and somewhat more likely to come from town schools. AR users were much less likely to come from suburban and city schools. This is an interesting pattern, but quite what the causes are is difficult to see.

TABLE 11.4 School Location of AR Users and the US National Population

School location	AR users	US national population
Rural	30%	15%
Suburban	27%	42%
City	25%	32%
Town	18%	11%

Spanish Books and Quizzes

It is possible to read books in the Spanish language and take AR quizzes on those books (but, of course, this happens only in the USA). However, it appeared that many students tried one or a few books in the Spanish language and quizzed on it in Spanish, but after that the numbers dropped off steeply (the students presumably preferring and becoming more competent to read in the English language). Table 11.5 has the data on QP, ERT, APC and ABL, the latter three factors relating only to QP.

In Spanish, of Quizzes Taken (n = 509,098), only 52% (267,218) were Passed. There were almost no QP after grade 8. In both QP, ERT, APC and ABL, Spanish quiz takers did much worse than English quiz takers. The differences between Spanish and English quiz takers were ES = 0.41 for QP, 0.48 for ERT, 0.29 for APC and 0.67 for ABL – all substantial. For all variables (QP, ERT, APC and ABL), mean Spanish language scores were lower than English language scores. This was particularly striking in the case of ABL, where Spanish books read were much easier than English books. Even given this difficulty difference, APC (quality of

TABLE 11.5 QP, ERT, APC and ABL on Spanish and English Books and Quizzes

Language	Number with Quizzes Passed	QP	ERT	APC	ABL
Spanish	267,218 (3.1%)	14.71	*8.73	0.75	2.71
		(29.82)	(12.07)	(0.19)	(1.16)
English	8,447,912 (96.9%)	32.77	**21.91	0.80	3.61
		(44.84)	(27.40)	(0.17)	(1.34)

*Only 1848 valid cases found **only 6265487 valid cases found

reading comprehension) was lower for Spanish books, although this was the smallest difference in terms of ES. Books read (and quizzed) in Spanish were easier but read with worse comprehension, while Spanish quizzes were much less frequently passed (QP), and ERT was much less. The picture here is not of students who speak the Spanish language fluently at home and preferring to read (and quiz) in Spanish. It is more of students whose parents speak Spanish at home but who appear more motivated to read and quiz in English. The Spanish numbers were too small to explore fiction vs. non-fiction. For the same reason, analysis by grade level was not done.

New Data on Reading Counts

Data on RC only for socioeconomically disadvantaged, Spanish-speaking, disabled and EFL students were not available. Data on Read 180 were available for socioeconomically disadvantaged, Spanish-speaking, disabled and EFL students, but, of course, this was not the focus of this investigation. Additionally, some demographic settings were set by the teacher, who may have chosen to hide the results, so even these data might not have been complete.

Chapter Summary

There have been ten studies of the use of AR in schools which had a higher-than-average proportion of students with some degree of social disadvantage, all of which indicated some degree of effectiveness, but high implementation quality might be needed. However, there were no direct comparisons of advantaged and disadvantaged students. Three studies mentioned disability, but again there was no comparison of disabled and abled students. It appears that AR can impact students with a disability, but high implementation quality might be needed. Only two studies of AR with EFL (or ESL) students could be identified – outcomes were positive, but the quality of evidence was weaker. Three studies mentioned race/ethnicity, but only one compared outcome for different races/ethnic groups, finding that Caucasians had the highest scores, followed by Asians, and Hispanic, African-American and Native American had the lowest scores.

In terms of new data, half of the students in the US were eligible for free or reduced-price lunch, so this index of disadvantage is probably not specific enough. In regard to race/ethnicity, African-Americans and Caucasians were somewhat over-represented in relation to the national population, and Native Americans and especially Pacific Islanders were greatly over-represented. Star Reading student growth percentile (SGP) showed that Native Hawaiians had the highest average score, followed by Caucasians, then Other, then Asians – all above average. African-Americans came out considerably worse than all of the above. On QP, Asians showed low numbers and Hispanics, Caucasians and (particularly) Native Hawaiians had high numbers. On book difficulty (ABL), Asians read the hardest books, hence their low QP numbers. However, Native Hawaiians and Caucasians had high QP and high ABL, so they appeared to be reading hard books *and* doing relatively well on quizzes.

For APC (quality of reading comprehension), Caucasians, Native Hawaiians and those of Multiple Ethnicities showed the highest numbers, and African-Americans showed the lowest overall, but Asians' numbers were nearly as low. For ERT, Native Hawaiians showed by far the highest numbers, and African-Americans by far the lowest. As ERT in school is not really under the control of the students but under the control of the teacher, one wonders why African-American students are not receiving nearly as much ERT as other ethnic groups.

Compared with the national population, AR users were much more likely to come from rural schools and somewhat more likely to come from town schools but much less likely to come from suburban schools and city schools. It is possible to read books in the Spanish language and take AR quizzes in Spanish on those books (but, of course, this happens only in the USA). However, it appeared that many students tried one or a few books in the Spanish language and quizzed on it in Spanish, but after that the numbers dropped off steeply (the students presumably preferring and becoming more competent to read in the English language). In Spanish, of Quizzes Taken (n = 509,098), only 52% were Passed. There were almost no quizzes passed after grade 8. In both QP, ERT, APC and ABL, Spanish quiz takers did much worse than English quiz takers.

References

Goodman, G. (1999). *The Reading Renaissance/Accelerated Reader program. Pinal county school-to-work evaluation report.* Tucson, AZ: Creative Research Associates, Inc. https://files.eric.ed.gov/fulltext/ED427299.pdf

Gorard, S., Siddiqui, N., & See, B. H. (2017). What works and what fails? Evidence from seven popular literacy 'catch-up' schemes for the transition to secondary school in England. *Research Papers in Education, 32*(5), 626–648.

Hamilton, B. (1997). Using Accelerated Reader with ESL students. *MultiMedia Schools, 4*(2), 50–52.

Holmes, C. T., & Brown, C. L. (2003, February 7). *A controlled evaluation of a total school improvement process, School Renaissance.* Paper presented at the National Renaissance Conference, Nashville, TN. https://files.eric.ed.gov/fulltext/ED474261.pdf

Johnson, R. A., & Howard, C. A. (2003). The effects of the Accelerated Reader program on the reading comprehension of pupils in grades three, four, and five. *The Reading Matrix, 3*(3), 87–96. http://www.readingmatrix.com/articles/johnson_howard/article.pdf

McGlinn, J., & Parrish, A. (2002). Accelerating ESL students' reading progress with Accelerated Reader. *Reading Horizons, 42*(3), 175–189. http://scholarworks.wmich.edu/cgi/viewcontent.cgi?article=1186&context=reading_horizons

Moyer, M., & Williams, M. (2011). Personal programming: Customizing Accelerated Reader helps Delsea regional high school encourage student reading. *Knowledge Quest, 39*(4), 68–73.

National Center for Educational Statistics (2021). *Racial/ethnic enrollment in public schools.* Washington, DC: National Center for Educational Statistics.

Pappas, D. N., Skinner, C. H., & Skinner, A. L. (2010). Supplementing Accelerated Reading with classwide interdependent group-oriented contingencies. *Psychology in the Schools, 47*(9), 887–902. DOI:10.1002/pits.20512.

Rodriguez, S. (2007). The Accelerated Reader program's relationship to student achievement on the English/Language Arts California Standards Test. *The Reading Matrix, 7*(3), 191–205. http://www.readingmatrix.com/articles/rodriguez/article.pdf

Ross, S. M., Nunnery, J., & Goldfeder, E. (2004). *A randomized experiment on the effects of Accelerated Reader/Reading Renaissance in an urban school district: Final evaluation report.* Memphis, TN: Center for Research in Educational Policy, The University of Memphis.

Samuels, S. J., Lewis, M., Wu, Y. C., Reininger, J., & Murphy, A. (2003). *Accelerated Reader vs. non-Accelerated Reader: How students using the Accelerated Reader outperformed the control condition in a tightly controlled experimental study.* Minneapolis: University of Minnesota. https://web.archive.org/web/20040902144751/http://www.tc.umn.edu/~samue001/web%20pdf/Final%20Report--Accelerated%20Reader%20vs%20Non-Accelerated%20Reader.pdf

Samuels, S. J., & Wu, Y. C. (2003). *The effects of immediate feedback on reading achievement.* Minneapolis, MN: University of Minnesota. https://web.archive.org/web/20060423031356/http://www.tc.umn.edu/~samue001/web%20pdf/immediate_feedback.pdf

Stringfield, S. G., Luscre, D., & Gast, D. L. (2011). Effects of a story map on Accelerated Reader postreading test scores in students with high-functioning autism. *Focus on Autism and Other Developmental Disabilities, 26*(4), 218–229. DOI:10.1177/1088357611423543.

Topping, K. J., & Fisher, A. M. (2003). Computerised formative assessment of reading comprehension: Field trials in the UK. *Journal of Research in Reading, 26*(3), 267–279.

Topping, K. J., Samuels, J., & Paul, T. (2007). Computerized assessment of independent reading: Effects of implementation quality on achievement gain. *School Effectiveness and School Improvement, 18*(2), 191–208.

Vollands, S. R., Topping, K. J., & Evans, H. M. (1999). Computerized self-assessment of reading comprehension with the Accelerated Reader: Action research. *Reading and Writing Quarterly, 15*(3), 197–211 (themed issue on Electronic Literacy).

12

Electronic Reading and Out-of-School Reading

School days are crowded and it is difficult to give students enough time to read independently, although some of them are good at finding time outside lessons to snatch a little time with a book. Having books go home with students creates a challenge for teachers, who may worry (in some cases, with good reason) that the students will forget to return them to school next day. Of course, extending school reading out of school is highly desirable, and hopefully students who are motivated by the books they have chosen will want to do this. One way of addressing this problem is to provide a wide range of books through an electronic reader, which can travel from home to school and enable reading in both places. Renaissance Learning has gone one step further and provides books and the associated Accelerated Reader (AR) quizzes in software which can be downloaded onto any device that the student has available (desktop, laptop, tablet or even phone). This software is known as myON. Because the device itself is owned by the students, they are more likely to look after it.

myON is thus a digital literacy platform that offers every student unlimited personalized access to a library of digital books, together with a dictionary and writing tools such as highlighting, note taking, and journaling. It works both alone, with AR and in conjunction with Star Reading (which, of course, can be administered multiply as it is item-banked) – all available electronically. At the moment, students can access up to 13,000 digital books (including graphic novels, picture books and Spanish language texts) in the US and up to 5,600 books in the UK. Audio narration is available with all texts. Also offered is myON News, which gives students age-appropriate reporting on timely topics and current events. myON is available 24/7 online and offline and so can support reading at home as well as school or any other place the student happens to be. In addition to generating helpful reports for educators, myON includes a Student Profile for at-a-glance information on individual student reading activity that can be easily accessed by students and shared with families (see Figure 12.1). There are also several YouTube videos about myON.

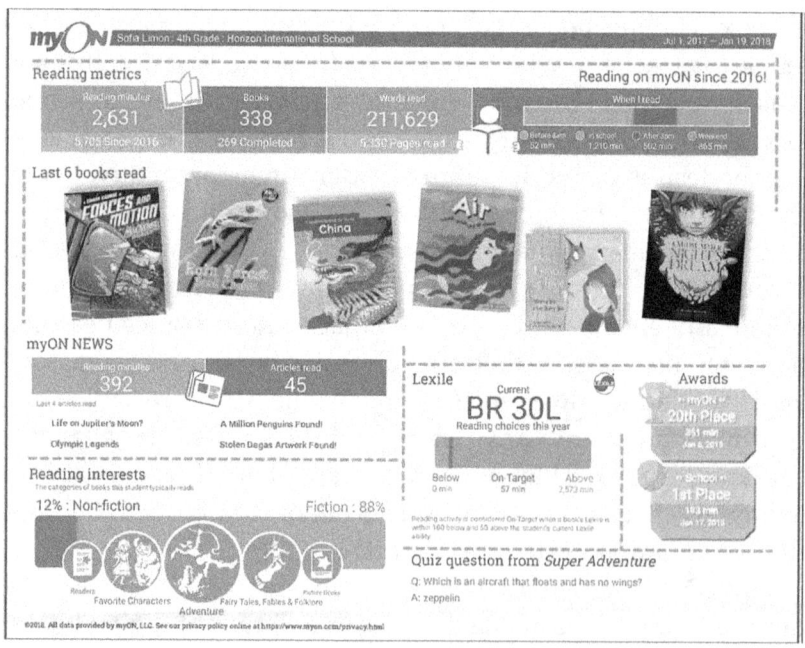

FIGURE 12.1 Screenshot from myON Reader

Research Literature on Accelerated Reader

Although myON is quite new, there is already some research literature on its effectiveness. The Lexile framework and myON Reader were described in detail by Sanford-Moore (2013), but no data on effectiveness were presented. Ortlieb, Sargent and Moreland (2014) randomly assigned three classrooms of fourth-grade students (n = 58) from three schools with 68% to 97% eligible for free lunch to one of three treatment conditions implemented during an after-school reading clinic. There were 12 tutoring sessions of 75 minutes each operated by pre-service teachers, who used printed materials, myON, or myON with printed materials with the students, but the teachers and not the students chose the books. Students in the myON-only group had significantly higher post-test scores than the print-only group (effect size [ES] = 0.90) on Lexiles but did not do better on a word recognition test (which seems an inappropriate measure if reading comprehension was the issue). Although this was a quasi-experimental study, the small sample size also raises concerns.

Alfageh and Demir (2018) investigated the usability of myON and the nature of student experiences. A set of predefined tasks were given to ten fourth- and fifth-grade elementary students (seven males, three females). Each investigative session with a participant lasted 45 to 90 minutes. Participants with less experience of myON took longer and were slightly less effective – but they recorded a 97% success rate in task completion. The consensus among the participants was that myON was appropriate for enabling students to read different books online.

A report on the use of myON to support English as a Foreign Language with 1,022 students in grades 5 through 8 in 44 schools over a whole school year was produced by the Education 2030 Research Group (2020). Three types of groups (optimum, minimum and control) participated in the research, which was based on voluntary participation. Teachers who undertook to teach optimum groups were expected to use the program at least weekly and the minimum group at least every two weeks, while the control group did not use the program with their groups.

Pre-post Star Reading tests bridged an initial period of traditional school-work and a second period of digital home-schooling. Optimum and minimum groups had significantly higher midterm and final-term scores than the control group. The largest ES was in the optimum group (ES 1.95), but the minimum group also increased (ES 1.50) compared with the control group. The average number of minutes spent reading per week had a significant moderating effect on achievement, especially in the case of the optimum groups. Although the Optimum and Minimum groups were very different at the beginning, they were equal at the end, suggesting that myON had compensatory effects and decreased inequality and disadvantage.

An eight-week trial of myON with 902 English as a Foreign Language students in grades 2 through 7 from 80 state schools was reported by the Ministry of National Education (2020) in Turkey. The audio narration of text by professionals was felt to be particularly useful for this population. There were positive gains in student reading ability in each grade. The ESs per grade ranged from 0.2 to 0.4 (and all gains but one were statistically significant), which was felt to be a good result for such a short intervention. As the number of books read, the number of words read, and the number of minutes read increased, so did the outcome scores, and number of words read showed the largest increase. The 85 teachers involved were surveyed, with a response rate of 83.5%, and generally the teachers were very satisfied with the myON device and its effects.

New Data on Accelerated Reader

In the USA, data indicated that reading in myON was associated with higher levels of annual growth in general reading ability. In the 2017–2018 school year, students who used myON and completed Star Reading pre- and post-tests numbered 108,752 students. Students who spent more time reading in myON (measured by both seconds spent reading and number of words read) experienced more growth in Star Reading. Analyses were for both the general population and lower-performing students

(Star Reading pre-test percentile rank 25 or less; in the bottom quartile). For the general population, Student Growth Percentile (SGP) rose from 45.6 at <2,500 seconds to 50.6 at >100,000 seconds and; SGP rose from 46.3 at <10,000 words to 49.2 at >200,000 words. For struggling readers, SGP rose from 46.6 at <2,500 seconds to 50.7 at >100,000 seconds: SGP rose from 47.3 at <10,000 words to 50.0 at >200,000 words. In the 2018–2019 school year, 105,518,942 openings of books in myON were examined. Overall, students read more than 827,885,052 minutes in myON – approximately 13,798,084 hours, 574,920 days, or 1,575 years of reading – and almost 2 billion pages over the school year.

From Table 12.1, it is clear that, in the UK, the top myON titles are quite different from those in the regular AR book lists and also those in the AR Favorite book lists. Some authors

TABLE 12.1 Top 20 Books Read with myON

Rank	Title	Author	ATOS level
1	Ballet Bullies	Emma Carlson Berne	3.6
2	The Legend of the Zombie	Thomas Kingsley Troupe	4.0
3	Volleyball Victory	Leigh McDonald	4.3
4	Victory Vault	Emma Carlson Berne	3.9
5	The Grin in the Dark	J. A. Darke	4.3
6	The Truth about Dogs: What Dogs Do When You're Not Looking	Mary Colson	2.4
7	Encountering Ghosts: Eyewitness Accounts	Mari Bolte	3.9
8	Say Cheese, Medusa!	Kate McMullan	3.8
9	The Truth about Hamsters: What Hamsters Do When You're Not Looking	Mary Colson	2.5
10	Do Not Watch	J. A. Darke	4.8
11	Gold Medal Swim	Thomas Kingsley Troupe	3.6
12	The Mummy at Midnight	Steve Brezenoff	3.5
13	The Legend of Bigfoot	Thomas Kingsley Troupe	3.4
14	Haunted Objects from Around the World	Megan Cooley Peterson	4.8
15	Hit the Road Helen!	Kate McMullan	4.0
16	Nice Shot, Cupid!	Kate McMullan	4.0
17	Striker Assist	Scott Welvaert	3.9
18	The Sinking of the Titanic	Matt Doeden	3.8
19	Blood in the Library	Michael Dahl	3.3
20	Doubles Trouble	Blake Hoena	4.0

appear frequently, so there are three books by Thomas Kingsley Troupe and two each by Emma Carlson Berne (including the top one), Mary Colson, Kate McMullen and J. A. Darke – none of these appears in the regular AR lists. Partially this is due to the much smaller number of titles available on myON at the moment, but it may be that reading digitally encourages students to read completely new books and authors. The average ATOS (Advantage/TASA Open Standard for Readability) is 3.8, compared with the UK average for all years of 3.6, so there is some initial evidence that reading digitally has the effect of raising the challenge level for students, which is important, especially in the case of secondary-aged students.

Chapter Summary

myON is software which can be downloaded onto any device the student possesses and gives access to the text of many books and the AR quizzes which go with them. It includes audio narration, a dictionary and writing tools such as highlighting, note taking, and journaling. It can also include the Star Reading test. There are 13,000 digital books (including graphic novels, picture books, and Spanish language texts). There are four studies of myON, all reporting positive effects. Much the same was found in the new data reported. The most popular myON titles are quite different from the regular AR popular book titles, perhaps due to the relatively small number of quizzes currently available for myON in the UK, although 13,000 is not that small. The average ATOS for myON texts is somewhat higher than for regular AR books, so perhaps myON encourages a greater challenge.

References

Alfageh, D., & Demir, F. (2018). The usability evaluation of a digital book application for elementary school students. *International Journal of Arts Humanities and Social Sciences*, 3(18), 27–33. http://www.ijahss.com/Paper/03082018/1079495654.pdf

Education 2030 Research Group (2020). *Using modern digital learning programs to scaffold learning in grades 5-8*. Eger, Hungary: Eszterházy Károly University.

Ministry of National Education (2020). *Trial of myON*. Ankara: Ministry of National Education.

Ortlieb, E., Sargent, S., & Moreland, M. (2014). Evaluating the efficacy of using a digital reading environment to improve reading comprehension within a reading clinic. *Reading Psychology, 35*(5), 397–421. DOI:10.1080/02702711.2012.683236.

Sanford-Moore, E. E. (2013). *The Lexile framework and myON Reader*. Bloomington, MN: myON. https://doc.renlearn.com/KMNet/R63032.pdf

13

What Bang for Your Buck? The Importance of Cost-Effectiveness

Of course, these programs have a cost, and teachers and especially education managers will be concerned about how much impact they are likely to get for each dollar (or other unit of currency) spent on them as well as whether any effects will continue in the longer term. Thus, this chapter is about cost-effectiveness – systematically comparing the costs and outcomes of alternative policies or interventions to aid decisions about the most efficient course of action.

Naturally, prices rise over time, and cost structures are different in different countries, so in the literature at different times we see comments on price structures which are now out of date or only of relevance to one country. Consequently, cost-effectiveness might be best estimated relatively, in relation to the cost at the same time of other methods and interventions.

Comparison with other methods and interventions is all very well, but at what level might these comparisons be made? At the level of very broad policy options regarding the management of education, at the level of other curricular options which are within the purview of the school, or at the level of a direct comparison between two or more programs which do almost the same thing?

Cost-effectiveness analysis seeks to look at the total costs of implementation of a program, not just the costs of buying it. Thus, teacher time to deliver the program and any other resources consumed are also factored in. Consequently, if a program enables teachers to do things more efficiently than they did previously, the saving in teacher time should also be factored in. Costs also include opportunity costs (i.e., the foregone benefits of the alternative use of the resources needed to implement an intervention).

Looking at Accelerated Reader (AR) first and considering the level of broad policy options first, Yeh (2007) compared the effectiveness and costs of rapid assessment, increased spending, voucher programs, charter schools, and accountability (high-stakes testing) systems. By "rapid assessment", he meant the AR program, coupled with the Star Reading test. However, Yeh (2007) used only two studies involving AR (Nunnery et al., 2006; Ross et al., 2004). These had quite modest effect sizes (ESs) (0.27 and 0.18).

However, the ESs were 0.08 for increased spending, 0.06 for vouchers, 0.05 for accountability and 0.01 for charter schools. AR was substantially more effective and less costly than the alternative interventions, resulting in an effectiveness–cost ratio that was between 57 and 23,166 times larger than for the alternatives. Yeh (2007) also interviewed an unspecified number of teachers in eight schools, who reported that the time saved by AR's student progress-monitoring features (which replaced the time-consuming tasks of grading homework and assessing reading comprehension) more than offset the time taken to help students select books and monitor student performance. As Yeh (2007) points out, AR was not designed to supplant regular instruction. However, to the extent that it increased the amount of time available for teaching, rapid assessment may have helped teachers whose aim was to spend more time on critical thinking activities.

A similar study by Yeh (2008) analyzed AR in comparison with 29 different Comprehensive School Reform (CSR) models, class size reduction and high-quality preschool. CSR ESs were small, ranging from 0.05 to 0.18, and the interventions which were most narrowly focused on the curriculum did best. The additional annual cost per student for the major CSR models ranged between $290 and $900. The annual cost of AR was $9.45 per student. As Yeh points out, one major difference was that one focused on teachers while the other focused on students. Class size reduction ES varied from 0.10 to 0.15, but reducing class size was vastly more expensive. The ES for children participating in high-quality preschool was 0.15, but high-quality preschool was even more expensive.

A further study of class size reduction by Yeh (2009a) found that the average ES of class size reduction across reading and math was 0.13 per year in Tennessee and negligible in California. The annual cost of class size reduction ranged between $197 and $211 for every single student reduction in class size. In contrast, AR gave an ES of 0.28, with unusually disadvantaged populations of students, at greatly reduced cost.

Yeh (2009b) then estimated the benefits and costs of nationwide implementation of AR, in terms of increased earnings, increased tax revenues, the value of less crime, and reductions in welfare costs. Results suggest that the social benefits would be 28 times the total social costs. Tax revenue benefits would exceed costs by a ratio of 93, and social benefits to each state treasury would exceed costs by a ratio of 286.

Yeh (2009c) similarly investigated the relative cost-effectiveness of AR and raising teacher quality – substituting high-performing teachers for low-performing teachers. The cost-effectiveness of requiring teacher applicants to meet a minimum 1,000 SAT test score, while raising teacher salaries by 45% in order to maintain an adequate pool of candidates, was determined. The ES of raising teacher quality was extremely small – between 0.01 and 0.06. AR was 1,008 times more cost-effective than raising teacher quality.

Yeh and Ritter (2009) then compared the cost-effectiveness of AR with voucher programs, charter schools, a 10% increase in educational accountability, CSR, quality preschool and rapid assessment. AR was ten times more cost-effective than CSR; 20 times more cost-effective than class size reduction, increased per-student expenditure, increased educational accountability or replacing the lowest quartile of novice teachers; 30 times more cost-effective than high-quality preschool or voucher programs; and 40 times more cost-effective than charter schools.

Yeh (2010a) then investigated the cost-effectiveness of 22 approaches intended to raise student attainment: CSR, cross-age tutoring, computer-assisted instruction, a longer school day, increases in teacher education, teacher experience or teacher salaries, summer school, more rigorous math classes, value-added teacher assessment, class size reduction, a 10% increase in per-student expenditure, full-day kindergarten, Head Start (preschool), high-standards exit exams, National Board for Professional Teaching Standards (NBPTS) certification, higher teacher licensure test scores, high-quality preschool, an additional school year, voucher programs, and charter schools – and AR. AR had an ES of 0.27, a cost per student of $9.45, and an effectiveness–cost ratio of 0.03. Just three of the other 21 interventions had larger ESs but were much more expensive: CSR, cross-age tutoring, and Head Start. Their effectiveness–cost ratios were 0.002, 0.001 and <0.001 respectively.

Further work by Yeh (2010b) showed that the cost-effectiveness of the NBPTS certification was less than that of a range of alternative approaches for raising student achievement, including CSR, class size reduction, a 10% increase in per-student expenditure, the use of value-added statistical methods to identify effective teachers, and AR, the last of which was the most cost-effective approach.

Yeh (2010c) then addressed factors influencing persistence and intrinsic motivation, including the notion of "learned helplessness". He argued that age-graded schools and group tests labelled students as 'below' and 'above' average, inadvertently demoralizing below-average students, depressing effort and achievement, and perpetuating the gap in achievement between poor students and their peers. AR could lead to individualized instruction, ensure that each student received objective assessment information confirming that he or she was successfully advancing to higher levels, and might be especially suited to remediate these differences.

These findings were further explicated in Yeh's (2015, 2018) subsequent papers but focused more on the issue of closing the attainment gap between advantaged and disadvantaged, and between African-American and Caucasian students. It should be noted that Yeh's assessments of ESs for rapid assessment in reading are all based on the two studies cited in his 2007 paper. His work has also been summarized in three books (Yeh, 2006, 2011, 2017).

Here we break our rule of excluding PhD dissertations (this will happen only once) by discussing the excellent work of Jessica Simon (2011), who offered "A Cost-Effectiveness Analysis of Early Literacy Interventions", by which she meant grades K through 3. Unfortunately, this thesis does not appear to have been translated into peer-reviewed published papers. In it, she gives a thorough critique of Yeh's (2007, 2009a, 2009b, 2009c) papers (and of several other prominent academics). Simon (2011) investigated four programs the What Works Clearinghouse had found to be "effective": AR, Classwide Peer Tutoring (CWPT), Reading Recovery (RR), and Success for All (SFA). She reported that AR, including all materials and 200 licenses, cost $2995 and that each additional license cost $4.25. She had a much more inclusive method of calculating cost per student than Yeh, involving all training costs, yielding a figure for AR of $716 per student per year. By contrast, CWPT cost $488 per student per year, RR $6,631 and SFA $11,706.

However, 60% of Simon's reviewed studies of AR were doctoral dissertations, and (remarkably) only US studies were considered. Only three studies were considered acceptable for meta-analysis (Nunnery et al., 2006; Ross et al., 2004, and a dissertation). Despite Simon's critique of Yeh, she came down to more or less the same studies. ESs for AR were 0.39, 0.71, 0.36, 0.25 and 0.33 (excluding the dissertation) – averaging to 0.41. ESs were 0.55 for CWPT (although from very few studies), 0.26 for SFA and very heterogeneous for RR, from −0.84 to +4.32. Thus, AR and CWPT, two relatively small add-on programs, appeared to be more cost-effective than RR and SFA, two relatively more intensive interventions.

We turn now to the actual costs of implementation.

Accelerated Reader

Early information about costs was based on how the program was marketed at that time. Now the program has a great many more quizzes which are all available to every student, has transferred operation to the cloud so all feedback emanates from the cloud, and operates on a subscription basis with a cost per student, as well as being bundled with Star Reading in the UK.

The USA
The Education Commission of the States (2000) reported that in 2000 the costs of AR plus the Star Reading Test were USD $2,999 for 200 students and 1,000 quizzes (i.e., $15 per student). Now (2021 prices) the cost with 205,000 quizzes for both elementary and secondary schools is USD $7.35 per student per year for AR only, plus $5.10 per student per year for Star Reading, making $12.45 per student per year. There is a minimum license package of 100 licenses and a one-time school start-up fee of $1,599.

The UK and Further Overseas
In England and Wales, 40,000 quizzes are available (the books read in the USA and the UK are largely different, with some obvious exceptions such as the Harry Potter books). The cost to an elementary school for 30 student licenses for a year for both AR and Star Reading is GBP£865, plus GBP£4.70 per additional student (2021 prices), giving a total of GBP£1,664 for 200 students (about GBP£8.32 per student, equivalent to USD $11.65, but the price per student declines after this). The cost to a secondary school for 40 student licenses for a year for both AR and Star Reading is GBP£1,026, plus GBP£6.20 per additional student (2021 prices), giving a total of GBP£2,018 for 200 students (about GBP£10.09 per student, equivalent to USD $14, but the price per student declines after this). The cost in Scotland and Northern Ireland is a little less. If schools commit to a multi-year contract, they can negotiate a discount. Similar pricing applies in the many other countries outside the USA which use AR/STAR, although there is some variation between countries.

Thus, in the UK and other countries, the cost of AR + Star Reading is very similar to the cost in the USA, but in the USA the two products are sold separately while in the UK they are bundled together. The cost of AR + Star Reading has relatively declined over the years (despite the upward pressure of inflation), while the value of the package has increased.

Comparison with Overall Educational Expenditure
In the USA, in 2019 (the latest date for which reliable figures are available), there were 48 million students in elementary and secondary schools, and total expenditure was $762 billion, or $15,875 per student per year (albeit with considerable variation between states) (National Centre for Educational Statistics, 2021; United States Census Bureau, 2021). AR + Star Reading at $12.45 per student per year represented 0.0008% of this.

In the UK, in 2019, there were 3.81 million students in elementary schools, and in 2021, the total educational expenditure was GBP£31,726 million (Institute for Government, 2021; Statista, 2021), giving an expenditure figure per student per year of GBP£8,327. AR + Star Reading at GBP£8.32 represented 0.001% of this. In secondary, there were 2.85 million students and expenditure was GBP£48,060, so expenditure per student per year was GBP£16,863. AR + Star Reading at GBP£10.09 represented 0.0006% of this.

In relation to relative expenditures on elementary and secondary education (secondary expenditure being higher), secondary schools still get AR + Star relatively cheaper, so you can see the logic in the price differentials for elementary and secondary. Thus, in both the USA and the UK, in relation to expenditure on education overall, AR + Star Reading is a tiny fraction of expenditure. In all schools in all countries, salaries and benefits for staff make up 80% of the expenditure.

Reading Counts

In 2010, the cost of Reading Counts (RC) Only was $9.50 per student per year for up to 999 students plus an annual subscription or Access Fee of $350, and a minimum requirement of 50 student licenses, plus sales tax unless exempt. Currently (2021 prices), the cost of RC Only is $8 per student per year. The Reading Inventory is additional to this at $4 per student per year, giving a total of $12 per student per year. Thus, RC Only has increased in price in recent years. The Teacher Kit is a one-off $60.50, but there are no other costs.

As of January 2017, the initial start-up cost of a Read 180 Universal package for 60 students was about $43,000. Included in this was one day of face-to-face professional development, a two-hour webinar, and eLearning courses. A Read 180 Universal upgrade kit for 30 students cost $11,000 and included teacher materials, two Houghton Mifflin Harcourt (HMH) Teacher Central licenses, 30 ReaL Books, six boxes of Independent Reading Library books, access to the online student application, and 30 HMH Student Central licenses. An upgrade kit with 60 student licenses costs $15,000. As would be expected, Read 180 is considerably more expensive than RC Only.

Chapter Summary

Yeh (2007) compared the costs and effectiveness of AR + Star Reading with increased school spending, voucher programs, charter schools, and accountability (high-stakes testing) systems and found AR to be by far the most cost-effective. However, he used only two outcome studies of AR. Later papers by Yeh (using the same two studies) compared AR + STAR with the following: 29 different CSR models, class size reduction, substituting high-performing for low-performing teachers, voucher programs, charter schools, quality preschool, cross-age tutoring, computer-assisted instruction, a longer school day, increases in teacher education, teacher experience or teacher salaries, summer school, value-added teacher assessment, a 10% increase in per-student expenditure, full-day kindergarten, Head Start (preschool), high-standards exit exams, NBPTS certification, higher teacher licensure test scores, high-quality preschool and an additional school year. In every case, AR was more cost-effective.

Simon (2011) investigated AR, CWPT, RR and SFA. CWPT and AR were the most cost-effective.

In terms of actual costs of the AR program today (2021), in the UK the cost of AR + Star Reading is USD $11.65 per student per year, but the price per student declines after this. The cost in the USA is $12.45 per student per year, but in the USA the two products are sold separately while in the UK they are bundled together. In the USA, the cost of AR + Star Reading represented 0.0008% of the annual expenditure on schools (elementary and secondary combined) (2021 prices). In the UK, as a proportion of the annual expenditure on schools, AR + Star Reading represented 0.001% in primary (elementary) schools and 0.0006% in secondary schools (2021 prices). Salaries and benefits for staff make up 80% of the annual expenditure on schools. The cost of AR + Star Reading has relatively declined over the years (despite the upward pressure of inflation), while the value of the package has increased by the addition of a great many more quizzes which are all available to every student and the transfer of operation to the cloud so all feedback emanates from the cloud.

RC costs $12 per student per year and so is about the same price as AR. Read 180 costs a great deal more but, of course, is known to be more effective.

References

Education Commission of the States (2000). *Accelerated Reader/Reading Renaissance.* Denver, CO: E.C.S. https://web.archive.org/web/20050414213152/http://www.ecs.org:80/clearinghouse/18/79/1879.htm

Institute for Government (2021). *Performance tracker schools.* https://www.instituteforgovernment.org.uk/publication/performance-tracker-2019/schools

National Centre for Educational Statistics (2021). *Public school expenditures: Preprimary, elementary, and secondary education.* Washington, DC: Institute of Education Sciences. https://nces.ed.gov/programs/coe/indicator/cmb

Nunnery, J. A., Ross, S. M., & McDonald, A. (2006). A randomized experimental evaluation of the impact of Accelerated Reader/Reading Renaissance implementation on reading achievement in grades 3 to 6. *Journal of Education for Students Placed at Risk*, 11(1), 1–18. https://www.researchgate.net/publication/233069439_A_Randomized_Experimental_EvaluationoftheImpact_of_Accelerated_Reader/Reading_Renaissance_Implementation_on_Reading_Achievement_in_Grades_3_to_6

Ross, S. M., Nunnery, J., & Goldfeder, E. (2004). *A randomized experiment on the effects of Accelerated Reader/Reading Renaissance in an urban school district: Final evaluation report.* Memphis, TN: Center for Research in Educational Policy, The University of Memphis.

Simon, J. (2011). *A cost-effectiveness analysis of early literacy interventions.* Ph.D. dissertation. Columbia University. https://academiccommons.columbia.edu/doi/10.7916/D8Z03G6B/download

Statista (2021). *Public sector expenditure on education in the United Kingdom (UK) in 2020/21.* https://www.statista.com/statistics/298910/united-kingdom-uk-public-sector-expenditure-education/

United States Census Bureau (2021). *US spending on public schools in 2019.* https://www.census.gov/library/stories/2021/05/united-states-spending-on-public-schools-in-2019-highest-since-2008.html

Yeh, S. S. (2006). *Raising student achievement through rapid assessment and test reform.* New York: Teachers College Press.

Yeh, S. S. (2007). The cost-effectiveness of five policies for improving student achievement. *American Journal of Evaluation*, 28(4), 416–436. DOI:10.1177/1098214007307928.

Yeh, S. S. (2008). The cost-effectiveness of Comprehensive School Reform and rapid assessment. *Education Policy Analysis Archives*, 16(13). http://epaa.asu.edu/ojs/article/viewFile/38/164

Yeh, S. S. (2009a). Class size reduction or rapid formative assessment?: A comparison of cost-effectiveness. *Educational Research Review*, 4(1), 7–15. DOI:10.1016/j.edurev.2008.09.001.

Yeh, S. S. (2009b). Shifting the bell curve: The benefits and costs of raising student achievement. *Evaluation and Program Planning*, 32(1), 74–82.

Yeh, S. S. (2009c). The cost-effectiveness of raising teacher quality. *Educational Research Review*, 4(3), 220–232. DOI:10.1016/j.edurev.2008.06.002.

Yeh, S. S. (2010a). The cost-effectiveness of 22 approaches for raising student achievement. *Journal of Education Finance*, *36*(1), 38–75. https://www.jstor.org/stable/40704405

Yeh, S. S. (2010b). The cost-effectiveness of NBPTS teacher certification. *Evaluation Review*, *34*(3), 220–241. DOI:10.1177/0193841X10369752.

Yeh, S. S. (2010c). Understanding and addressing the achievement gap through individualized instruction and formative assessment. *Assessment in Education*, *17*(2), 169–182. DOI:10.1080/09695941003694466.

Yeh, S. (2011). *The cost-effectiveness of 22 approaches for raising student achievement*. Charlotte, NC: Information Age Publishing.

Yeh, S. (2015). Two models of learning and achievement: An explanation for the achievement gap? *Teachers College Record*, 117, 120308.

Yeh, S. S. (2017). *Solving the achievement gap: Overcoming the structure of school inequality*. New York: Palgrave Macmillan.

Yeh, S. (2018). Evaluation of a new theory of the racial achievement gap. *Teachers College Record*, *120*, 120301.

Yeh, S. S., & Ritter, J. (2009). The cost-effectiveness of replacing the bottom quartile of novice teachers through value-added teacher assessment. *Journal of Education Finance*, *34*(4), 426–451. https://www.jstor.org/stable/40704368

14

Summary and Conclusions

This brief chapter offers a Summary and Conclusions. This may be suitable for busy politicians or even school managers to read next if the Executive Summary excites their interest.

Summary

This book is about a single kind of software, designed to improve reading comprehension of real books through computer assessment and feedback. But this is no ordinary software – it is used by about nine million school students in 100 countries around the world. There is great emphasis on evidence-based education, and this book summarizes *independent, peer-reviewed* research evidence and new research freshly done. Additionally, it gives extensive guidance on good-quality implementation which enhances results.

Of course, schools have long had programs to encourage independent reading of self-chosen books which could have an element of accountability, through book discussion groups, book reports, and so on, but this becomes a problem when students are choosing their own very diverse books and is very time-consuming. By contrast, computer-based systems for managing independent book reading encourage students to choose a real book of their own choice (adequately challenging for their age and ability), read it, then self-test their comprehension with a quiz on a computer. Their performance is automatically scored and analyzed, and results are swiftly fed back to the student. Results are also fed back to the teacher, who can guide the student towards more-effective book choices. Teachers and librarians are enabled to manage the reading experiences of students with far greater efficiency than before.

There are two main programs which deliver computer assessment and feedback on the reading of real books: Accelerated Reader (AR) (published by Renaissance Learning in the USA and the UK and available worldwide) and Reading Counts (RC) (published by Houghton Mifflin Harcourt [HMH] and available only in the USA). There are three other programs which do somewhat similar things: Book Adventure by Sylvan Learning, ReadnQuiz by IntraData and Book It by Pizza Hut. There is no published literature on any of these. These three companies were contacted to request their cooperation but did not reply.

This book gathers all the independent research studies in peer-reviewed journals on these programs, not mentioning studies done by the manufacturers. Books, chapters, doctoral dissertations and master's theses were also excluded, as not subject to peer review and very diverse in quality. Five research databases were searched. "Accelerated Reader" generated many hits, "Reading Counts" very few. However, Read 180 (in which RC is now embedded) generated many hits. Studies which combined the computer programs with some other intervention and did not disentangle the effects were also excluded. The book adds new analyses of fresh data supplied by the relevant companies but analyzed independently by the author. Because the academic years 2019–2020 and 2020–2021 had been severely disrupted by the Covid pandemic, additional data were requested from 2018–2019, but HMH could provide data for 2015–2016 only. Better-designed studies were investigated for effect size (ES) (a quantitative measure of the magnitude of effect).

Accelerated Reader

AR enables individual computer-based assessment of comprehension of self-chosen independently read real books (fiction and non-fiction) for pre-K to 12th grade and provides instant feedback to the student, which encourages metacognition. AR also helps teachers accurately and efficiently monitor student progress in quality of comprehension, quantity, difficulty of books read and quiz scores. Teachers can then take whatever action is needed (e.g., shape subsequent reading instruction, guide individual students, or discuss choosing books with the whole class). The Star Reading computer-based adaptive reading comprehension test is often used to indicate the student's starting reading level. Renaissance Learning recommends a minimum of 30 minutes of daily independent reading time for elementary schools and 20 minutes for secondary schools. They are very clear that AR is not an instructional program and not a reward program. Nor do they recommend that AR be linked to grades in schools.

Comprehension quizzes comprise 5, 10 or 20 multiple-choice items and are literal rather than open-ended (for reliability). Quizzes are available for more than 200,000 books. Pass rates are 60% for short quizzes and 70% for longer ones, but an 85% rate is recommended for optimal reading growth. AR allows teachers to develop custom quizzes. There are also Literacy Skills quizzes (covering 24 specific higher-order comprehension and thinking skills), Spanish quizzes (based on Spanish books), Recorded Voice and Vocabulary Practice quizzes. Available titles are found using AR Bookfinder, and a school's book stock can be compared with AR quizzes available. Book difficulty level (usually marked on the book) is determined by ATOS (Advantage/TASA Open Standard for Readability), which scans the whole book and determines readability by average sentence length, average word length, word difficulty level and the total number of words in the book. Students can set goals for themselves. Students can rate the book after they have read it, and student choices of Favorite Books are recorded. Reports for parents can also be generated, and Home Connect allows parents and guardians to monitor what their children are reading. Both remote and face-to-face training sessions are available. It is possible to cheat with AR, so teachers should be careful that all AR quizzes be taken at school.

Reading Counts

RC is similar to AR but has some additional features. It has about 75,000 book tests and is based on the Lexile measure of difficulty. Students take the computer-adaptive Reading Inventory and then select books of the appropriate level from the Book Expert information database. Quizzes are cheat-proof because each has a randomly selected set of questions from a 30-item bank, so no two tests are alike (but there might be an issue about comparability of items). Points are awarded based upon the percentage of test questions answered correctly. The pass rate is 70% by default, but students are encouraged to aim for 80%. Reading goals can be set.

Teachers can customize tests to suit individual students by doing the following: modifying the number of questions per test, setting a new passing rate, setting the number of test attempts allowed (a 10-question test can be taken three times, because there are 30 questions in the item bank), deciding the number of days between retakes, and adjusting point allocation. Many of these features are not found in AR, but the proportion of teachers using them is small. RC allows teachers and students (with teacher supervision) to develop custom quizzes. RC has congratulations screens, certificates and the Read-O-Meter device for indicating the extent to which students liked the book. RC is available separately, but mostly it is embedded in Read 180, which includes small group teacher instruction and independent reading and is targeted mainly to lower-ability readers. RC offers a range of mostly online professional development initiatives. RC is not an instructional program (but Read 180 certainly is) and is not a reward program. So, AR and RC are not in competition but are different.

AR and RC have been criticized, but criticisms are often based on misconceptions of what the programs do, and often attribute defects of implementation to the programs when they reflect independent decisions about implementation by teachers (often despite advice to the contrary). Paradoxically, at the same time, there is a complaint that the program robs teachers of their right to make decisions about education. Many of these critiques cite only other papers antagonistic to AR and RC as "evidence", and almost all are conspicuously lacking in evidence. However, improvements to both AR and RC could be made.

AR Research Literature

Previous studies (n = 64; 51 from the USA) were divided into the following: Reviews (n = 14), Randomized Controlled studies (n = 7), Controlled studies Not Randomized (n = 4), Many Schools with Reading Tests (n = 10), Single Schools with Reading Tests (n = 4), Many Schools with No Reading Tests (n = 9) and Single Schools with No Reading Tests (n = 16). The average ESs were +0.28 for Reviews, +0.35 for Randomized Controlled studies and +0.35 for Controlled studies Not Randomized.

Many so-called reviews included very few studies. The Randomized and Controlled studies all reported positive effects for AR and were much more satisfactory in quality than the reviews, as were almost all other categories (except for one negative result with very poor implementation and two which were not really evaluations of AR). However, the Single Schools with No Reading Tests section had several studies with severe design or methodology problems: three studies had a neutral result and in two cases results were not clear, but the remaining 11 studies reported positive effects for AR. Overall, of 64 studies, four reported no effects and four were not clear. Thus, 56 (88%) out of 64 studies reported positive effects for AR.

RC Research Literature

There was very little research literature about RC alone, except for two studies. Greer (2003) directly compared AR and RC but offered no data. Biggers (2010) offered a very weak study with very poor implementation. However, Read 180 (in which RC is embedded) had a good deal of literature. Reviews by Slavin et al. (2008) indicated an average ES of 0.59, while a What Works Clearinghouse review (2016) indicated an ES of only 0.10 (both reviews included nine studies). Thus, while it certainly appears that Read 180 is an effective program, it is impossible to extract the independent effect of RC from these data.

AR New Data

Data were available for 8,745,130 students for the academic year 2018–2019. Quizzes Taken averaged 37.83, while Quizzes Passed (QP) averaged 32.77. The Pass Rate was 87%. The Average Book Level (ABL) (measure of difficulty) was 3.61, the Average Percent Correct (APC) (measure of comprehension quality) 0.79 (or 79%), and the average Engaged Reading Time (ERT) was 21.91 minutes.

There were slightly more males than females, and females performed slightly better on the Star Reading test, passed slightly more quizzes, and had higher ERT and higher book difficulty. However, APC was markedly higher for females than for males. In regard to differences between countries, Canada had the highest score on the Star Reading test, followed by the UK, the USA and Australia. Differences in QP were very large: the USA was highest, Canada was next and the UK was much lower. Differences in APC showed the US high and the UK low. Differences in ERT also showed the US high and the UK low, although both were low in relation to recommended reading time. However, in difficulty of books read (ABL), the UK was well ahead of the USA, which partially explains the difference in QP. Canada did well on all these variables.

RC New Data

RC-only data were available for 14,567 students for the academic year 2015–2016. The difference between initial and final Lexiles gave an ES of 0.23. Tests Taken overall were 307,912 and *Unique* Tests Taken were 278,495, so in only 9% of cases did teachers allow students to retake tests and this did not happen successfully in more than 7% of cases. The average Tests Passed was 16.04. The Pass Rate averaged 72%. The Average Test Score was 71. The Average Reading Level of books was 4.03, and the Average Lexile of books read was 603.74. There was more Fiction than Non-fiction reading, at a ratio of 3:2 (ES = 0.59).

Data for RC + Read 180 were available for 26.921 students, again for 2015–2016. Initial to Final Lexile gave an ES of 0.36, larger than for RC Only students. Tests Taken were considerably lower than for RC Only. Compared with Tests Taken, Tests Passed were 92% of the total and the Pass Rate averaged 70. The Average Test Score was 70, only slightly less than RC Only. On QP, 168,666 were passed on first try (66%), much less than RC Only. The Average Reading Level of Books was 3.03, considerably less than for RC Only. Fiction and non-fiction reads were 50% each.

Implementation

RC seems to be somewhat more complex than AR and has more customizable features. While this ability to customize might appear intuitively appealing to teachers, the amount of time this would involve is likely to prove prohibitive. Indeed, the number of teachers using these extra features is very small. There was evidence of variability in implementation in both AR and RC, and there were special concerns about RC. Secondary schools showed the worst implementation. A checklist of implementation quality variables has been developed (asterisked items are for action by students) (see Appendix A):

1. Assign reading time in class
2. Ensure ease of access to class and school library or other sources
3. *Student selects books of high interest (teacher helps if needed), *and*
4. *Student selects books of appropriate difficulty (teacher helps if needed)
5. *Use AR Book Guide as needed
6. Allow books to be taken home
7. STAR placement test or RC Reading Inventory
8. Sustain high reading volume in and out of school
9. Sustain high number of books in lower grades but not in higher grades
10. Counsel students about interests and/or have class or peer discussion
11. Targeted book recommendations given (RC Only)

12. Assess appropriateness of interest level of book to student maturity
13. Include non-fiction as well as fiction
14. *Students read independently
15. Use varied quiz question formats (embedded cloze, modified cloze, direct questions, and complete-the-stem questions) (RC Only)
16. Sustain difficulty of books in relation to student ability, particularly in secondary grades
17. Allow students to read above notional reading level if highly motivated
18. *Students use computer to take quizzes on books
19. *View personalized and printable Congratulations Screen (RC Only)
20. Retake a different version of the quiz if score is below 70% (RC Only)
21. Teacher modifies the number of questions per quiz (5–30; default is 10) (RC Only)
22. Teacher modifies passing rate for the quiz (0%–100%; default is 70%) (RC Only)
23. Teacher decides number of quiz attempts allowed (1–6 times; default is 3) (RC Only)
24. *Students create own reading lists (teacher helps if needed)
25. *Student sets personalized goals for relevant variable (teacher helps if needed)
26. Teachers talk to students about books they are reading
27. Counsel students as to what feedback means
28. Sustain high average percent correct (AR) or average test score (RC)
29. Sustain APC/Average Test Score at or above 85%
30. Teachers can write their own quizzes
31. Monitor student reports (especially At-Risk) carefully and regularly
32. Monitor males more closely than females
33. Teacher intervenes with struggling students
34. Respond to alerts about student struggling or cheating
35. Praise where merited and modify system where not

36. Encourage students to recommend favorite books to each other
37. Reading progress reports sent home to parents
38. Teacher reviews progress of individual student and whole class regularly
39. Teacher gives feedback to class on progress of individuals and whole class
40. Teacher encourages student to read a harder book
41. Consider use of electronic readers if available (AR only)
42. STAR test at end of semester or year to evaluate progress (AR only)
43. Sustain high implementation quality, particularly in secondary grades
44. Sustain high implementation quality for less-able students (lowest quartile)
45. Sustain high implementation quality for more-able students (highest quartile).

Elementary vs. Secondary Schools

Many studies of AR focused on the elementary grades, which performed considerably better than secondary schools. This may be due to differences between sectors in implementation quality, to changes in the preferences of students as they grow older, to some other factor, or to all of these. However, six of seven other studies did find gains in secondary schools. New data on AR showed maximum use in grades 3 through 5, and there was some use extending into the first two grades of secondary school but much less after this. Book difficulty (ABL) rose steadily through elementary school but much less in secondary school. Quality of comprehension (APC) remained above 0.80 through elementary school but declined at the secondary level. ERT in minutes per day was much higher in elementary schools than secondary schools. New data on RC showed a similar but even more erratic picture. Book difficulty and Average Lexile plateaued in the early grades, rose sharply in the later elementary years, then plateaued again in secondary. This again indicated problems with implementation, not only at secondary but also in the early elementary years.

Low- vs. High-Ability Readers

With AR, two studies found that low-ability students made the largest gains, while two studies noted major differences between low and high groups (with high groups doing better). A further two studies found that performance depended very much on participation and quality of implementation. The general picture is that high-ability readers do better on AR than middle-ability or low-ability readers. Low-ability readers can make large gains but probably only if participation and implementation quality are high.

Favorite Books

In both AR and RC, readers can vote for their Favorite book after completing a book. For grades 1 through 4, AR students were reading Favorite books at a difficulty level far above their actual age but still maintaining a high rate of comprehension (high APC). In grades 5 and 6, relative difficulty declined somewhat, but there was a marked difference after grade 6 (secondary school transfer), when favored books were no longer above chronological age and a rapid decline in difficulty set in. New data were available only from the UK, which confirmed these findings. Quality of comprehension (APC) rose to 0.94 in grade 5 and did not decline after this. Voting for favorite books was much less common in secondary school than elementary school.

Fiction vs. Non-fiction Reading

Of three AR studies, one found no differences between boys and girls, but the other two found marked differences. Girls preferred fiction and boys preferred non-fiction, and this was especially marked at secondary school. However, boys' reading of non-fiction showed a lower quality of comprehension (APC) than girls. New AR data showed that three times more fiction books than non-fiction books were read. The book difficulty for non-fiction was markedly higher than for fiction, and again the APC for non-fiction was much lower than for fiction. New data on RC showed that there was much more fiction than non-fiction reading, at a ratio of 3:2, but clearly there was more non-fiction reading in RC than in AR.

Social Disadvantage

There were ten studies of AR in schools with a higher-than-average proportion of students with social disadvantage, and all of these indicated some degree of effectiveness, but it might be that high implementation quality would be needed. There were no direct comparisons of advantaged and disadvantaged students. Three studies mentioned disability, but again there was no comparison of disabled and abled students. In two studies of AR with English as a Foreign Language (or English as a Second Language) students, outcomes were positive. Three studies mentioned race/ethnicity, but only one compared outcome for different groups, finding that Caucasians had the highest scores, followed by Asians, while Hispanic, African-American and Native American students had the lowest scores. Half of the students in the US were eligible for free or reduced-price lunch, so this index of disadvantage is probably not specific enough.

In terms of new data, in regard to race/ethnicity for AR in relation to the national population, African-Americans and Caucasians were somewhat over-represented; Native Americans and especially Pacific Islanders were greatly over-represented. Star Reading SGP showed that Native Hawaiians had the highest average score, followed by Native Hawaiians, students with Multiple Ethnicities, Caucasians, then Other, then Asians – all above average. African-Americans came out considerably worse. On QP, Asians showed low numbers and Hispanics, Caucasians and (particularly) Native Hawaiians had high numbers. On book difficulty (ABL), Asians read the hardest books, hence their low QP numbers. However, Native Hawaiians and Caucasians had high QP and also high ABL, so they appeared to be reading hard books *and* doing relatively well on quizzes. For APC, Caucasians, Native Hawaiians and those of Multiple Ethnicities showed the highest numbers. African-Americans showed the lowest numbers overall, but the overall numbers of Asians were nearly as low. For ERT, numbers for Native Hawaiians were by far the highest, and numbers for African-Americans were by far the lowest.

It appeared that many students tried one or a few books in the Spanish language and were quizzed on it in Spanish, but after that the numbers dropped off steeply (the students presumably preferring and becoming more competent to read in the English language). Of Quizzes Taken, only 52% were Passed, and in both QP, ERT, APC and ABL, Spanish quiz takers did much worse than English quiz takers.

Electronic Reading

myON is software which can be downloaded onto any device the student possesses and gives access to the text of many books and the AR quizzes which go with them. It includes audio narration, a dictionary and writing tools such as highlighting, note taking, and journaling and can also include the Star Reading test. There are 13,000 digital books (including graphic novels, picture books, and Spanish language texts) (2021 numbers). There are four studies of myON, all reporting positive effects. Much the same was found in the new data reported. The most popular myON titles are quite different from the regular AR popular titles. The average ATOS is somewhat higher than for regular AR books.

Cost-effectiveness

Yeh (2007 and later studies) compared the costs and effectiveness of AR plus Star Reading with increased school spending; voucher programs; charter schools; high-stakes testing systems; 29 different Comprehensive School Reform models; class size reduction; substituting high-performing for low-performing teachers; quality preschool; cross-age tutoring; computer-assisted instruction; a longer school day; increases in teacher education, teacher experience or teacher salaries; summer school; value-added teacher assessment; a 10% increase in per student expenditure; full-day kindergarten; Head Start (preschool); high-standards exit exams; National Board for Professional Teaching Standards (NBPTS) certification; higher teacher licensure test scores; high-quality preschool; and an additional school year. In every case AR was by far the most cost-effective. However, he used only two outcome studies of AR. Simon (2011) investigated AR, Classwide

Peer Tutoring (CWPT), Reading Recovery, and Success for All. CWPT and AR were the most cost-effective.

In the UK, the cost of AR + Star Reading was USD $11.65 per student per year (2021 prices), but the price per student declined after this. The cost in the USA was $12.45 per student per year. In the USA, the cost of AR + Star Reading represented 0.0008% of the annual expenditure on schools (2021 prices). In the UK, AR + Star Reading represented 0.001% of the annual expenditure in primary (elementary) schools and 0.0006% in secondary schools (2021 prices). Salaries and benefits for staff make up 80% of the annual expenditure on schools. The cost of AR + Star Reading has declined over the years in relation to the real value of money, while the value of the package has increased by the addition of a great many more quizzes. RC Only (including the Reading Inventory) costs $12 per student per year and thus is more or less the same price as AR. The price has risen in recent years.

Conclusions

So, can AR and RC Only be compared? If we look at the quantitative indices common to the programs, we see (Table 14.1) the following:

- AR and RC Only cost about the same. AR has more quizzes, more participating students, a higher pass rate, a higher number of QP, a higher APC, better implementation, a higher proportion of studies with a positive outcome, and a higher ES. RC Only has students reading harder books (which may partially account for the lower pass rate and lower APC but not for the far lower number of QP) and a more equivalent ratio between fiction and non-fiction. For both AR and RC Only, there was evidence of a decline in difficulty in secondary school. This was at least partially due to poorer implementation in secondary schools. For RC Only, only 9% of tests were retaken

TABLE 14.1 Comparing AR and RC Only on Common Indices

Program	Year of new data	Readability measure	Number of book quizzes or tests	N	Pass rate Quizzes Passed (QP) or Unique Quizzes Passed (UQP)	Average Percent Correct (APC) or Average Test Score (ATS)	Average Book Level (ABL) or Average Reading Level (ARL)	Implementation	Fiction/non-fiction ratio	Proportion of studies with positive outcome (total n of studies)	Effect size*	Cost per student per year+
AR	2018–19	ATOS	205,000	8,745,130	87% 32.77	79.00%	3.61	Variable	3:1	88% (64)	0.33	$12.45
RC Only	2015–16	Lexiles	75,000	14,567	70% 16.04	71.23%	4.03	Poor	3:2	(1)	0.23	$12.00

* Effect sizes not comparable as on different measures
+ Includes AR and Star Reading Test; RC Only and Reading Inventory

and only 7% were passed on the second or third try, so teachers are not using RC Only's greater flexibility to any great extent. Quizzes cannot be retaken in AR. Fiction/non-fiction ratios were very different between AR and RC Only. In the latter case, proportionately twice as many non-fiction books were read. However, RC Only is a minority use of the RC program, which mostly operates as part of the wider Read 180 and System 44 programs. In fact, AR and RC are not really in competition.

The following are improvements that could be made:

1. Implementation of both AR and RC Only could certainly be improved, especially in secondary schools, and hopefully the implementation checklist will assist in this.
2. The status of points as a form of feedback rather than anything else could be made clearer and this might enhance student metacognition.
3. The inappropriate attribution to Vygotsky is inaccurate and this should be clarified.
4. More information about the other kinds of quizzes which test higher-order thinking should be made available to schools, but these may remain a minority interest unless the nature of the curriculum changes.

References

Biggers, P. S. (2010). *Reading counts toward success: A program evaluation*. Paper prepared for Vila Rica Middle School. http://stu.westga.edu/~sayers1/8480_FinalReport_psb.docx

Greer, J. (2003). Point: A positive experience with Accelerated Reader. *Teacher Librarian*, 30(4), 32.

Simon, J. (2011). *A cost-effectiveness analysis of early literacy interventions*. Ph.D. dissertation. Columbia University. https://academiccommons.columbia.edu/doi/10.7916/D8Z03G6B/download

Slavin, R. E., Cheung, A., Groff, C., & Lake, C. (2008). Effective reading programs for middle and high schools: A best-evidence synthesis. *Reading Research Quarterly*, 43(3), 290–322.

Yeh, S. S. (2007). The cost-effectiveness of five policies for improving student achievement. *American Journal of Evaluation*, *28*(4), 416–436. DOI:10.1177/1098214007307928.

What Works Clearinghouse (2016). *Read 180: WWC intervention report*. Washington, DC: U. S. Department of Education. https://ies.ed.gov/ncee/wwc/Docs/InterventionReports/wwc_read180_112916.pdf

Appendices

Appendix A: Implementation Quality Checklist

	IMPLEMENTATION FACTOR	CHECK
1	Assign reading time in class	☐
2	Ensure ease of access to class and school library or other sources	☐
3	*Student selects books of high interest (teacher helps if needed), *and*	☐
4	*Student selects books of appropriate difficulty (teacher helps if needed)	☐
5	*Use AR Book Guide as needed	☐
6	Allow books to be taken home	☐
7	STAR placement test or RC Reading Inventory	☐
8	Sustain high reading volume in and out of school	☐
9	Sustain high number of books in lower grades but not in higher grades	☐
10	Counsel students about interests and/or have class or peer discussion	☐
11	Targeted book recommendations given (RC only)	☐
12	Assess appropriateness of interest level of book to student maturity	☐
13	Include non-fiction as well as fiction	☐
14	*Students read independently	☐
15	Use varied quiz question formats (embedded cloze, modified cloze, direct questions, and complete-the-stem questions) (RC only)	☐
16	Sustain difficulty of books in relation to student ability, particularly in secondary grades	☐
17	Allow students to read above notional reading level if highly motivated	☐
18	*Students use computer to take quizzes/tests on books	☐

From *Improving Reading Comprehension of Self-Chosen Books through Computer Assessment and Feedback* by Keith James Topping, Copyright © 2023, Routledge

	IMPLEMENTATION FACTOR	CHECK
19	*Students view personalized Congratulations Screen (RC only)	☐
20	Retake a different version of the quiz if score is below 70% (RC only)	☐
21	Teacher modifies the number of questions per quiz (RC only)	☐
22	Teacher modifies passing rate for the quiz (default 70%) (RC only)	☐
23	Teacher decides number of quiz attempts allowed (default 3) (RC only)	☐
24	*Students create own reading lists (teacher helps if needed)	☐
25	*Student sets personalized goals for relevant variable (teacher helps if needed)	☐
26	Teachers talk to students about books they are reading	☐
27	Counsel students as to what feedback means	☐
28	Sustain high Average Percent Correct (AR) or Average Test Score (RC)	☐
29	Sustain Average Percent Correct/Average Test Score at or above 85%	☐
30	Teachers can write their own quizzes	☐
31	Monitor student reports (especially At-Risk) carefully and regularly	☐
32	Monitor males more closely than females	☐
33	Teacher intervenes with struggling students	☐
34	Respond to alerts about student struggling or cheating	☐
35	Praise where merited and modify system where not	☐
36	Encourage students to recommend favorite books to each other	☐
37	Reading progress reports sent home to parents	☐
38	Teacher reviews progress of individual student and whole class regularly	☐
39	Teacher gives feedback to class on progress of individuals and whole class	☐
40	Teacher encourages student to read a harder book	☐
41	Consider use of electronic readers if available (AR only)	☐
42	STAR test at end of semester or year to evaluate progress (AR only)	☐
43	Sustain high implementation quality, particularly in secondary grades	☐

From *Improving Reading Comprehension of Self-Chosen Books through Computer Assessment and Feedback* by Keith James Topping, Copyright © 2023, Routledge

	IMPLEMENTATION FACTOR	CHECK
44	Sustain high implementation quality for less able students (lowest quartile)	☐
45	Sustain high implementation quality for more able students (highest quartile)	☐
	DO NOT:	☐
	Link AR or RC to external rewards	☐
	Link AR or RC to grades or any other form of official assessment	☐

AR = Accelerated Reader (AR) only; RC = Reading Counts (RC) only; all others both R and RC.
* = Student action; all others Teacher action.

From *Improving Reading Comprehension of Self-Chosen Books through Computer Assessment and Feedback* by Keith James Topping, Copyright © 2023, Routledge

Appendix B: Reports Authored by the Manufacturers

These are not peer reviewed and are not referred to in the book.

Accelerated Reader

Renaissance Library USA https://research.renaissance.com

In-house reports tend to be referred to as "White Papers"

Noble, M. L. (2001). Arkansas school sees schoolwide improvements in reading achievement. https://doc.renlearn.com/KMNet/R001178921GDA8CD.pdf

Renaissance Home Connect®: Connecting parents and extending practice (2008). https://doc.renlearn.com/KMNet/R004122813GH637F.pdf

Accelerated Reader: Understanding reliability and validity (2009). https://doc.renlearn.com/KMNet/R003580612GF885B.pdf

AR, reading comprehension, and critical thinking (2011). https://doc.renlearn.com/KMNet/R001183909GDE62C.pdf

Gordon, E. (2011). Cleveland Metropolitan School District reading scores transformed by Accelerated Reader. https://doc.renlearn.com/KMNet/R0045891E9441ABD.pdf

Milone, M. (2011a). Student comprehension of books in kindle and traditional formats. https://doc.renlearn.com/KMNet/R0054730029120B5.pdf

The design of Accelerated Reader® assessments (2011). https://doc.renlearn.com/KMNet/R001184509GD7209.pdf

From *Improving Reading Comprehension of Self-Chosen Books through Computer Assessment and Feedback* by Keith James Topping, Copyright © 2023, Routledge

Text complexity: Accurate estimates and educational recommendations (2012). https://doc.renlearn.com/KMNet/R00548821C95879F.pdf

The research foundation for Accelerated Reader® goal-setting practices (2012). https://doc.renlearn.com/KMNet/R001438603GC81D6.pdf

Using Renaissance Learning programs to support vocabulary development (2012). https://doc.renlearn.com/KMNet/R0055230B02EBE69.pdf

Guided independent reading (2012). https://doc.renlearn.com/KMNet/R005577721AC3667.pdf

Milone, M. (2014). Development of the ATOS® Readability Formula. https://doc.renlearn.com/KMNet/R004250827GJ11C4.pdf

Using readability levels to guide students to books (2014). https://doc.renlearn.com/KMNet/R001005421GD6336.pdf

The research foundation for the Accelerated Reader (2015). https://doc.renlearn.com/KMNet/R0057375D0FDD7A8.pdf

myON

Brekhus, T. (2011). Building proficiency through personalized reading: Capstone Digital's myON reader. https://doc.renlearn.com/KMNet/R63034.pdf

Milone, M. (2011b). Student comprehension of books in kindle and traditional formats. https://doc.renlearn.com/KMNet/R0054730029120B5.pdf

Renaissance myON meets the "evidence-based" requirements of ESSA (2018). https://doc.renlearn.com/KMNet/R62045.pdf

Trends in student outcome measures: myON® and student achievement (2019). https://doc.renlearn.com/KMNet/R62687.pdf

Mid-trial report: Trial of myON by Renaissance (2020). https://research.renaissance.com/research/632.asp

From *Improving Reading Comprehension of Self-Chosen Books through Computer Assessment and Feedback* by Keith James Topping, Copyright © 2023, Routledge

Reading Counts

HMH Research Library www.hmhco.com/research/library

Houghton Mifflin Harcourt (2011a). The value of independent reading. Research Professional Paper. Boston, MA: HMH.
Houghton Mifflin Harcourt (n.d.-a). HMH Reading Counts; Grades K-12. Inspire reading success for all students. Boston, MA: HMH. https://www.hmhco.com/programs/reading-counts
Houghton Mifflin Harcourt (n.d.-b). Reading Counts: A measurable independent reading program to raise reading achievement. Program Guide Grades K-12. Boston, MA: HMH.
Houghton Mifflin Harcourt (2011b). Reading Counts: Educator's guide. Boston, MA: HMH. https://www.hmhco.com/product-support/content/techsupport/src/documentation/ReadingCounts_Educators_Guide.pdf

Read180

Houghton Mifflin Harcourt (n.d.-c). Read 180: Grades 4-12. Unlock whole-brain reading through blended learning intervention. Boston, MA: HMH. https://www.hmhco.com/programs/read-180-universal
Fields, M. M., Alexander, F., & Endo, A. (2019). Read 180: 20 Years of evidence and efficacy. Boston, MA: HMH. https://www.hmhco.com/research/read-180-20-years-of-evidence-and-efficacy

From *Improving Reading Comprehension of Self-Chosen Books through Computer Assessment and Feedback* by Keith James Topping, Copyright © 2023, Routledge

Appendix C: How to Use This Book in a Professional Development or Study Group

Teachers learn best from other teachers, and it is hoped that the reader will be able to be part of a small group who meet periodically to discuss issues arising from this book and to compare their subsequent experiences. This would be true for pre-service teachers as well as in-service teachers. This group might be from the same school or university or it might be a group from several schools (or perhaps even several countries), in the latter case meeting virtually. Early meetings might be to discuss key issues arising from the book; later meetings are likely to be reviewing experience from trying to put principles into practice and seeking suggestions from colleagues about some of the thornier problems that have arisen.

Early meetings could focus on each person reviewing the Implementation Checklist in Appendix A. Does everybody agree with this list? What changes would they like to see? Is there anything that should be added? By all means, produce your own version of the Implementation Checklist. Which of these many items do you manage to do regularly and consistently, which are done less often when you get round to it, and which are never done at all? Mark each item "R" for Regularly, "I" for inconsistently, and "N" for Never. You can discuss these in a group, or if you are brave enough, put them online first so everyone has the opportunity to compare and contrast their own responses to everyone else's. You are likely to find different patterns of R, I and N in different people. Discuss and debate. Of course,

From *Improving Reading Comprehension of Self-Chosen Books through Computer Assessment and Feedback* by Keith James Topping, Copyright © 2023, Routledge

the aim is to get all group members doing more of the implementation items regularly, but as classes and ages of students are different, some differences may remain. Each person should target one to three items which they will seek to improve over the next month. When the group meets again, each member can report back on how their attempts to improve implementation went – what went well and what not! Of course, this cycle can be repeated.

Implementation is probably the most important thing to work on, but once you have done this (remembering it will need doing again from time to time, with more experienced teachers helping out less experienced teachers), you might want to look at the more academic items in the book. Apart from Implementation, the other big thing was Evidence. Accelerated Reader (AR) had by far the greatest amount of evidence, and there was some new data on Reading Counts (RC), but none on the other programs mentioned. You don't have to use AR or RC, but if you are using one of the other programs, you could think about doing an evaluation in your own school and then publishing the results, which would be very valuable because there is nothing at the moment. Even with a heavily researched program like AR, there are many opportunities to add to the knowledge base. If you find one of the Implementation items which you (or others) think is controversial, you could set up a study which compares AR with that item to AR without that item (perhaps in two separate but similar classes) and then see which works best. This would be much better than just operating on the basis of opinion. Again, you could publish the findings. Try to get friendly with someone from a university who might help with the write-up and publication. Or even if you can't manage publication, you could see if ERIC (Education Resources Information Center - https://eric.ed.gov) would accept your research as an item for its database and then the whole world would have access to it.

From *Improving Reading Comprehension of Self-Chosen Books through Computer Assessment and Feedback* by Keith James Topping, Copyright © 2023, Routledge

However, to start you off (or to continue your meetings once you have done all of the above), a number of Study Questions are offered below. Some of them will seem relevant to your school; others will seem completely irrelevant. Just chose the ones that fit.

1. How do AR and RC compare with book reports, book discussion groups, and other ways of creating accountability for independent reading in the classroom? What are the advantages and disadvantages of each?
2. During the pandemic, was it possible for your students to continue doing quizzes and tests on AR and RC? If they were able, how concerned were you about the possibilities for cheating, especially with AR? Did you have any students who were able to use myON or any similar electronic reading device? In post-pandemic times, do you think AR and RC will be more or less used?
3. Some students get obsessed with earning points (irrespective of whether any extrinsic reward is attached) and, for example, might try to read a lot of easy books to rack up points. How do you think points could be modified to be more clearly a form of feedback which conveys how successful the reading was? Is there a need for questions to be attached to points for students to reflect upon as they consider their next strategic move?
4. AR and RC should not be linked to grades in schools. But then how are the students to be motivated? What exactly are grades supposed to be measuring anyhow? Discuss the advantages and disadvantages of linking and not linking.
5. AR and RC Only are not instructional programs. So what instructional program(s) in reading should they most effectively be linked with?

From *Improving Reading Comprehension of Self-Chosen Books through Computer Assessment and Feedback* by Keith James Topping, Copyright © 2023, Routledge

6. AR and RC are not reward programs. If you choose to link extrinsic rewards to points gained in either program, this is your own decision. Will you set goals leading to potential extrinsic rewards for some or all students? Which students and why? Based on which of the implementation variables (points, yes, but other things – Average Percent Correct [APC], Average Book Level [ABL], Engaged Reading Time [ERT], for example)? And what kind of extrinsic rewards – a book? More reading time?
7. Thinking of AR's Literacy Skills quizzes, which seek to develop higher-order reading and thinking skills, can you see a way of using them with or instead of the regular quiz (bearing in mind they are not as reliable). If you ask students to do both, might they get "quiz fatigue"?
8. We have noted that both AR and RC refer to the "zone of proximal development" in a way that Vygotsky (the originator of the term) would not have recognized. Can you think of a better term for this concept in AR and RC which does not take Vygotsky's name in vain?
9. Both AR and RC have tools that enable teachers to relate the school stock of books with those books which have quizzes or tests. Has this been done in your school? Of course, you have a better chance of relating books to quizzes with AR, which has many more quizzes.
10. What role should parents play with either program? Both have tools to generate reports for parents. But what happens to these reports when (or if) they get home? Should there be some guidance for parents on how to react when they get a good (or bad) report?
11. Favorite Books show very high difficulty with very high rates of comprehension, especially in the early elementary grades. How can teachers encourage students to recommend these books to other students? Through

From *Improving Reading Comprehension of Self-Chosen Books through Computer Assessment and Feedback* by Keith James Topping, Copyright © 2023, Routledge

wall displays, through peer group meetings, through class group meetings, or what?
12. Girls like fiction better, and boys like non-fiction better (but do not read it with any greater comprehension). How can we develop non-fiction reading skills (especially in boys)? How much of the reading curriculum should this take up?
13. Obviously, it takes teacher time to vary the RC system (by enabling test retakes, changing the pass score, etc.). For what students do you think this expenditure of teacher time is worth it? Does the extra work lead to improved student performance?
14. Secondary schools have worse implementation than elementary schools, even though secondary schools have more funds per student than elementary schools. Why do you think this is? What can be done about it?
15. Does your school (or do you) allow books to be taken home? If yes, what is the loss/damage rate with AR and RC books? If no, do your students use myON or some similar electronic device. If no, do you allow extra reading time in school?
16. How do you monitor At-Risk reports? Do you have a set time each week to look at this? If you don't have a set time, how do you arrange it? What actions do you take if a student is At-Risk? List them.

Low-ability readers probably need more careful monitoring than other readers. How do you keep an eye on them? And do you watch males more closely than females? And socially disadvantaged more closely than otherwise? And African-American students more than otherwise? And disabled students more than otherwise? And Spanish language speakers taking Spanish quizzes more than otherwise?

From *Improving Reading Comprehension of Self-Chosen Books through Computer Assessment and Feedback* by Keith James Topping, Copyright © 2023, Routledge

Subject Index

This subject index shows where terms are discussed substantively, rather than every occurrence of a term in the text, as some terms (and their abbreviations) are used very often.

Accelerated Reader (AR) xi, xii, 4, 50, 77, 98, 105, 108, 118, 120, 129, 131, 138, 139, 143, 146, 150, 151, 165, 166, 175, 183, 185, 186
accuracy rate 17
African-Americans xiii
AR Bookfinder xi
assessment xi, xiii
ATOS (Advantage/TASA Open Standard for Readability) xi, xiii, 17, 18, 19, 20, 40
Average Percent Correct (APC)/ comprehension quality xi, xiii, 78, 107, 110

best practices xi, xiii, 20
Book Adventure by Sylvan Learning 6
book discussion groups 3
books excluded from studies 6, 8
Book Expert xi, 25, 26
Book Finder 17, 18
Book Interest Screen 28
Book It by Pizza Hut 6
book reports 3, 13
BookSharp 6
books, number of 106

Carter, Rosalie 5
Caucasians xiii
challenge 3, 21
cheating 23, 26, 30
Classwide Peer Tutoring (CWPT) xiii
comparison xiii, xiv, 6, 26, 192
competition xi, xiii, xiv, 6, 26, 192
comprehension quality/ Average Percent Correct (APC) xi, xiii, xiv
computer xiii
controlled studies xi, 4, 11, 49, 57
cost xiii, xiv, 175, 176
cost-effectiveness xiii, 12, 170, 192

countries xi, 78, 175
customize xi, xii, 23, 27

difficulty level of books (ABL) x, xi, xii, xii, xiii, xiv, 11, 78, 106, 110
difficulty level of non-fiction xii
disability xiii, 149, 150, 191
disadvantage 12, 149, 150, 152, 191
Drop Everything and Read (DEAR) 3
Duolog Reading 14

educational interventions, other xiii
Effect Size (ES) x, xi, xiv, 10, 49
effectiveness x, xii
Electronic Bookshelf 5
electronic reading xiii, 12, 98, 163, 192
elementary schools xi, xii, 11, 118, 189
Engaged Reading Time (ERT) xi, xii, xiii, 109, 118
Engaged Reading Volume 105
English as a Foreign/Second Language xiii, 149, 150, 157, 191
ERIC 8
evidence xi, 2, 3
excluded papers, chapters, books, dissertations 6, 7
expenditure on schools, percentage of xiii, 176

Favorite Books xi, xii, 12, 14, 137, 190
feedback x, xi, xii, xiv, 13, 14, 17, 26, 37
females/girls xi, xii,12, 77, 108
fiction xii, xiv, 12, 25, 143, 190
free or reduced-price lunch (USA) 149
free school meals (UK) 149
Free Uninterrupted Reading (FUR) 3
Free Voluntary Reading (FVR) 3
funding 23, 30

gender: see females and males
goals xi, 14, 25, 42
Google Scholar 8
grades xi, 21

Hedges' g 10
high-ability readers xii, 12, 106, 129, 190
high/secondary schools xii, xiv, 11, 118, 189
Home Connect 15
home-schoolers 6
Houghton Mifflin Harcourt (HMH) ix, 5, 8

implementation x, xii, xiii, xiv, 2, 11, 42, 98, 105, 108, 118, 187
implementation checklist xiv, 12, 101, 102, 114, 187, 197
Independent Reading Time (IRT) 3
instructional program, not x, xi, 21, 30

JSTOR 8

Lexiles xi, 5, 20, 25, 26, 28
librarians 3
Literacy Skills Quizzes 17
literal xi, 16, 38, 39
location of school 151, 157
low-ability readers xii, 11, 106, 129, 190

males/boys xi, xii, 12, 77, 108
manufacturer studies 6, 199
mean, arithmetic or average 9
meta-analyses 11
metacognition xiv, 14
monitoring 13, 23, 107
myON xiii, 163

Native Americans xiii
Native Hawaiians xiii
non-fiction xii, xiv, 12, 15, 25, 143, 190
number of observations (n) or (N) 9

parents xi, 3
Pass Rate xi, xi, xiii, xiv, 5, 17
Paul, Judi 4
Paul, Terry 4
peer-reviewed x, 2, 4
percentiles 9, 10
phonological skills 4
points 15, 16, 22, 23, 37
positive effects xi, xiii, xiv

practice, reading 4
preferences, student xii
professional development/study group 202

quartiles 9
quizzes xi, xiii, xiv, 4, 16, 23
Quizzes Passed xi, xiii, xiv, 78, 109
Quizzes Taken xi, 109

race/ethnicity 151, 152, 191
randomized controlled trials/studies (RCTs) xi, 4, 11, 49, 53
range 9
Read 180 x, xi, 5, 25, 76, 85
reading comprehension x, xii, 26
Reading Counts (RC) x, xi, xii, 5, 23, 75, 81, 85, 102, 111, 126, 147, 159, 176, 184, 185, 186
Reading Counts (RC) Only xi, xii, xiii, xiv, 5, 81, 147, 159
Reading Inventory xi, 26
reading logs 13
Reading Renaissance 21
reading tests 11, 49, 60, 67, 69, 72
ReadnQuiz 6
Read-o-Meter 25, 28
real books (self-chosen books) x, 3
Recorded Voice quizzes 17
Renaissance Learning ix, 4, 8
retaking tests 5, 24
reviews xi, 11, 49, 50
rewards x, xi, 21, 22, 30, 36, 37, 41, 43, 44

sample size 9
Scholastic 5
Scopus 8
secondary/high schools xii, xiv, 11, 118, 189
self-image/self-concept 14, 42
social disadvantage xiii
Spanish xiii, 25, 149, 157, 192
Spanish quizzes 17, 149, 157, 192
SQUIRT (Sustained Quiet Uninterrupted Reading Time) 3
standard deviation (s.d.) 9
Star Reading Test x, 5, 14, 111
statistical significance 9
Student Growth Percentiles (SGPs) 10, 111
Sustained Silent Reading (SSR) 3, 42
System 44 xiv, 5, 25, 85

Tests Passed xi
Test Score xi
Tests Taken xii
That's a Fact, Jack! 6
thinking, higher-order xiv
time commitment 3, 20, 42, 43
tracking 3, 14, 23
training 21, 29
t-test 9

Uninterrupted Sustained Silent
  Reading (USSR) 3

Vocabulary Practice Quizzes 17
Vygotsky name xiv, 40

Web of Science 8

"zone of proximal development" 15, 40

Author Index

Alfageh (2018) 165, 168
Algozzine (2006) 58, 92
Anderson (2001) 73, 90

Balajthy (2007) 51, 90
Benjamin (2012) 19, 34
Betebenner (2011) 10, 12
Bettinger (2012) 22, 34
Biggers (2001) 40, 46
Biggers (2010) 75, 88, 90, 185, 195
Bonds-Raacke (2012) 71, 92
Borman (2004) 64, 90
Brem (2005) 59, 74, 90, 92
Brimmer (2002-2003) 73, 93
Brindger (2009) 22, 34
Brown (2003) 58, 92, 100, 104, 150, 161
Brown (2006) 58, 92
Burns (1987) 57, 90
Burns (1991) 57, 90

Camarata (2000) 39, 40, 48
Camarata (2005) 39, 40, 48
Carter (1996) 39, 47
Ceprano (2002) 73, 90
Chambers (2009) 51, 95
Chase (2010) 70, 90
Chenoweth (2001) 73, 90
Cheung (2008) 51, 76, 95, 196
Cheung (2009) 51, 95
Cipielewski (2002–2003) 41, 47, 73, 93
Clark (2016) 71, 90
Collins (1987) 57, 90
Collins (1991) 57, 90
Collins (2009) 52, 91
Cox (2012) 14, 34
Cuddeback (2002) 73, 90
Cunningham (2016) 71, 90

Daley (2014) 76, 93
Davis (2009) 51, 95
Demir (2018) 165, 168
Dewalt (1994) 41, 48, 50, 53, 93, 119, 127

Dowling (2004) 64, 90
Dresang (2005) 70, 91
Duggan (2005) 59, 74, 90, 92

Education 2030 Research Group (2020) 165, 169
Education Commission of the States (2000) 50, 90, 175, 178
Esposito (2006) 74, 91
Evans (1999) 41, 48, 57, 96, 162
Everhart (2005a) 69, 91
Everhart (2005b) 70, 91

Fisher (2003) 64, 96, 150, 162
Florida Center for Reading Research (2004) 50, 91
Foster (2014) 68, 91, 119, 127
Fryer (2011) 22, 34
Fulgham (2012) 44, 47

Gardiner (2014) 22, 34
Gardner (2014) 76, 93
Gast (2011) 70, 95, 162
Goldfeder (2004) 51, 53, 55, 94, 162, 179
Goodman (1999) 67, 91, 119, 127, 150, 161
Goodson (2003) 41, 47
Gorard (2016) 56, 95, 128
Gorard (2017) 53, 91, 119, 127, 150, 161
Gorard (2020) 53, 94
Greer (2003) 75, 88, 91, 185, 195
Groce (2005) 42, 47
Groff (2008) 51, 76, 95, 196

Hamilton (1997) 72, 91, 150, 161
Hansen (2009) 52, 91
Häubl (2010) 14, 34
Hejny (2017) 72, 95
Henk (2004) 69, 92
Holmes (2003) 58, 92, 100, 104, 150, 161

Holmes (2006) 58, 92
Houston (2008) 19, 34
Howard (2003) 64, 92, 150, 161
Huang (2012) 68, 92, 119, 127
Husman (2005) 59, 74, 90, 92

Institute for Government (2021) 176, 178

Johnson (2003) 64, 92, 150, 161

Kerns (2003) 41, 47
Kettle (2010) 14, 34
Kohn (1993) 38, 47
Kohn (2010) 38, 47
Kotrla (2005) 70, 91
Krashen (2003) 41, 42, 47
Krashen (2005) 41, 42, 47
Kulik (2003) 50, 92

Lake (2008) 51, 76, 95, 196
Lake (2009) 51, 95
Lawson (2000) 72, 92
Leider (2014) 76, 93
Lewis (2003) 54, 94, 162
Liben (2012) 20, 34
Long (2012) 71, 92
Louick (2014) 76, 93
Luscre (2011) 70, 95, 162

McCarthy (2003) 41, 47
McDonald (2006) 56, 93, 179
McGlinn (2002) 73, 92, 150, 161
McQuillan (1996) 21, 34
Madden (2008) 51, 95
Madhuri (2008) 43, 48
Malette (2004) 42, 47, 69, 92
Melnick (2004) 69, 92
Ministry of National Education (2020) 165, 169
Moreland (2014) 165, 169
Moyer (2006) 74, 92
Moyer (2011) 74, 93, 150, 161
Murillo (2016) 44, 47
Murphy (2003) 54, 94, 162

National Center for Educational Statistics (2021) 152, 161, 175, 178
Nelson (2012) 20, 34
Nunnery (2004) 51, 53, 55, 94, 162, 179
Nunnery (2006) 56, 93, 171, 174, 179
Nunnery (2007) 59, 93, 118, 127

Ortlieb (2014) 165, 169

Pappas (2010) 74, 93, 150, 162
Parrish (2002) 73, 92, 150, 161
Paul (1999) 61, 96, 128, 136
Paul (2007a) 65, 96
Paul (2007b) 66, 96, 106, 108, 116, 119, 128, 130, 137, 162
Paul (2008) 66, 96, 118, 148
Paulsell (1991) 57, 91
Pavonetti (2002-2003) 41, 47, 73, 93
Peak (1994) 41, 48, 50, 53, 93, 119, 127
Penuel (1997) 60, 93
Perfetti (2012) 20, 34
Persinger (2001) 98, 104
Pfeiffer (2011) 74, 93
Poock (1998) 98, 104
Proctor (2014) 76, 93
Putman (2005) 22, 34

Reininger (2003) 54, 94, 162
Rejholec (2002) 73, 94
Ritter (2009) 172, 180
Rodriguez (2007) 68, 94, 119, 127, 130, 135, 151, 162
Rosenheck (1996) 72, 94
Ross (2004) 51, 53, 55, 94, 150, 151, 162, 171, 174, 179
Ross (2006) 56, 93, 179
Ross (2007) 59, 93, 118, 127
Rudd (2006) 50, 94, 118, 127

Samuels (2003a) 14, 34, 50, 54, 94, 135, 150, 162
Samuels (2003b) 54, 150, 162
Samuels (2004) 98, 104
Samuels (2007a) 65, 96
Samuels (2007b) 66, 96, 106, 108, 116, 119, 128, 130, 136, 162
Samuels (2008) 66, 96, 148
Sanders (2000) 62, 96, 106, 107, 117, 119, 128, 130, 136, 143, 148
Sanford-Moore (2013) 165, 169
Sargent (2014) 165, 169
Sawilowsky (2009) 10, 12
Schall (2016) 44, 47
Schmidt (2008) 43, 48
See (2016) 56, 95, 128
See (2017) 53, 91, 127, 161
See (2020) 53, 94
Shannon (2010) 52, 95
Shannon (2015) 56, 95

Shaughnessy (2012) 44, 47
Siceloff (2010) 52, 95
Siddiqui (2016) 56, 95, 119, 128
Siddiqui (2017) 53, 91, 127, 161
Simon (2011) 174, 178, 179, 192, 195
Skinner (2010) 74, 93, 162
Slavin (2008a) 51, 76, 88, 95, 185, 196
Slavin (2008b) 51, 95, 185
Slavin (2009) 51, 95
Small (2012) 44, 47
Smith (2006) 74, 91
Smith (2011) 70, 95
Smith (2017) 72, 95
Solley (2011) 75, 95
Souto-Manning (2010) 44, 48
Stanovich (2017) 135, 136
Statista (2021) 176, 179
Stefl-Mabry (2005) 42, 48
Stevenson (2000) 39, 40, 48
Stevenson (2005) 39, 40, 48
Stiegemeier (1999) 60, 95, 129, 136
Stringfield (2011) 70, 95, 150, 162
Styers (2010) 52, 95

Tardrew (2003) 41, 47
Taylor (2008) 43, 48
Thompson (2008) 43, 48
Topping (1999a) 50, 96
Topping (1999b) 41, 48, 57, 96
Topping (1999c) 61, 96, 118, 128, 130, 136
Topping (2000) 62, 96, 105, 106, 107, 117, 119, 128, 130, 136, 143, 148
Topping (2003) 64, 96, 150, 162
Topping (2007a) 65, 96
Topping (2007b) 66, 96, 106, 108, 116, 119, 130, 136, 151, 162
Topping (2008) 66, 96, 143, 148
Topping (2015) 138, 142, 144, 148
Topping (2017) 106, 108, 116, 119, 128, 130, 136
Topping (2018) 105, 107, 108, 116, 119, 128, 130, 136

Trelease (2001) 43, 48
Triplett (2004) 42, 48

United States Census Bureau (2021) 176, 179

Vollands (1999) 41, 48, 57, 96, 150, 162
Vygotsky (1978) 40, 48

Wade (2006) 50, 94, 118, 127
Warschauer (2009) 52, 91
Westberg (2011) 70, 95
Westberg (2017) 72, 95
What Works Clearinghouse (2008) 51, 96
What Works Clearinghouse (2010) 76, 88, 96
What Works Clearinghouse (2016a) 52, 97, 185
What Works Clearinghouse (2016b) 76, 88, 185, 196
Willekes (2014) 44, 48
Williams (1979) 138, 142
Williams (2011) 74, 93, 150, 161
Wu (2003a) 14, 34, 50, 54, 94, 162
Wu (2003b) 54, 94, 130, 135, 150, 162
Wu (2004) 98, 104

Yeh (2006) 174, 179
Yeh (2007) 106, 107, 117, 171, 174, 177, 179, 192, 196
Yeh (2008) 171, 179
Yeh (2009a) 172, 174, 179
Yeh (2009b) 172, 174, 179
Yeh (2009c) 172, 174, 179
Yeh (2010) 14, 34, 52, 97
Yeh (2010a) 173, 180
Yeh (2010b) 173, 180
Yeh (2010c) 173, 180
Yeh (2011) 174, 180
Yeh (2015) 174, 180
Yeh (2017) 174, 180
Yeh (2018) 174, 180

For Product Safety Concerns and Information please contact our EU representative GPSR@taylorandfrancis.com
Taylor & Francis Verlag GmbH, Kaufingerstraße 24, 80331 München, Germany

www.ingramcontent.com/pod-product-compliance
Lightning Source LLC
Chambersburg PA
CBHW062221300426
44115CB00012BA/2158